Would Jesus Vote For Trump?

D1533777

Doug Giles and Brandon Vallorani

Published by Flag and Cross Network, LLC
Dallas, Georgia, USA

Printed in the United States of America

ISBN 978-1-64570-209-2

Cover art and design by Doug Giles & David Bugnon

Wholesale Inquiries Contact HQ@fcnetworkllc.com

Dedication and props.

This book is dedicated to all the liberty-loving #MAGA folks who were dead-on in their assessment of how Donald Trump would govern once he dusted Hillary in 2016.

Pat yourselves on the back, ladies and gents, because you were right and CNN and all the screeching NeverTrumpkins were wrong. As in, dead wrong.

In addition, we'd also like to thank Wes and Karen Walker for their research, writing and editing skills in helping us put this terrific and timely tome together.

Finally, we'd like to thank President Trump for kicking proper ass and taking names for God and Country. You, Mr. President, are a breath of fresh, Constitutional, air. Especially after the odious, anti-American, administration of Barack Hussein Obama. And for that President Trump ... we salute you.

Doug Giles & Brandon Vallorani
4/1/2019

CONTENTS

If You Embrace Christianity's Values, Then Trump's Your Best Buddy

Brandon Vallorani

But Jesus knew their thoughts, and said to them:
"Every kingdom divided against itself is brought to desolation,
and every city or house divided against itself will not stand."
Matthew 12:25, NKJV

What, exactly, is it that Trump's supporters see in him when so many others can't stand him? Are they deceived? Dumb? Or do they see something in Trump the haters don't? Something that other politicians just don't offer?

Remember Rachel Maddow's tragi-comic reaction to Trump's election?

> You're awake, by the way. You're not having a terrible, terrible dream. Also, you're not dead and you haven't gone to Hell. This is your life now. This is our election now. This is us. This is our country. It's real.[1]

That was the reaction of a supposedly serious news personality. That might help explain why the media is the least trusted institution of any except Congress in a recent poll.

Maddow's lament was not an unusual reaction among media talking heads. There are plenty of mashups online with people freaking out as the results roll in. CNN had some good ones. The best one might be the one that featured Cenk Uygur from *The Young Turks* gradually shifting from smug arrogance to near-panic[2] as he watched Hillary's comfortable lead slip away in real time.

The militant Left with their Trump Derangement Syndrome despises everything the man stands for. They despise the party he leads. And they despise everyone who dared to vote for him. No surprise there. They've hated others before him. Remember George W. Bush, back before the media rehabilitated him and had him sharing candies with Michelle Obama? Back then, they called him a "war criminal." Leftists daydreamed out loud about him being tried at the Hague. Maybe even hung. They've always hated the Right. But something has changed this time. The hatred has intensified by orders of magnitude. And one of the complicating factors that really has them wrapped around the axle is the question Hillary used as a book title: *What Happened?*

It goes deeper than just the broad question of why would *anyone* vote for him – that's the starting point of everyone from the screaming "No!" at the sky on Inauguration Day protester to the media establishment that was just as gob-smacked as Maddow with Trump's triumph over Hillary. They're wondering, how could this *possibly* happen? And they were mystified by the question: "How could Christians elect someone like ... *him*?"

The party that has bankrupted Christian bakers and florists, that has slandered us as racist and sexist at every turn, that booed God at their national convention, redefined marriage, and is on board with literal infanticide still can't figure out why anyone would possibly vote for Trump.

Remember the movie clip with Hitler freaking out in his bunker -- the one that has been redone into a thousand different memes? That almost perfectly captures the mood and frustration of the Left when Evangelicals – and Christians more generally – showed up on Election Day and pulled the lever for Trump.

Democrat activists did everything by the book, didn't they? They made sure Hillary ran through the Primaries without any real opposition so that she wouldn't face any damaging Blue-on-Blue mudslinging.

Didn't you find it curious how not a single Democrat was remotely interested in running against Hillary in 2016? Not a soul, besides Bernie Sanders, made any serious challenge to rival her nomination. Not Bloomberg. Not Biden. Not Elizabeth Warren. Only Hillary was interested in the job. Who could have guessed there was so little ambition among the Democrats? It's certainly not the case as the Democrats prepare for 2020. The field is so crowded that virtual no-name candidates running on a single issue as well as actual mid-term losers are tossing their hats into the ring.

Back in 2016, it was a completely different story. Only the "Democratic Socialist" senator that normally sits as an Independent dared challenge the rightful heir, Hillary Rodham Clinton.

Their PACs and donors dropped big dollars – and time will tell whether they broke a lot of rules in the process – putting together opposition against Trump, and then weaponizing it against him. The Steele Dossier is an obvious one. The conveniently-timed discovery of the Billy Bush tape was another one.

Criminal charges have been laid in Ukraine against officials there accused of trying influence the 2016 elections, specifically attempting to help Hillary and producing dirt on ... Paul Manafort.

Democrats then trotted out a last-minute parade of women alleging Trump was a bad person. Was it merely a convenient coincidence that these accusers were a made-to-order fit with Hillary's "I'm With Her" slogan and the playing the woman card and the "Trump's a misogynist" narrative?

They found a woman who had once won Miss Universe 1995. Trump supposedly called her "Miss Piggy," when she put on weight during her tenure. Claiming to be insulted, she signed up as a Hillary surrogate to attack him. Sure, this new surrogate had gone on to be a porn star. And, yes, a Cartel Kingpin was her baby-daddy. And, yes, she was credibly accused of being an accomplice in the attempted murder of a judge.

In Hillary's big picture, though, none of that really matters. The only thing that really mattered is that Trump might have called her overweight. An observer might easily conclude that to Hillary, Alicia Machado wasn't a person, so much as an opportunity to exploit in the pursuit of a goal. (But, *shhh* – let's not talk about the video that shows Trump standing up for her against critics on CNN[3], saying the people behind the camera, himself included, were in no position to point fingers, even though she'd been criticized in the media for the same thing.)

But wait, there's more! At the eleventh hour, Lisa Bloom was paying women to accuse Trump of harassment. Money changed hands, with offers of more still, with one condition. It was being offered so long as they went public before election day. After election day, that offer of cash dried up.

All the polls pointed to Hillary coasting to victory, the insiders keeping their positions of power, the secular/socialist agenda going ahead as planned. The media played its role in attacking Trump tirelessly. But in the end, none of those things mattered.

When Hillary asked America that question "Having said all this, why aren't I fifty points ahead, you might ask?"[4] people throughout the insulated blue bubbles in New York, the Left coast, and Washington D.C. – or at least the media who claim to speak for those regions – were pretty much wondering the same thing. How do we stop this guy?

For all the careful preparation poured into to propping her up and dragging him down, Trump just wouldn't say die. He might even do the unthinkable – he might actually win!

And win he did.

This impossible situation left the so-called experts scratching their heads. How could a thrice-married, loudmouth billionaire with a sketchy moral past possibly stand in the way of Hillary Rodham Clinton?

Team Hillary and her most rabid supporters found their scapegoat: it was those pesky deplorable Christians. How dare they? How dare they put that MAGA-hat-wearing, plain-talking, hard-tweeting offense to every single leftist sensibility ahead of sweet, loveable and ever-so-wise Hillary Clinton?

To them, Christians are just that annoying group of curious people who have strong opinions about sex – that prostitutes shouldn't be called "sex workers." That homosexuals getting married is the beginning of a slippery slope that diminishes the God-ordained institution between one man and one woman that is the primary foundation of civil society. That adultery – even if it's in the Oval Office – inexplicably bothers their 'Invisible Friend in the sky'.

Oh, they'll invoke religion when it serves their purpose – especially when they can club someone else over the head with it. But so far as being actually governed by it? Not so much.

With all the dirt they dug up to smear Trump, why is it that Christians weren't leading the charge to defeat him? They checked all the boxes in destroying him and making him hateful – it was a slam dunk. What could they possibly have missed?

They missed a few things. Christians have wised up to exactly where they stand with the Democratic party. They've figured out exactly how interested the Democrats are in supporting Christian priorities. They watched the Democrats rope-a-dope Christian traditions and institutions. Demonize them. Call them bigots. They noticed that the only refugees Obama didn't want in this country was the German Christian family – the Romeikes – who had been awarded religious asylum when they were being harassed by their own government for choosing to homeschool their children. Even after the courts had awarded asylum, the Obama administration went to court (and lost) trying to send them packing.[5]

Christians noticed that the government went to court against religious institutions. That the government sued a church school for firing a teacher that had violated one of its religious tenets. (And lost.) That they fought the Little Sisters of The Poor, insisting that the nuns there provide contraception coverage in their government-mandated health care insurance.

Christians have noticed that standards and traditions have been changed by someone who had promised to fundamentally transform America – without explaining exactly how he planned to accomplish that change.

Christians have noticed that America was no longer a country whose leaders loved and appreciated the hard-working First Responders the way we traditionally had. Right from the beginning, we had a President that rushed to judgment assuming the worst about them. Remember the Beer Summit? Obama automatically *knew* the cop had "acted stupidly" and assumed the cop had been unfair. Remember that time in Texas, where officers – who had just finished providing a legal escort for a Black Lives Matter protest – were shot dead by a cop-hating black supremacist? At the memorial, where Obama should have offered comfort to the families, he instead blamed "the system" for being "systemically racist."

The voters remembered. There wasn't too much they could do during those last 4 years. But they could get ready for 2016 – and that's exactly what they did.

The voters remembered Hillary, too.

The "Basket of Deplorables" comment didn't do her any favors. Nor did her ugly record of organizing the "Bimbo Eruptions" war room shutting down women accusing Bill of sexual harassment – especially when she made a big show of playing the woman card as the great defender of women. She came across as more than a little inauthentic. The electorate noticed that Hillary couldn't tell the truth to save her life, even when the lies she told did nothing to benefit her – claiming to have landed in Bosnia under sniper fire, for example, when the historical footage shows young girls handing her flowers as she lands.

The electorate noticed that the same Hillary Clinton who now claims that same-sex marriage should be a Constitutional right held a very different position in 2004:

> I believe that marriage is not just a bond but a sacred bond between a man and a woman. I have had occasion in my life to defend marriage, to stand up for marriage, to believe in the hard work and challenge of marriage. So I take umbrage at anyone who might suggest that those of us who worry about amending the Constitution are less committed to the sanctity of marriage, or to the fundamental bedrock principle that exists between a man and a woman, going back into the mists of history as one of the founding, foundational institutions of history and humanity and civ-

ilization, and that its primary, principle role during those millennia has been the raising and socializing of children for the society into which they are to become adults.[6]

She takes umbrage at anyone who worries that she might amend the Constitution. Umbrage is a strong word. Then she gave the sort of robust defense for traditional definitions of marriage that would later lead to Mozilla Firefox's CEO being thrown out of his job. You'd almost think Hillary has some really rock-ribbed principles there; until her donors drive the winds of change, when we all saw just how quick she was to adjust her sails. Does she have any rock-ribbed principles, other than what the critics have claimed about her dogged pursuit of power and wealth?

She's never seemed to waver on the abortion issue. But even there, she hasn't been entirely straight with us. Either she has always been for "safe, legal, and rare" – as she and Bill framed it during his presidency – or she thinks it should be "on-demand and without apology" like the philosophy driving the Shout Your Abortion crowd, new no-limits state laws concerning abortion, and Virginia Governor Northam's harrowing Infanticide statements (which were almost instantly eclipsed with a Blackface/KKK yearbook scandal).

Is the *real* Hillary Clinton the "safe, legal, and rare" one? Or is it the Hillary Clinton who stood on stage with Cuomo as he announced his new State laws removing all obstacles to third-term abortion?

Throw a couple of big scandals – Benghazi and her missing emails into the mix, where even former FBI Director James Comey testified under oath that Hillary's statements to the

FBI had been lies – and Hillary has a whole lot more than three strikes against her.

After years of marches, city riots, and increasing tension between political and racial factions, having another President go out of her way to drive more wedges between competing groups was not a particularly attractive option. For many Christians, Hillary being the nominee changed the game. The options were no longer Republican or Democrat at that point, so much as Republican, Other, or stay home.

Republicans had seventeen options to choose from. Among them, were the pro-life female CEO of a Fortune 500 company, a black came-up-from-nothing neurosurgeon, together with several well-known GOP politicians, Ted Cruz, Marco Rubio, Bobby Jindal (Rhodes Scholar and son of Indian immigrants), another son of the Bush Dynasty as well as a handful of others. Keen observers would notice that these seventeen contenders do not fit with the "racist, sexist" claims the media loves to paint Republicans with. Each one would have consulted an exploratory committee before running for office to know they've at least got a shot before throwing money away. And still, they ran.

Then came the debates.

One by one, candidates started to stumble or fall away. Carly Fiorina was doing well until she tripped over her own feet. Dr. Carson was indisputably one of the smartest guys in any room he walks into but didn't have the same capacity to rally a crowd that others did. Rubio stepped away from being himself and tried to trade punches with Trump. He wound up looking foolish and destroying himself in the process. Others like Christie and "low-energy Jeb!" just couldn't keep up. In the end, it came down to two contenders. Ted Cruz and Donald J. Trump.

Ted Cruz was a stand-up guy, in the model of traditional by-the-book politics. Donald Trump was an entirely different creature. He was an iconoclast. He didn't care what the "traditional" method of success was. He didn't squeeze himself into any traditional mold. He watched the previous two elections just like the rest of us. He saw how the press chewed up and spit out the last two Republican candidates before him. Playing nice didn't help them any. He didn't run as a gentleman. He ran as a political knife-fighter. He fought to win. Period. He was willing to color outside of the lines to do it. When Trump spoke to the press, it wasn't with a supplicant's timidity. He knew them for the weasels they are and – often as not – he bent them to play by his rules. That was exactly the kind of pushback the Right had been craving for so long. Someone who could hold a hostile media accountable, and shut them down when they behave as the open partisans we all know them to be.

For too long our leaders have been trying to win over the media and the left by moving to the middle and being "nonpartisan"... only to be slapped in the face by those same people when we want them to respect our priorities.

The Right wanted someone who would stand up as a voice for the people who sent him to Washington in the first place ... not to compromise, but to be as aggressive in upholding traditional American values as the Left has been in pushing their agenda.

We'd tried the consensus-builder, the war hero, and the choirboy. Now it was time for a political gladiator. But that was only half the story. It wasn't just what he was fighting against ... but what he was promising to fight *for*. Those little red Make America Great Again hats stood for something. This is the guy who showed up after a flood, meeting the victims in Louisiana and handing out supplies while Obama and Hillary were busy golfing or hanging with their donor-class friends.

He spoke with the gravitas of someone who truly believed in America's natural greatness – the greatness that springs from a free people. He was proud of American institutions. He was proud of our military. He was proud of our flag. He was unafraid to talk about American exceptionalism. He was not going to spend his time in office apologizing to the world for who and what the American people are. These are the kinds of ideas that can unite a country. To bring us together. To unify us in a common purpose – ramping up the economy so that good jobs would be there for people who need them. Respecting our police and prioritizing the rule of law. Recognizing people suffering from opioid addiction and prioritizing solutions to that problem. Recognizing ISIS as a rabid beast needing to be put down, rather than dismissing it as a "J.V. team," and standing by while it spread like cancer across the Middle East.

He identified the various threads that together made America great as a nation and drew them together into one binding cord. America was founded upon ideals of Life, Liberty and the Pursuit of Happiness. The American Dream serves as a magnet that draws people from around the world with the hope of a shot at a better life.

It is an environment that has allowed enormous freedom of artistic expression, musical innovation, scientific advancement, technological revolutions, and medical discoveries while placing few, if any, restrictions on the personal religious views of its citizens. We are once again at an inflection point in history, one many of us old enough to remember the Cold War would never have imagined possible. America is now flirting with Socialism.

Never have President Reagan's words of warning seemed more relevant than now:

> Freedom is never more than one generation away from extinction. We didn't pass it to our children in the bloodstream. It must be fought for, protected, and handed on for them to do the same.[7]

The Left, in the name of such things as "compassion" or "justice" claim theirs is the nobler or more just direction ahead. Some even dare to dress it up in religious terms, as though socialism in history has any history of *not* crushing religion under the sole of its boot.

They even go so far as to scold Christians for pulling a lever for Trump and wearing a MAGA hat, convinced that they can only choose Trump's vision of America over their own by turning their back on every Christian principle.

This book sets out to explain why that isn't just a weak argument, but one that is completely unjustified by every conceivable metric.

The Democrats' Divide and Conquer politics of grievance and victimhood pitting one petty interest against another isn't just a violation of the 10th Commandment, it even fails by the simple principle in Jesus' own words:

And if a kingdom be divided against itself, that kingdom cannot stand. And if a house be divided against itself, that house cannot stand. (Mk. 3:25, KJV)

CHAPTER ONE

God Chooses The Base And Despised To Shame The "Wise"

Doug Giles

The Son of man is come eating and drinking; and ye say, Behold a gluttonous man, and a winebibber, a friend of publicans and sinners!
Luke 7:34, KJV

I n 2015, I read a column on a major conservative news portal I used to write for that told Christians not to vote for Trump, should he win the GOP ticket, because Donald didn't pass the Word of God litmus test. I bet that man feels like a fool now because, after two years of the Reign Of Trump, DJT has become, from a policy and appointment standpoint, the biblical believer's best buddy. Of course, I'm assuming that the "Christian" truly embraces the biblical *weltanschauung*.

Anyway ... The Christian scribe said evangelicals shouldn't support The Donald primarily because Trump mocked the disabled NYT reporter Serge Kovaleski. That, for said writer, was a divine deal breaker.

He also pointed out that Trump was cocky, cheeky, and brag-gadocious and that, my dear brethren, was why he counseled the faithful to not play the Trump card in 2016. The author went on to say that we needed a "statesman" like Winston Churchill which made me spew my dirty Martini all over my dirty MacBook.

Now ... before anyone thinks I'm anti-Churchill, allow me to allay any concerns because I'm a huge Churchill fan and a painting I did of Winston adorns my epic man cave at Casa de Giles. (If you'd like to see my personal Churchill art go to DougGiles.Art. #boom)

The thing that struck me as weird after the columnist trounced Trump for his arrogance, insults and his blistering quips was the Captain Obvious fact that I know of no one on the planet who was more adept and acerbic in their verbal cut-downs of their political opponents than my curmudgeony hero, Sir Winston Churchill.

Matter of fact, Churchill makes Trump look truly measured compared to the way the British bulldog wielded his caustic verbal whip. If you don't believe me give *The Wicked Wit Of Winston Churchill* a cursory glance.

In the aforementioned slim tome, you'll quickly get schooled that the colossal Prime Minister, who crushed Nazis like a narc at a biker party, was also a man who had a laugh-out-loud sense of humor. Much of it was devilish. And God help you if he pointed his verbal guns at you. However, a lot of Winston's mischievous maledictions are lost in his historical/famous sayings, but true Churchill enthusiasts know he was the King Of Cut Downs, jibes, jokes, and aphorisms which were often parlayed at his opponents' expense. And his slams also included his female opponents.

Yep, I know of no other modern "Statesman" like Churchill who was a combination of a great heart, brilliant talent, political savvy, who was ferociously funny and concretely conceited.

Oh, and one more thing, Churchill used to do his dictation naked or, "nekkid," as we say down here in Tejas. I wonder if the hailer of the "Churchill statesman model/Trump's the Devil motif" would be cool with Winston free-ballin' while he's spitballin' his musings to his terrified female secretary who had the displeasure of recording Winston's thoughts while his pink *wienerschnitzel* dangled in the damp British breeze? CNN and Christine Blasey-Ford would have a field day with that nugget, eh?

Anyway, back to the Biblical acid test for Trump because our standard is not Winston but The Wonderful Counselor.

So ... would Jesus dare to choose and use an unsanctified, gruff billionaire, with an epic gold comb-over and a sordid past to right the ship of our great state? Well, little children, we'll have to go to the Book of Books to answer that riddle, won't we?

The short answer is, my dear pearl-clutching NeverTrumpkin inquirer, God has always used the man or the woman whom the self-righteous wouldn't choose, nor even consider.

But God would.

Paul, the apostle, put it this way ...

> *For consider your calling, brethren, that there were not many wise according to the flesh, not many mighty, not many noble; but God has chosen the foolish things of the world to shame the wise, and God has chosen the weak things of the world to shame the things which are strong, and the base things of the world and the despised God has chosen, the things that are not, so that He may nullify the things that are, so that no man may boast before God.* (1 Co. 1:26-29, NASB)

Did you get whom God chooses and why?

Huh?

No?

Read it again *real* slowly.

I'll give you a few extra seconds because reading can be a high hurdle for some nowadays.

Did you re-read it, Dinky?

You did?

Well, good for you.

Before I dissect Paul's text, here's an idea: why don't you print out that scripture and duct tape it to your 'fridge and try to memorize it so when God chooses someone else to do an epic task and they don't fit in your miniscule monochrome mold, the Holy Spirit can bring to remembrance this verse and hopefully it'll make you shut your mouth at a pivotal historical moment, so that you don't sound like an anti-biblical smellfungus who's opposing the person whom God is promoting. Wouldn't that be neat?

Okay, let's get busy and dissect Paul's assessment of the person whom God often chooses and why Jehovah digs shaking up the know-it-alls.

It's clear from 1st Corinthians that Christ calls the bad boy. The one that, according to the powers that be, be not "good enough" according to "them."

It's also crystal clear that God enjoys shaming the "wise" and the "strong." Did you catch that? A loving God *loves* shaming "experts." As in humiliating them. Ouch, baby. Very *ouch*. Indeed, prior to Trump's election, both "the wise and the strong," on The Left and The Right, were mocking Trump and boldly stating that there's no way in Hades he would get elected. Many smarmy and religious conservative "big shots" said he was too stupid, too base, too weak, too unsavvy, too unsavory and poorly politically connected, etc ... and blah, blah to be "worthy" of The White House. They made bold predictions of how he should and would lose. They ridiculed the ground Trump walked on. They labored to derail him. They prophesied his demise and in the final analysis, they were more off-base than Pete Rose on a wild pitch. I laughed on election night and I'm still laughing now at those who were so sure of themselves and their beclouded crystal ball. How these "experts" still have talk shows and are still courted and paid for their opinion on cable news and opinion shows is beyond me. From a punditry standpoint, I'd quit if I were that damn daft.

Especially if I claimed to be a Christian because fundamental to the believer's funky-bottom-line-bass-note is the fact that God *always* chooses the person that'll give the hoity-toity a stroke while he nullifies the things that "are."

Since God loves to shame and quash the experts, He always goes a-lookin' for the man or the woman who the dipsticks think is the least likely to succeed. He said there be not many who are wise, mighty, and noble who do his bidding. But the base? Well, he uses them in abundance.

I know that some of you are thinking this refers only to a person's salvation and not their spiritual calling, purpose, vocation or office and that somehow Christ calls the imperfect to salvation but He only promotes the perfect to places of power. To that sentiment, me and Jesus say, "Uh, no."

Matter of fact, I don't think most of Christendom's biblical protagonists would pass the fussy evangelical muster if we held them to stringent scriptural standards that some Never-Trumpkins applied to Trump in the 2016 election.

For instance: would any of the NeverTrumpkins vote for...

King David. King David was a hot mess. He had seven wives, shagged Bathsheba and then had her husband Uriah murdered. Isn't that special? In addition, he danced nude before the Ark of The Covenant. Every Church Lady pundit on the planet would be caterwauling about all of that crud, eh? Also, can you imagine the field day CNN and the coven of The View would have with that intel? Good Lawd! We'd never hear the end of it. Oh, I almost forgot. David and his boys cut the foreskins off two-hundred Philistines. I wonder what the now-defunct Weekly Standard would think about that? Not very presidential, eh? In addition, before David became the giant-slayer we all now know him to be, nobody and I mean nobody, including the prophet Samuel, thought God would use him and yet, he was God's pick to crush Israel's foes and restore the glory of God back to Zion. Let that sink in a bit. Oh, lastly, this scandalous man, who was used to restore Israel's greatness, and write some of the most amazing, Spirit inspired prayers and songs known to mankind, was written up in Holy Writ as a "man after (God's) own heart" (Acts 13:22). Indeed, The Holy Spirit wrote up this adulterer, conspirator to commit murder and spiritual rapscallion as a God's special boy. Aren't you glad God writes you up in the end instead of some graceless jerkmeister? You are? Me too. Dang it, I nearly forgot to mention that David killed a lion and a bear. That alone is enough for the effeminate fragile amongst us to forever write him off as an "evil hunter who kills Disney characters."

No one would've picked David. But God did. He chooses the foolish things to shame wise. Boom.

Moses. Moses wasn't some squeaky clean, Mitt Romney-like bearded bro from antiquity. Moses was a murderer on the lam, who married a black chick, stuttered like Simple Jack, had a very non-presidential job and massive anger issues. Can you say "deal breaker" for most NeverTrumpkins? Also, Moses was eighty years old when he got God's nod. Do you know any eighty-year-olds? Are they still dreaming? Are they up for becoming Liberator and Lawgiver and the most noted historical figure next to Jesus? Are they jonesing to be the personal emancipator of millions of people? The person who gets to tell the world's most formidable foe that God's going to kill them and their horses? Uh, no. Most eighty-year-olds are trying to remember if they took the right amount of pills this morning, how to get the nude pic of Kim Kardashian off their iPhone's screensaver, where they put their Powerball tickets, and how and when The Grim Reaper's finally gonna rock up with his sickle and transport their soul to the Otherworld. They're not looking for "The Call." They're not on a '"vision quest." They're grabbing onto stair-rails and holding on for dear life and both themselves and others do not believe that God would ever elect them to be The Player to open up the major can of whoop ass on an insidious and implacable enemy.

I bet being chosen by God to lead Israel in their grand exodus was the last thing on Moses' mind. Remember, prior to Moe's call, cries are going forth to God for freedom! I'm sure a lot of dolts were predicting whom would get The Gig as the epic freedom-fighter and I'm equally certain no one was looking at old Moe to mow down Pharaoh and his forces, Moses included.

Let's recap the particulars of the person God chose to free his folks from Pharaoh's phalanges, shall we? Moses was a murderer; a rager; an outlaw; with a crap job; who is old as dirt. There you go, folks. That's who God chose. He's more akin to Whitey Bulger than Billy Graham and yet to God ... he was perfecto. What would be a dealbreaker for the pusillanimous and the fastidious amongst us was no big whoop to God. The choice of Moses looked foolish to all who looked on, even Moses. He wasn't bringing anything of virtue, verve, vision, or talent and tenacity to the table. He's a washed-up old fart. Imagine George Costanza's old man on Seinfeld. However, one encounter with a holy God on one cold and lonely night walking through the wilderness and it was on like Donkey Kong. No one would've picked Moses. But God did. And through this unqualified, washed up old bro he shamed the wise and the mighty and none of "the experts" schlepping this rock back then would've picked him to do it. I wonder if The Trump Haters would've chosen Moe, given his past track record, to lead Israel into freedom and vanquish their foes?

Samson. Question: What if Samson were on the GOP's ticket for the NeverTrumpkins to vote for? Would Samson be "good enough?" Would Sam pass "The Statesman/Character/ True Conservative Test" the NeverTrumpkins foisted and are still foisting upon Trump? Let's dissect Samson's CV, shall we? Let's see ... he dated a hooker, killed Cecil The Lion, and sported dreadlocks. Can you imagine the melee that would ensue should some candidate have this Nazirite's track record? OMG. Scandal aplenty for the punctilious among us. But ... he was God's choice and God's Judge to lead ancient Israel for a time.

Yep, Samson had *serious* issues and yet, he was chosen by God to lead a nation. Let's tumble through Samson's infractions and malfunctions, shall we?

Samson married a Philistine (Jg. 14). That would be akin to Franklin Graham marrying Miley Virus. Can you say, "Not Kosher?" Hello. That would not be "very presidential" for the frozen chosen amongst us. Scandalous, eh? That's the kind of stuff that greases up the D.C. gossip wheels really well. Samson's marriage to the Philistine chick was directly forbidden by the Law of Moses but Samson was like, "eh ... I like the unsaved chicks over church girls, so ... sue me." That's Billy Joel stuff, baby. Oh, I nearly forgot, God was cool with his wife selection. See Jg.14 if you don't believe me.

Samson killed a lion. He killed a lion?! Yes, he killed a lion. Can you imagine the cacophony coming from the pussified

Left and Right if Number Forty-Five shot a lion? Look what The Media(D) did to both Donald Jr. and Eric Trump for hunting non-endangered dangerous game in Africa. They went hashtag, Twitter and Facebook nuts even though the Trump boys' hunt was legal and the meat, plus a big chunk of the money, went to impoverished blacks whom The Left supposedly cares so much about. Oh, by the way, after Samson killed his lion he just left it there to rot and turned its death into a brainteaser for his buddies. How calloused of him, right? Can you picture PETA's outrage? I can hear Don Lemon and Shepard Smith screaming like a female cappuccino machine at the gall of Samson to slay Cecil the Lion and not eat it or at least send its skin over to the Smithsonian to be taxidermied and preserved for viewing by obese, man-titted, adolescent, soy boys who'd never venture out to Africa to see a real lion because it's so scary and it requires walking.

Samson not only slayed Simba but he also "abused foxes." Three-hundred of them, to be exact. What? You never heard that before? Did you miss that story during your, "Aren't We Special," youth group meeting? Look, if The Left went apoplectic over Romney taking his pooch for a ride in a dog crate on the top of his Mormon wood-paneled station wagon they would crap a twenty-eight-pound cinder block over what Samson did to a sleugh of foxes. For the uninitiated, Samson caught 300 foxes and tied their tails together in pairs and then attached torches, yes ... torches, to their bodies and then sent them, burning alive, through The Philistines' vineyards and olive groves, roasting both the foxes and the uncircumcised heathens' livelihood down to the ground. That's Beavis & Butthead stuff, y'all. Would you choose him to be your leader? Would you vote for Samson in 2020? Huh? No? Well, God did back in the day. His ways aren't our ways and His thoughts aren't our thoughts (Is. 55:8, 9).

Between Samson's naughty nuptials and his time with another unwashed broad named Delilah, Samson shagged a Stormy Daniels. Yep, he bumped uglies with a pirate hooker. (Jg. 16:1). Question: would you vote for him after that revelation? Would you say, "Yep! Samson's my boy!" No? Well, God did. God's call remained on this Nazirite even after his dalliances and that's the big difference between you and God. He chooses the base and the corrupt to shame and nullify the "wise."

Samson sucked at keeping trade secrets. He had to tell Delilah where his strength lay.

Samson killed one-thousand people with a donkey's jawbone (Jg. 15:16). Thank God there weren't any smartphones and YouTube around back then because I guarantee that wouldn't replay well on HuffPo.com, eh? Zuckerberg would, no doubt, ban that video and Samson for violating that twit's "rules."

Samson's hairdo was unconventional. If you think Trump has wild hair, Samson had uncut dreadlocks (Jg. 16:13). You could probably smell this Rasta before you could see him. He was a seven braid Bob Marley from antiquity. Surely, God would never ordain such an obtuse man to a position of leadership with such unsavory hair, would he? Yes, he would and yes, he did.

The last mention of Samson. I think it's fascinating how God writes Samson up. Check it out:

> *And what shall I more say? for the time would fail me to tell of Gedeon, and of Barak, and of Samson, and of Jephthae; of David also, and Samuel, and of the prophets: Who through faith subdued kingdoms, wrought righteousness, obtained promises, stopped the mouths*

of lions. Quenched the violence of fire, escaped the edge of the sword, out of weakness were made strong, waxed valiant in fight, turned to flight the armies of the aliens. Women received their dead raised to life again: and others were tortured, not accepting deliverance; that they might obtain a better resurrection: And others had trial of cruel mockings and scourgings, yea, moreover of bonds and imprisonment: They were stoned, they were sawn asunder, were tempted, were slain with the sword: they wandered about in sheepskins and goatskins; being destitute, afflicted, tormented; (Of whom the world was not worthy:) they wandered in deserts, and in mountains, and in dens and caves of the earth. And these all, having obtained a good report through faith, received not the promise: God having provided some better thing for us, that they without us should not be made perfect.
(Heb. 11:32-40, KJV)

In case you missed it, God didn't say diddly squat about all the crap that we get wrapped around the axle about regarding Samson and his sins. God said Samson died in faith, did epic stuff for God and country and is an example of what New Testament believers should aspire towards.

Most religious idiots would focus on Samson's foibles.

God focused on his faith and his finale.

Noah. Here's a question for all the self-righteous, pearl-clutching, dipsticks tongue-wagging Trump's past peccadilloes and previous penchants. What if Trump got wasted and fell down with his balls out for all his family to see? How 'unchristian', eh? Who would trust such an undisciplined lush? Getting so inebriated that you pass out pantless? For those who never heard this story via their lame church let me lay it out for you. Check it out ...

> *Then Noah began farming and planted a vineyard. He drank of the wine and became drunk, and uncovered himself inside his tent. Ham, the father of Canaan, saw the nakedness of his father, and told his two brothers outside. But Shem and Japheth took a garment and laid it upon both their shoulders and walked backward and covered the nakedness of their father; and their faces were turned away, so that they did not see their father's nakedness. When Noah awoke from his wine, he knew what his youngest son had done to him. So he said, "Cursed be Canaan; a servant of servants he shall be to his brothers. He also said, Blessed be the LORD, The God of Shem; And let Canaan be his servant. May God enlarge Japheth, And let him dwell in the tents of Shem; And let Canaan be his servant."*
> (Ge. 9:20-27, NASB)

What did we learn from this nifty Bible nugget, my little children? Well, we learned the following about the man who God chose to save creation from the flood waters.

Noah got drunk.

Noah got naked.

Noah passed out.

Noah's son, Ham, has got a big mouth and is a self-righteous little tattletale and would've probably gone on CNN, if it existed back then, and blathered his pop's drunkenness to every dipstick who liked to listen to gossip and slander.

Noah's other sons wouldn't even look at Noah but instead, they took care of their old man and covered his nakedness.

Noah wakes from his bender and proclaims doom to his gossipy son, Ham. Here's a little ditty worthy of note, namely, God's gifts and callings are without repentance. Noah getting blitzed did not remove the prophetic gift or God's call on the man. Suck on that nugget all you self-righteous gnat strainers.

Noah's son, Ham, was cursed forever for his fault-finding spirit.

Noah's other boys, Shem and Japheth, were blessed forever for covering their dad's faults versus exposing them.

It appears, little kiddies, in this biblical lesson, that Ham's finger pointing was actually worse than Noah's deep love of the fruit of the vine.

Oft times, I wonder when the woodlice attack Trump and others for their bad choices in their past, if God looks down from heaven at such graceless finger pointing and pronounces a similar curse on the person and their offspring who seemed to have forgotten that they too are beset with sins and are in need of mercy, forgiveness, and grace?

Oh, by the way, God wrote up Noah, in the end, as a "preacher of righteousness" (2 Pet. 2:5). The Holy Spirit said nada about him getting wasted and passing out with his junk out. I wonder how you would've written up Noah?

Abraham. Do you need another example of the eccentric and sin beset critters God used because they're thick in the scripture? I know ... let's take another leader lauded by the big three religions namely ... Abraham. Everyone knows and loves old Abe. However, if Abraham were held to the NeverTrumpkins' standards of "statesmen-like worthiness" this cat would crash and burn like Hillary trying to juggle bobcats while working a seven-foot-tall unicycle after downing six Mexican martinis. Succinctly, Abraham was a liar and a coward, who had sex with his maid, who scoffed at God, who had no problem stabbing his son after hearing voices, who was old as dirt and had a nephew who had an affinity for cities that celebrated sodomy. In other words, he was just like a Kennedy.

Let's take the aforementioned apart one by one, shall we?

Abraham was a liar. What did ole Abe fib about? Well, he lied about being married to his wife, twice (Ge. 12:11-13; 20:1-2, 5)! That's not very presidential, is it? I wonder what CNN would do with that scandalous revelation? Would the Gang of 22 NeverTrumpkins draft an intricate blog about Abraham's proclivity to prevarication and, ergo, that's why he should be shunned like the sit-up bench at Rosie O'Donnell's house?

Abraham was a coward. The reason Abraham lied about being married to Sarah was he was scared Pharaoh would kill him, so he told his wife he was going to sell her out, give her to Pharaoh, and tell King Tut Sarah is his frickin' sister. Wow. Oh, and pardon my redundancy, he did that *twice*. Like in, one-two, times. Once with Pharaoh and again with King Abimelech. That's *House of Cards* crap, right there, folks. HuffPo and National Review would have a field day with that juicy McNugget.

Abraham had sex with his maid (Ge. 16). In Genesis 12, God promised old man Abraham that, via his equally old wife's dusty baby-maker, that he was going to birth nations. After eleven years of nada, Abraham and Sarah, not seeing the promise of birthing nations fulfilled, decided, like good sinners, to take things into their own hands and make stuff happen because God can be oh-so-slow sometimes, right? Their motivations moved from waiting on the Lord to, "God helps those who help themselves." So, at Sarah's behest, Abe boinks their Egyptian maid, Hagar, and the rest is Middle-Eastern mayhem history. By the way, when Sarah suggested that Abraham bump uglies with their female personal assistant, Abraham didn't protest. He didn't say, "Get thee behind me Satan!" Oh, no. He went full *coitus maximus* with Hagar and she got preggers. Arnold Schwarzenegger, you see, isn't the only one who tapped his hired help and had an illegit son. Abraham preceded him by several thousand years with that bad idea.

Abraham scoffed at God (Ge. 17:17; 18:10-12). This pooh-poohing of God's promise is also called, "unbelief." and unbelief is a Texas-sized sin. I know it doesn't get the press that the "more vile" vices do, but according to the scripture, it's huge. It makes God a liar (1 Jn. 5:10). Dang, eh? What did he scoff at God about? Well, God said, through Abe and Sarah, who were 99 and 90 respectively, that they would figure in greatly in populating the planet, essentially. This is way before Viagra and Cialis and it wasn't normal back then for dusty sex organs to make babies at the near century mark. So, when God said brace yourself, you're going to have a baby, Abraham and Sarah said, "yeah ... right."

Abraham had no problem with the thought of stabbing his son after hearing voices (Ge. 22:1-18). Anti-Trump Anti-theists would have a field day with this ditty. Imagine if President Trump was caught sneaking out of the West Wing with

Barron and a machete in tow and the Fake News champions, CNN, intercepted him en route to the sacrifice? "So, where are you going Mr. Trump?" "Well, I'm off to sacrifice my son Barron because God told me to." "Really? God told you to off your kid? How long have you been speaking directly with God and hearing voices telling you to filet your child?" The Twitterverse would melt down overnight. Don Lemon would pass out from hyperventilating that Trump must be Baker Acted. Rachel Maddow would go hoarse screaming, "25th Amendment! 25th Amendment!" In addition to that melee, Sam Harris would devote an entire week of podcasts highlighting how weird Trump is for a). Thinking he's actually talking to God. b). That "God" would want him to sacrifice his son. And c). That Trump, like Abe, was like, "Okay. No problemo."

Abraham was old as dirt. I love it when those beset with Trump Derangement Syndrome talk about how old Trump is (72) and he's losing/lost his mind. It's especially amusing to me in light of the fact that Bernie Sanders who, at this writing, is 77, Pelosi's 78, and Biden's 76 and all three of them are nuttier than a squirrel turd. And yet, "Trump's too old?!?" Abraham was 75 when he began his calling, 86 when Ishmael was sired, and 100 when Isaac popped out of Sarah's 90-year-old womb. Evidently, age ain't no big thang, either young or old, when God picks a leader.

All the aforementioned glaring foibles from the Father of our Faith, if fixated upon, would be a bridge-too-far for the religiously fastidious amongst us. "Why, Beauregard ... we can't support an old cowardly leader that lies about his wife, shags and impregnates his maid, scoffs at God and hears voices that want him to slay his only son. That's not statesmanly. That's not cricket. He's not the man we need to forge a path to greatness." The way the anti-Trump pundits blast the president's past you can bet your ass *Morning Joe* would be grinding a Paul Bunyan-sized axe against Abe's various harmatiological hang-ups. But God didn't. Matter of fact, in the apostle Paul's Holy Spirit inspired homage to the old man in Romans chapter four, Paul mentions *nada* about Abe's blunders. But he does deep dive into the man's faith and tenacity when cards were ridiculously and deeply stacked against him. Check it out. Of Abraham, Pablo says ...

Abraham believed God, and it was credited to him as righteousness. (Ro. 4:3, 5, 9)

Abraham is the father of all who believe. (Ro. 4:11)

Abraham believed God gives life to the dead and calls into being that which does not exist. (Ro. 4:17)

Abraham, in hope against hope he believed, so that he might become a father of many nations according to that which had been spoken, "So shall your descendants be." (Ro. 4:18)

Abraham, without becoming weak in faith, he contemplated his own body, now as good as dead since he was about a hundred years old, and the deadness of Sarah's womb; yet, with respect to the promise of God, he did not waver in unbelief but grew strong in faith, giving glory to God. (Rom. 4:19, 20)

Abraham was fully assured that what God had promised, He was able also to perform. (Ro. 4:21)

Therefore it was also credited to him as righteousness. Now not for his sake only was it written that it was credited to him, but for our sake also, to whom it will be credited, as those who believe in Him who raised Jesus our Lord from the dead,

He who was delivered over because of our transgressions, and was raised because of our justification. (Ro. 4:22-25)

So what did we learn, little kiddies, about father Abraham? Did he screw up? Yep. Did he let that keep him from moving forward? Nope. Stupid and petty humans only focus on one's jacked up past and present. God, on the other hand, wants to know if you'll believe when it seems like you got a snowball's chance in Miami of accomplishing what He's called you to.

Paul said this man, this very flawed man, didn't become weak in faith, didn't waver in unbelief, but grew strong in faith and had hope *against* hope. I wonder if all the pearl-clutching NeverTrumpkins can be thusly characterized? I doubt it. Oh yeah. Here's an aside: I wonder if Trump's critics could hold up to the same scrutiny they're laying on Trump for his past Trumpness? I doubt it. But I digress. Back to Abraham.

Paul was fascinated by this flawed critter and how he cracked the code way before Moses and his buddy Peter graced the scene. Paul didn't even mention what The Daily Mail would solely focus on, mainly, Abraham's mistakes.

Look folks, Trump could heal the blind, walk on water and turn clay pigeons into mourning doves, and those beset with Trump Derangement Syndrome (TDS) would blame him for putting braille publishers, bridge-builders, and skeet ranges all out of business. There's no pleasing them that be bedeviled with TDS.

As stated, there are some who claim "piety keeps them from supporting a character like Trump with such a naughty past." What I would like to ask them is if they would've chosen King David, Moses, Samson, Noah or Abraham as a leader of their nation after their deep dives into the superfluity of naughtiness? For those who have short term memory problems, here's a succinct synopsis of the scandalous acts of the five dudes we just scanned, of whom God chose to lead His people.

Marrying seven women. I said, seven.

Committing adultery.

Conspiracy to commit murder.

Trying to hide your adultery and murder.

Dancing naked during a worship service.

Cutting the foreskins off 200 of your enemy's penises.

Killing a lion and a bear.

Murder.

Running from the Law.

Having sex with a hooker.

Marrying a pagan.

Wearing dreadlocks.

Killing a lion and leaving it to rot.

Murdering 1000 people with the lower mandible of a donkey simply because they don't hold your view of God.

Lighting 300 foxes on fire.

Burning an olive grove to the ground.

The inability to keep trade secrets.

Extreme inebriation to the point of passing out nude.

Lying about being married, twice.

Giving your wife to another man, twice.

Cowardice.

Hearing voices.

Pulling a knife on your son with intent to kill him because a "voice" told you to.

Scoffing at the promises of God.

Committing adultery with your housekeeper and getting her knocked up.

That's just the sins of five of God's elected leaders, ladies and gents. I could literally write a big book on the blunders God's people committed before-during-and-after their call to kick butt for Him and mankind. Indeed, the list could go on and on regarding the massive unholy incongruities of fallen men and women, both redeemed and damned, whom God utilized to shake and shape nations for his righteous purposes. Their sinful pasts and current cruddy conditions, when called, obviously wasn't that big of a deal to God because he worked with them and through them and he forgave when they were repentant.

It's all about grace folks, in salvation and in our spiritual vocation. If you want God to be merciful to you, then you should be merciful to others and that includes Trump. If you don't understand that, then that's your problem. I have neither the time, desire, nor the crayons to further explain it to you.

I'll never forget seeing a Crisco-sweating, obese minister on Facebook deride Trump for his multiple marriages and his past penchants as he stood aghast over the possibility that the president might've shagged Stormy Daniels or Karen Mc-Dougal a decade ago. They were shocked. Shocked, I tell you! Me? Well ... I'm not. I'm like, "What did you expect from a billionaire Playboy, you daft idiot?" In addition, I'm sitting there thinking, "Hey Jabba, if you were an unsaved, sixty-year-old Richie Rich and had porn stars and Playboy bunnies sticking their boobs into your triple chinned melon-head do you think you could resist?" I doubt it. I'm 99.9% sure I don't think I'd be able to traverse those dicey rapids without jumping in head first and butt-naked. I think it's convenient for this particular bloated evangelical to feign outrage at Trump's sins when no one wants to sleep with him because he's ugly, broke, fat, drives a crap car, and smells like Cool Ranch Doritos. Oh, by the way, gluttony is a sin, chunky butt. Google it if you don't believe *moi*.

For the Leftist, who makes zero claims to personal saintliness being the basis of their bellicosity towards Trump, ask them if they equally grill their glory boys and girls with the same merciless scrutiny they've given The Donald? I doubt they do. Matter of fact, I know they don't because we've been covering the quadruple standards they've been affording their reps

36

for several years, equating 250 Million page-views, over at my website, ClashDaily.com. Just look at how they don't say shizzle about Hillary's high crimes and misdemeanors. That old chick could stand butt-naked on top of The Pope, while screaming aloud the contents of *Mein Kampf,* as she drank blood from the slit throat of the last Tasmanian Tiger and CNN would call her "America's *zeitgeist* ... a poet of extraordinary talent."

Oh, crap. What is wrong with me? I forgot about God's favorite leader, the man, Christ Jesus. I seriously doubt many today would vote for Him because He definitely was not politically correct. He roasted evil politicians and religious leaders; called them wicked names, and lambasted the lovelies of His day and even called a woman a dog. Can you imagine what the harpies on *The View* would do with that one?

Bottom line: good luck finding Mr., Ms., Miss, or Mrs. Perfect when voting for president or looking for a leader for any station in life, you dipstick. If they're human ... they're sinners and sinners, last time I checked, sin. So, shut the front door on who someone has or hadn't boinked twenty-years ago and focus, primarily, on whether or not said Presidential candidate has a high view our founding docs. Duh.

Personally, I think Christians who are groping for a good "Christian candidate" according to their politically correct, neutered, self-righteous, and totemic standards are silly. I believe the last "good evangelical" candidate that evangelicals got giddy over was the squeaky clean Jimmy Carter. How'd that work out for you?

No, what I'm looking for is some quasi-decent person who loves our Constitution and our original intent.

Yes, I want a leader who can convince me that they revere our founding docs, they'll keep us secure, jack up our economy, plug our porous borders and bounce our enemies into a fiery hell. Call me a simple man. And if he or she doesn't perform according to what they promised us, I'll devote my voice and pen to keeping them out of office.

CHAPTER TWO

Evangelical NeverTrumpkins Said Trump Would "Flip-Flop" Once Elected. They Were Wrong

Brandon Vallorani

"But what do you think? A man had two sons, and he came to the first and said, 'Son, go, work today in my vineyard.' He answered and said, 'I will not,' but afterward he regretted it and went. Then he came to the second and said likewise. And he answered and said, 'I go, sir,' but he did not go. Which of the two did the will of his father?"
They said to Him, "The first."
Jesus said to them, "Assuredly, I say to you that tax collectors and harlots enter the kingdom of God before you."
Matthew 21:28-31, NKJV

D onald J. Trump is a man who – between the time he registered as a Republican in 1987 until registering as a Republican (again) in 2012 – has changed his party affiliation a total of five times. In 1999 it was to join the Independence Party of New York, in 2001 he joined the Democrats, in 2009 it was Republican, in 2011 it was "no party affiliation" and finally in 2012, he was back to the Republicans.

It should come as no surprise, then, when Conservatives doubted whether he could ever be the standard-bearer for the entire Republican Party. More than a few people wondered if even Trump himself really knew what he stood for. Others didn't bother with the wondering, they went straight to the accusations.

Some of his old interviews didn't help win the skeptics over to his cause, either. There was, for example, one interview with Wolf Blitzer in 2004.

> "In many cases, I probably identify more as Democrat," Trump told CNN's Wolf Blitzer in a 2004 interview. "It just seems that the economy does better under the Democrats than the Republicans. Now, it shouldn't be that way. But if you go back, I mean it just seems that the economy does better under the Democrats. ... But certainly we had some very good economies under Democrats, as well as Republicans. But we've had some pretty bad disaster under the Republicans."[8]

Going back further still, and raising greater alarm bells was when he had a very different answer on the abortion question than the one he has now. "I am very pro-choice," Trump told NBC's Tim Russert back in 1999. "I hate the concept of abortion. I hate it. I hate everything it stands for. I cringe when I listen to people debating the subject. But you still – I just believe in choice."

Back in those days, Trump was so close to the pro-choice movement that he co-sponsored a dinner for the president emeritus of the National Abortion Rights Action League at the Plaza hotel, which he owned at the time. This seems an unlikely beginning for someone who cast himself as a hard-charging Republican President. It became a case of, "Will the *real* Donald Trump please stand up."

Have Trump's convictions really shifted that much over time? Was he just not giving much thought to certain political issues before now, and giving off-the-cuff answers? Was this the coy answer of yet another greasy politician with an instinct for which babies he'll have to kiss when it's time to get out the vote? Was it all for show? Is he just a pragmatist saying what needs to be said? Or is this the Trump we really would get if we elect him? It left people wondering – who are we actually getting here? But that wasn't even the whole question. We all know he's very keen on the deals he makes. What happens if the Democrats get hold of the levers of power and they try to threaten, flatter or otherwise convince him to defect to their way of thinking on this issue or that ... can he be trusted to hold his ground, seeing how recently he's started standing on it?

Later, in 2018, when Nancy got her mitts on that gavel again, that question became tested in real life as Republicans looked on nervously to see exactly how he would interact with the new divided Congress. Would he drift to the center, or would he take the same strong stands? Is he a guy who has your back in a fight? Or will he defect if someone gives him a better offer?

The Washington Post ran a story about a year into his presidency – just after the Stoneman Douglas shooting – saying that the Democrats' new strategy on gun control would include "flattering Trump on TV."

It didn't help that he was a political neophyte, either. He had no political track record to which he could point. We had only the word of a guy who tends to, shall we say, make embellishments to the story when it suits him. Because so much was riding on this, there was a real sense of uncertainty. Sure, he's a strong showman, a great fighter, and he's talking about some great ideas with his Make America Great Again agenda ... but what happens when he actually *goes* to Washington. Does he get sucked in like so many others? Is it better to go with Ted, the known entity and proven politician?

Looking back at politics over the last few decades, is it any wonder people are gun-shy about a politician's real motives? Let's look at a few other people we've sent to Washington.

There was this one guy, he was a relative newcomer to politics, a Senator for Illinois. He blew into Washington on promises of being winsome, transparent, and generally beneficial to Americans from sea to shining sea. So convinced of his own virtue was he that he proclaimed that his election would be the point from which they would claim the waters began to recede and the Earth began to heal. Maybe you've heard of him.

He came to the White House in 2008 with zero mandate to redefine marriage – he even claimed to associate with the traditional views on the topic – but in just a few short years he wasn't just splashing the White House in rainbow colors to celebrate a Supreme Court decision, but threw the nation into a debate about transsexual bathroom use. That wasn't all.

He also had some really off-putting religious tics. As someone who attended the racist church of Jeremiah Wright for decades, Obama identified in some loose, utilitarian definition of the word as a "Christian." But you'd never know it by comparing how he treated Islam and Christianity.

Islam, for example, could do no wrong in his eyes. He walked on eggshells around terror attacks, desperate to find some other explanation for why a jihadi would murder innocents in cold blood. Referring to the horrific 2009 Fort Hood Islamic terror attack as "workplace violence" was among the more cynical of his dodges. He gave a bizarre mandate to NASA, according to their top official. Mr. Bolden said:

> "When I became the NASA administrator, he [Mr. Obama] charged me with three things. One, he wanted me to help reinspire children to want to get into science and math; he wanted me to expand our international relationships; and third, and perhaps foremost, he wanted me to find a way to reach out to the Muslim world and engage much more with dominantly Muslim nations to help them feel good about their historic contribution to science, math, and engineering." He added: "It is a matter of trying to reach out and get the best of all worlds, if you will, and there is much to be gained by drawing in the contributions that are possible from the Muslim [nations].[9]

Then, days after Benghazi, he stood in front of the UN and said, "the future must not belong to those who slander the prophet of Islam."

But where was the "Cool clock, Mohamed" guy when it came to Christianity? He routinely insulted Christians: "They get bitter, they cling to guns or religion"... he used the occasion of the National Prayer Breakfast to invoke the Crusades ... he tried to throw the homeschooling Romeike family out of the country *after* the American courts had decided they qualified for religious asylum from a hostile secular nation ... and of course, he took nuns to court over birth control.

As for that pen and phone of his? He used it to not only circumvent Constitutional spheres of authority with his open-borders policy towards DREAMers, but he went against every public statement he had made as a Senator about the importance of secure borders and legal immigration.

What about George W. Bush? He was a consensus-builder who didn't ever seem to figure out that his party was the only one ever crossing the aisle over domestic issues.

Remember McCain? After Dubya was considered too "extreme" to do well in another election, we went with a "moderate" with a pedigree as a War Hero. That courage and character was all well and good in the privation and pain of a POW cell, but it takes a different kind of courage in the midst of comfort, privilege, and acclaim. He was a man who was prone to petulant grudges and put his own grievances before those he was elected to represent; going so far as to become the deciding vote against his own solemn campaign promise just so he could "stick it" to the President.

No wonder McCain was the willing accomplice Comey & Co. would use to give an air of "bipartisanship" and legitimacy to the bogus, salacious Steele Dossier. "Mr. Integrity" got played and we all paid the price. In the end, did he even step aside so that another Senator could faithfully uphold the duties of office when his illness was in its final stages? Or did he stubbornly and uselessly remain in office for personal and selfish reasons? And to think we might have made this man president.

You could go on down the list. Romney is as likely to stab you in the back as look at you. All of the Bushes sided against Trump, some even voted for Hillary. What about some of the Tea Party members who pledged to drain the swamp, only to become denizens of it? Who could forget the sad display of the aptly-named Jeff Flake? He wrote an anti-Trump book while in office and used his position on the Judiciary Committee to personally block the advancement of 21 judicial nominations and 32 confirmations – nominations including vacancies on the 9th Circuit. He blocked them because he wanted Congress to usurp Article II Presidential powers and make it illegal for Trump to fire Mueller. Everyone not named Flake might notice that for all his bluster and contempt for the investigation, the President has never once blocked it. Don't shed any tears for Flake, though. That former "Tea Partier" got his 30 pieces of silver and a new job. He's working for CBS.

There have been plenty of supposedly "authentic" Republicans that have fallen over and slid into the swamp ... what's to say the Johnny-come-lately who stepped off that escalator and into the public fray would fare any better?

When he was campaigning, it was at least partly just a gut-check. Do you think this guy really means what he says, or not? Does he really care about America and the preservation of its institutions or not? Will he be swayed and pressured by public opinion or not?

There is one "yuge" advantage he has over all the other guys – he owes nobody any favors or debts of gratitude for having made him the man he is in the political world. He won despite the best efforts and interests of many big players in the donor class, not because of them. His connection was to the people themselves. You saw that at the rallies. You saw it again when the floods hit Louisiana during the campaign. Hillary was visiting donors and telling other people where and how to give their money, but Trump took his own cash, filled an 18-wheeler with supplies, donated $100k of his own money, and personally met with the people in the affected region. At his rally later that day, he challenged Obama to get off the golf course and go visit them.

The voters in their red MAGA hats attending those enormous rallies obviously felt confident that he really meant what he said.

Even before he took office, there was another way we could measure his credibility. All you need to do is take a good look at the things he was saying. Was Donald Trump saying things that are easy and non-controversial? Yeah, he's a real shrinking violet. Of course not! People liked him because he didn't say *safe* things. For instance, after years of cynical politicians trying to be religiously neutral, he went out of his way to mention spiking the Johnson Amendment. It isn't something that would endear him to the more secular regions of America at all, and he didn't have to go there – other Republican Presidents hadn't – but this was an issue worth sticking his neck out over.

Once in office, what did he do, hold the line or tack to the center in the name of "bipartisanship"?

If there was ever a window for him to move to the center, that bridge was burned early on by the "literally Hitler" crowd on the left, who were lying and disparaging him at every turn. Even before he took office, people in his inner circle had been put under surveillance and had been illegally unmasked.

He was picked for the job of President partly to disrupt the old boys' network of the swamp and partly because they figured he had enough steel in his spine and cojones to actually hear and act on the demands of the base, instead of doing what some play-it-safe insider donor-class expected of him.

We were tired of electing people on Conservative platforms who governed with Purple Policies. It was time for a conservative who would *act* like a conservative. They chose as their representative, a billionaire in a red trucker's hat. And you know what? That gamble paid dividends.

He's governed as the most consistently conservative President since Ronald Reagan. He is the guy who stood up in a State of the Union speech and dropped the gauntlet against the rise of socialism.

He is the guy who ripped up the Iran agreement.

He is the guy who pulled out of the "non-binding" Paris Accord and *still* led a country that did a better job of reducing various emissions than other signatory countries because of the good work of our *private* sector, without resorting to any federal government arm-twisting.

He is the guy who has nominated a string of Originalist judges who will – depending on the district – slow or even stop the trend of activist judges chipping away at our laws. Not to mention the rebalancing of the Supreme Court that happened under his watch, with what is being called the first Republican-friendly SCOTUS in at least 50 years.

He has been as rock-ribbed as they come on the issue of abortion, taking that issue head-on, even more robustly than his Republican predecessors. Not bad for a guy who was panned for being pro-choice. He's even showcasing the difference between his pro-life position and the Left's new aggressively pro-abortion stand that extends right to the moment of birth. (Or, if you're the Democrat Governor from Virginia with that blackface/KKK photo in his yearbook, even later than that.)

We were tired of electing people on Conservative platforms who governed with Purple Policies. It was time for a conservative who would act like a conservative.

Look at some of Trump's other priorities. Conservatives have long said that Red Tape is an enormous drag on our economy and hamstrings business. How many Republicans who gave lip service to that issue actually DID something about it? Trump specifically directed that any new federal law that goes on the books must be balanced by at least two old ones coming off. This is one of many changes he's initiated to get government out of the way of individuals and businesses.

He is reducing taxes, reducing the burden of the government on the shoulders of its citizens so that they can put their money in priorities of their own choosing. As a result of this change, we are seeing employment growth numbers we have never seen even among some of the most vulnerable groups in our nation. This includes women, ethnic minorities, and those with disabilities. Folks with criminal histories or limited experience are getting opportunities they may not have had in poorer economies because of this increased demand for able workers.

His domestic policy has focused, among other things, on cracking down on opioid dealers, including dishonest doctors and pharmacists.

He's pushed all his chips in on the issue of securing the border – that's the first time he's needed to invoke his veto prerogative.

His foreign policy has been very proactive. His first trip abroad was not – as in Obama's case – an apology tour. It was a trip that pointedly visited Riyadh, Jerusalem, and the Vatican before heading to Belgium, the head of the EU.

It's too early to say for sure what will eventually happen in North Korea. But here's what we can say: some hostages were returned, the remains of some soldiers have been repatriated. The tensions between North and South have been eased, and we've gone more than a year since the last missile test or threat of a strike. All the critics who said Trump was ginning up a war ... were wrong. Those who said he would fail by giving away the store to Kim ... were wrong. Then they covered by saying Trump had "failed" when he walked away from the bargaining table ... even though there was no change conceded in the leverage he's got on the sanction side. In the meantime, he is using his own particular skill-set developed over time – that of a negotiator in one-on-one dealings to push for non-violent settlement of disagreement.

When a show of force is needed, he'll drop a MOAB and drive the point home, or drop an air strike in Syria when they'd crossed the red line that Obama described but never enforced. But mainly, he is using *non*-military means of projecting American political power. He is using things like trade negotiations and sanctions to get the attention of foreign nations. And isn't that what a good leader *ought* to do when it's still an option on the table?

When an opportunity arises to reduce or withdraw an American military presence, Trump looks carefully at that option, preferring to take our troops home when we can. Say whatever you like about his Twitter talk and blustery rhetoric, when you're looking at his actual promises, even acknowledging the pushback he sometimes got from his own party, he's pulled every lever at his disposal to deliver on those promises. Compared to the shysters who run on what they think you want to hear and then do the opposite, did President Trump hold true to his conservative pledges in these first two years? I think his record is quite clear.

CHAPTER THREE

Is Trump's Politically Incorrect Crassness Biblical?

Doug Giles

*Jesus went away from there, and withdrew into the district of
Tyre and Sidon. And a Canaanite woman from that region
came out and began to cry out, saying, "Have mercy on me,
Lord, Son of David; my daughter is cruelly demon-possessed."
But He did not answer her a word. And His disciples came
and implored Him, saying, "Send her away, because she keeps
shouting at us." But He answered and said, "I was sent only to
the lost sheep of the house of Israel." But she came and began
to bow down before Him, saying, "Lord, help me!" And He
answered and said, "It is not good to take the children's bread
and throw it to the dogs." But she said, "Yes, Lord; but even
the dogs feed on the crumbs which fall from their masters'
table." Then Jesus said to her, "O woman, your faith is great;
it shall be done for you as you wish."
And her daughter was healed at once.*
Matthew 15:21-28, NASB

Can you imagine if Jesus were here today, in bodily form, and He floated that "dog" insult to a hurting female minority in our "woke," hashtag, immediately offended 21st-century social media milieu?

Holy crap.

Today's online lynch mob would expedite His crucifixion, PDQ. There'd be no three-year earthly ministry after He played that derisive dig.

Maybe three months.

Tops.

For certain, the keyboard-ragers would demand that God, The Father, fire Him immediately from being Lord and Savior and require Jesus to spend at least a twelve-month stint being re-educated at The Syrophoenician School Of Sensitivity before He's ever allowed to show His face again, and that would be on Oprah where He'd trip over Himself apologizing to the planet with a sad, "Michael Cohen before Congress," look upon His face. Right after that, He would then have to forever prove that He's officially one of the woke by starting a 501(c)3 organization with Alyssa Milano that provides shelter, Sloppy Joe's, and free exorcisms for Syrophoenician women who have kids who're full of the devil.

Yep, I think today's Thought Police would swallow their whistle, hyperventilating, trying to blow "foul, foul, foul" at The Nazarene if He were to launch that verbal missile at some needy female minority who's currently cruisin' this blue marble.

For giggles, let's breakdown Matthew's take on one of The Son of God's most "shocking insults."

Jesus, after rebuking the spiritually blind religious leaders and having to deal with His daft disciples (Mt. 15:1-20), looks for a place to chill and bumps into a non-Jewish lady screaming for Him to cast demons out of her daughter who's acting like Miley Cyrus.

The lady cries out for mercy and Jesus, seemingly, blows her off.

Jesus' boys tell Him to get rid of her because she's making too much noise.

Jesus then informs the lady that He's not dolling out favors for her kind but for Jews only.

The woman, undaunted at His rebuff, presses in for His help. At this juncture, Jesus jabs her with the dog jibe ... "It is not good to take the children's bread and throw it to the *dogs*."

Strangely, the lady didn't call TMZ or go on Twitter and Face-book and report a "hate crime" and hashtag the MeToo movement for support. What she did do was extend His riddle by replying, "Yes, Lord; but even the dogs feed on the crumbs which fall from their masters' table" and walked off impressing Christ with her answer and in turn, He healed her kid.

No matter how theologians and pastors try to clean this text up, the fact remains that sweet and cuddly Jesus called this chick a dog. A vomit-eating, crotch-licking, butt-sniffing dog.

Dogs, back in Jesus' day, weren't these bedazzled, four-legged accoutrements the *Real Housewives of Orange County* carry to the bar nowadays when they go get wasted with their abhorrent buddies.

Nope, dogs weren't worshipped in ancient times. Nobody back then gave a crap about a one-eyed, lonely and hungry, cold dog that needed rescuing even if Sarah McLachlan tried to guilt trip them into adopting one by crooning, *In the arms of the angel*. Matter of fact, in the Old Testament ...

Smacking a dog was quasi-normative (1 Sam. 17:43; Prov. 26:17).

Dogs in the OT were like turkey buzzards, in that they didn't mind at all scarfing down dead bodies (1 Ki. 14:11; 16:4; 21:19, 23-24; 22:38; 2 Ki. 9:10, 36).

Ergo, calling someone a dog was not flattering (Ex. 22:31; Dt. 23:18; 1 Sam. 24:14; 2 Sam. 3:8; 9:8; 2 Ki. 8:13; Prov. 26:11; Eccl. 9:4).

In addition, in the New Testament, calling one a dog equated to being considered one of El Diablo's buddies (Phil. 3:2; Rev. 22:15).

So, why did I pick this text to display Christ's crassness? Well, it's principally because everyone gets Jesus laying into the Pharisees, crooked politicians or His disciples when they were acting the fool, but not Him busting the chops of a needy female foreigner. That's not very "Christ-like" according to our politically correct culture that's been cowed by, and now beholden to, the grievance industry.

Here's a mega-dose of reality for all of you who're trying to turn Jesus into a non-offensive bearded lady.

When Jesus Christ got injected into the human mix two thousand plus years ago, from the cradle to the cross, He was a lightning rod of controversy. His incarnation heated up the culture war more than Trump could ever dream of doing.

Immanuel's arrival upon the scene caused-demon inspired political idiots to try to kill Him while He was still cooing and pooping in His pampers. The dragon no likey his party getting ruined -- and ruin it the Prince of Peace did.

The initial message the Wonderful Counselor preached, according to Dr. Luke's take, ticked off the crowd He was addressing so thoroughly that they attempted to throw Him off a cliff. He nailed that haughty mob for the crud they were practicing—and He did so publicly. That, too, is not very "Christian" of our "Nicer-than-Christ" 21st-century Jesus.

In reality (on this planet), Jesus received minimal accolades. No lucrative gigs with the Premier Speakers Bureau; no "isn't He so nice let's put Him on Oprah" invite; no fat, Creflo Dollar-like honorariums; no limousine chariot services. He got *nada* and, for those who haven't seen *The Passion of the Christ* yet, it got even rougher.

Today in our radically pussified, politically correct state of bland, we won't embrace this Jesus because He'd so get under our skin. And we like our skin. The truth of the matter is that what Jesus said and did caused more discomfort to man's me-monkey human spirit than cheap Tequila and three bags of pork rinds drenched in hot sauce would to Gwyneth Paltrow's colon.

It's funny that a bunch of churchgoers who "worship" Jesus probably wouldn't hire Him to be their pastor today because He was too much of a hellrazer. His solid/acidic, anti-*bovine scatology* posture toward politicians, priests, pet sins, oppressors, and others who were playing games with God and man, equates to a résumé that most pastoral search committees wouldn't touch with a ten-foot pew.

Y'know, most of us forget the above when we see sweet baby Jesus lying in a manger during Christmas time. Because of our rank illiteracy regarding scripture, our prejudiced and politically correct approach to the Bible that's custom-tailored a Christ of our own imaginations, we have developed a deep distaste for anything but a bespoke and neutered little "g" god.

Yep, the creation of a feckless, Lysol-disinfected, Jesus of our own imagination who, supposedly, mollycoddles all of humanity (even if they're blatant liars) makes us stand aghast and clutch our pearls when Trump slams CNN, Jim Acosta or Rosie O'Donnell even though he stands on solid biblical ground when it comes to blasting bullshit artists.

WWJD, indeed.

Look, when whiners wince over Trump's epic takedowns, especially NeverTrumpkin evangelicals, and decry them as "untoward," I'm like, "have you guys never noticed the weighty, satirical, and hilarious modes of communication Jesus and other biblical badasses employed?" They roasted people, folks. A literate myopic cyclops, who's given *verbum Dei* a mere cursory glance, can see that.

As I see it, much of the clergy, the church, Christian music, and Christian literature have become pathetically soft and have lost their holy verbal punch. This, in turn, is causing our nation to go down the crapper and souls to be forever lost because we've lost or tossed away the Christ-like, prophetic art of what The Puritans called, "Plain Dealing."

If you don't think the church is becoming politically correct then take this challenge: From now on when you read the scripture, pay close attention when you land on a chunk of text in which Moses, Joshua, David, Elijah, Jeremiah, Ezekiel, John the Baptist, Paul or Jesus is engaged in dialogue with a corrupt impenitent politician, an idiotic idolater, a pompous Pharisee or a vacillating vixen. You won't see these searing saints doling out nicety-nice stuff 24/7/365. Nope, they'll be challenging, oft times ridiculing, the very ground the impenitent unbeliever or the feigned professor stands on. Not only that, you will rarely see God's holy ones repenting of the verbal invectives they have aimed at their audience's willful blindness.

Concerning these greatest of biblical characters, we not only see amazing acts of compassion toward the repentant; we also see an unapologetic verbal "gloves-off" approach with someone God wants and needs His spokesman to offend. These Holy Spirit inspired men of the Bible were godly figures of great antagonism who insisted on battling bogus belief systems and telling the truth, frequently at the expense of a person's person. And get this: It was God who egged His vessels on to give offense. Give it – it's a gift.

The greats of the Bible excelled not only at biblical insight and break-through-to-the-other-side intercession; they also had a wry wit about them that God didn't mind at all. In fact, He joyfully endorsed and eternally preserved it in the canon of scripture for future generations to read and chuckle over.

From a communication standpoint, the prophets, patriarchs, warriors and wildmen of scripture were more like sandpaper than a wet wipe to society's soft little bottom. Many of our biblical heroes, especially the emcees of the various main events, were holy smartasses – mental and spiritual heavy-weights with a verbal whip that they didn't mind using on whomever, whenever it was necessary.

One of the chief signs of the Church's abysmal condition is its refusal to call a spade a spade (in love, of course) both in-side and outside the Church, and have a side-splitting, obe-dient, good time doing it. Both in scripture and in the an-nals of church history we have great examples of reformers who made their nation great again because they obeyed God through tornadic use of tongue and pen.

If, if, we truly desire revival, reform, and a national renais-sance, then get ready for the spiritual wrecking cranes, i.e., the prophets, to come in and wield their abrasive speech inside our churches, inside The Beltway and outside in the broader public square.

When the prophets poked the pompous, when they mocked the haughty and religiously arrogant, when they wreaked havoc on stale religious and political symbolism: they were clearing the ground for fresh, godly growth. I know it may seem ugly at times, but it can be fun, and it can effect change. That is, if we understand it, cheer it on and yield to it – espe-cially when it's aimed at us.

As you can imagine, after reading this chapter, I'd say from a biblical standpoint, obviously, Trump's on solid ground when it comes to him blasting the ubiquitous slingers of *stercore tauri*. As we have seen, Jesus did it, the prophets did it, and the apostles did it and all of them upset the world by upending bad dudes peddling bad ideas.

CHAPTER FOUR

Jesus, Trump, And Our
Southern Border

Brandon Vallorani

A merica is a diverse country built through many decades of hard work by generations of immigrants like my grandparents – and very likely yours. These immigrants came to America to become members of "one nation, under God, indivisible, with liberty and justice for all."

It was their love for American ideals and their pursuit of the American Dream that brought them together to form a society that would become what we today often refer to as a melting pot.

My great-grandfather, Luigi Vallorani, left his home in Italy for America because he believed the streets here in the New World would be paved with gold. After he left the military in Italy, he knew he did not want to scratch a living from the rocky mountain terrain like the rest of his farming family.

When he arrived, however, he quickly learned the truth about the streets of America. They were not paved with gold, and it was the Italians who were doing the paving! Undaunted by challenges and hardships, Luigi worked hard in the steel mills and coal mines of Pennsylvania and Kentucky, alongside many others from a myriad of countries who had also come here to make a better life.

Saving every penny to get him closer to his goals, eventually, Luigi opened and operated a restaurant and a grocery store — bringing the riches of his culture to the American economy.

Like most immigrants during this time in America's history, Luigi was processed quickly upon arrival and immediately considered to be an American. He embraced his American citizenship with pride and committed to learning all about his new nation — its history, language, laws, and culture. His goal was to assimilate as quickly as possible.

Although assimilation had its challenges, this was a great time in American history. People put a high priority on being an American rather than just exploiting their ethnicity for personal gain. The American flag was respected, not burned. People stood for the national anthem, rather than knelt.

While communities were often knit together in segments of Old World commonality, it was ultimately patriotism and religion that brought ethnic varietals together, as evidenced by the varied mix most of us find when we process a DNA test. Communities banded together to help each other in times of need.

None of my immigrant ancestors would have taken a dollar from the government. It would have been against their principles. Their attitude was a simple, "No thanks. We earn our own, and we take care of our own." We've lost a lot of that sense of self-reliance and replaced self-governance with handouts and bailouts.

Immigration looks much different today, as well. Illegal immigrants are breaching our southern border, exploiting the American catch-and-release loophole by claiming asylum, and adding themselves to the millions already living here illegally.

Those who try to enter legally must often wait years and years, spending thousands of dollars and even hours, navigating an unwieldy maze of documentation and red tape. Even then there are no guarantees of citizenship.

I have met people from all over the world—not just Latin America but also Ireland, Australia, and Canada—who simply cannot start the new life they dream of having in this country despite the value they could bring, all because of long-standing government policy that I believe needs reform. But I also believe reform can only come when security is first established.

Few politicians or political parties have properly articulated a sound plan for immigration that is efficient while also ensuring the safety of the current citizenry. Republicans want immigrants to follow the law, despite the fact that we lack the resources to enforce those laws. Democrats call for open borders, granting amnesty to immigrants who arrive illegally and subsidizing them with taxpayer dollars. Why?

The answer is simple. Democrats want to replace America's Republican voters with new Democrat voters from third world countries. It all began with Ted Kennedy's Immigration Act of 1965. Ann Coulter exposed their frightening agenda when she said:

> Most Americans don't realize that, decades ago, the Democrats instituted a long-term plan to gradually turn the United States into a Third World nation. The country would become poorer and less free, but Democrats would have an unbeatable majority!
>
> Under Teddy Kennedy's 1965 immigration act, our immigration policy changed from one that replicated the existing ethnic population to one that strictly favored unskilled immigrants from the Third World. Since 1968, 85 percent of legal immigrants have come from what is euphemistically called "developing countries."[10]

Democrats need voters because Americans won't give them enough votes to win. They've been caught voting for dead people, bribing and bussing voters to the polls, voting multiple times, and even manufacturing votes out of thin air. It's been proven that Democrats will stop at nothing to win: even if it requires manipulating the system meant to ensure these very things cannot happen.

The hunger for more votes demands that Democrats turn a blind eye to human trafficking, drug trafficking, criminal activity, and even those bent on committing terroristic acts that are crossing the southern border in droves. In 2010 alone, Amnesty International reported that as many as 60% of women and girls are sexually assaulted while attempting to cross our southern border illegally.

Many argue that not all illegal immigrants are criminals, but they ignore a vital point: by entering this country illegally, a crime has already been committed. In 2018, ICE reported out of 158,581 administrative arrests 66% of the undocumented illegal parties were convicted criminals. Of the 257,085 removed from this country, 57% were convicted criminals. Further research conducted by the federal government oversight organization, Judicial Watch, indicates that 50% of all crimes were committed near our border with Mexico. The General Accounting Office documents that criminal immigrants have committed 25,604 murders between 2003 and 2009.

There is also a question of fairness to all of the immigrants — past and present — who worked and waited and put great effort into legally entering our country and seeking citizenship that is destroyed when illegal entry is ignored – and even rewarded.

The Democratic platform insisting illegals receive amnesty and the full benefits of citizenship in the United States without following legal and lawful due process is giving Democrats access to even more votes. It is a blatant attempt to shift the balance of power from the conservative American values that made us great to the quagmires of failed socialist regimes like Venezuela.

Conservatives, led by President Trump, aren't opposed to immigrants as the liberals would have you believe. This is a straw man argument created by the left to control the narrative through the mainstream media -- in fact, the vast majority of the legal immigrants I am acquainted with hold conservative views. Conservatives are against *illegal* immigration, believing that a wall on our southern border is a necessity.

Democrats want you to believe that building a wall is insane, cruel, and even racist (but of course, they say everyone and everything is racist). Barack Obama and Nancy Pelosi supported the wall a mere number of years ago, as did Bill and Hillary Clinton. What changed? They are against it now because President Trump — and conservatives – are in support of it.

Jesus says, "When a strong man, fully armed, guards his own house, his possessions are safe." (Lk 11:21, NIV) Just ahead of this verse, He states "Any kingdom divided against itself will be ruined, and a house divided against itself will fall." (Lk 11:17, NIV). While Jesus is referring specifically to spiritual matters in these passages, the principle can be applied to all areas of our society.

If we are going to move America past these divisive issues, we must have a new immigration policy that is humanitarian and biblical. The new policy must respect and secure our borders and the rule of law, while giving skilled and motivated people in other nations the opportunity to become citizens. Citizens who contribute to our economy and have the opportunity to pursue and achieve the American dream for themselves and their families.

When President Trump was elected, he knew that America was at a critical crossroads. The road offered by the Democrats simply kicks the can down the road to future generations. Ironically, just like the city of Troy opening its gates to the Trojan horse, Democrats will be voted out of office by the children of the very people they allowed into our nation.

The second road is dominated by fear of those who are different and leads to xenophobia. Thankfully we have a President who is taking the third and wisest road of all. President Trump wants to enforce our laws and secure our borders, work with other countries to eliminate illegal immigration, and create a new system which welcomes high-skilled immigrants and temporary workers to improve our economy. This third road is mutually beneficial to the current citizens and to those who seek to become legal citizens. It is a return to the "Glory Days" of America being a city on a hill, a beacon of hope to thousands across the globe.

I implore our leaders and our country's citizens to welcome immigrants into this country, legally and efficiently, with reasonable requirements: understand and agree to uphold the Constitution of the United States, honor its laws, create income through gaining employment or building a business, pay taxes, commit to learning our language, and peacefully and lawfully integrate into our society.

Those who come with a hatred for America or wish to overthrow our government or harm our citizens, however, should be forever barred.

Our country is as strong as it is today because our immigrant ancestors risked everything to come here, and were more than willing to work hard to make their dreams come true. The American Dream is still alive and well. I believe this is what makes — and will keep — America great.

Of course, America is a work in progress. She has learned from earlier mistakes such as slavery and the mistreatment of Native Americans, and we are still self-correcting. Ultimately it has been our belief in God and our God-given rights that has and will continue to guide us into becoming a better nation through the times.

CHAPTER FIVE

Jesus And Trump – What Their Enemies Have In Common

Doug Giles

If the world hates you, you know that it has hated Me before it hated you.
John 15:18, NASB

Y ou can tell a lot about a person by the company they keep *and ...*

By the enemies they attract.

Speaking of enemies, all the impenitent creepy people who collided with Christ when He was kicking up dirt on the mean streets in the Middle East many moons ago loathed Him. Yep, they hated the Prince of Peace and for good reason: He rocked their little self-righteous, self-preening world of self-love and the well-sculpted veil of bollocks they hid behind.

No one was safe from His scathing rebuke if they were peddling lies, hype, and spin. Young, old, fat, skinny, male, female, stupid, smart, robed, naked, politician or priest yay, any and all, who were playing games with God and the lives of other people by spewing heretical smegma to themselves or the masses were awarded the unpleasurable dress-down by the Son Of God.

Heck, even before Jesus formally stepped into his earthly ministry, when He was a wee little baby, merely cooing and pooping in his swaddling clothes and breastfeeding off the Virgin Mary's mammaries He had King Herod try to kill Him (Mt. 2:1-18).

Herod was an insecure, toady little leader, who was extremely paranoid that someone was going to take his authority from him. Herod killed anyone, including friends, family, and foes, who he deemed a threat to his control. Google it if you don't believe me. His paranoia was the stuff of movies. He makes Jim Carrey, Charlie Manson, Zelda Fitzgerald, Syd Barrett, Van Gogh, Jussie Smollett, and Brian Wilson look centered, gracious, and easy-going compared to him. Ergo, when Herod found out that there was a baby who was born King of The Jews, well ... he was having none of that.

At first, Herod feigned respectful interest in Jesus but that was a hot steaming pile of *stercore tauri*. Herod wanted to kill that baby because he thought He was going to eventually take his political position which he had connived so long and hard for. His supremacy was on thin ice with this Christ-kid around and he'd kissed too much Roman butt to let some Galilean grab his gavel. Yep, this power hungry dude was threatened by a baby birthed into the prophetic purposes of God and the rest is bloody history, how he had slaughtered all the male children in the greater Bethlehem area just to get at Jesus.

Herod was the consummate, jealous/power hungry politician, who'd stop at *nada* to preserve his power. Kind of like the envious, soulless and specious political swamp critters on The Left and The Right who've made a very comfortable living off average American taxpayers during their near eternal feckless stints inside the Beltway. They too, don't want to lose their power, their control, their luxury condo, their hookers, their lifestyle, their special interest mega-money, their CNN gigs or anything else they are clinging to and they'll come after anyone who threatens their dream, starring them as the center of the universe, with razor blades and lemon juice. Indeed, they too are driven by the same pathetic envious fear that saddled satanic Herod.

Let's see. Aside from insanely insecure political leaders, who else hated Jesus with perfect hatred? Ah … I know. How could I forget? The religious leaders of His day definitely didn't dig The Son of Man. Yep, Christ clashed with the Pharisees saving some of His most bellicose *bon mots* for these boneheads.

The religious hoity-toities of His day hated Him and He loved provoking them to self-expose their very deep and ubiquitous stupidity and hypocrisy. Matter of fact, nearly every chapter of Matthew, Mark, Luke, and John has Jesus fish-slapping these supposed "spiritual leaders" into next week over some load of crap they spewed and it's delicious, very entertaining, reading. I hope God has videos of His rebukes to watch once I get to heaven. How fun! Anyway …

Yep, these supposed men of God were, according to Jesus, "Blind leaders of the blind," whom He warned every average Joe in earshot of His exhortations to do the exact opposite of what these sad and evil religious rapscallions did.

Like Herod, the religious leaders of Jesus' day, had worked long and hard, romancing Rome for their little piece of power and prestige and they weren't about to let this thirty-year-old rebel threaten their security, their wallet and their vaunted place as religious control freaks over us po' ... po' ... sinners.

Succinctly, the reasons why they hated Jesus and why Jesus constantly and sometimes violently jostled their warm, gooey and damnable Hot Tub Religion were as follows:

Jesus had authority and they didn't. They had been up-staged and these envious twits couldn't stand being bettered. Christ's authority was divine, their authority was a derivative of being Rome's useful idiots.

Jesus wasn't two-faced and they were. Jesus was the genuine article and they were about as real as Bruce Jenner's jugs.

Jesus cared about the common man and they didn't give a hootie-patootie about the plight of the "unwashed." Indeed, if you didn't jump through their superficial religious hoops then you were *persona non grata* to them.

Jesus had a true and powerful relationship with God and it had zero to do with their ridiculous rules.

Christ was humble before God and they were arrogant dorks.

They were into browbeating and Jesus was into burden lifting.

They loved setting traps for people and Christ loved setting folks free from Satan's snares.

They loved Rolexes and Jesus loved relationships.

They loved religious titles, Jesus loved the Father.

They separated from sinners and Jesus was a friend of sinners.

At that's why they opposed The Son of God and why, to the masses at least, Jesus was appealing and the religious leaders were appalling.

Matter of fact, Jesus' last podcast, before His crucifixion, was a holy jet blast to these particular religious dillweeds. He wanted to make certain everyone, forever, knew not to follow their weird cult or ever be like them. Oh, by the way, Jesus rebuked them to their faces and in public. This is why they had to kill Him: He threatened their credibility and career.

Finally, I'd be remiss (I don't know what that means but it sounds bad,) if I didn't mention the enmity between Jesus and the malevolent one ... *El Diablo.*

It's an understatement to state Beelzebub wasn't benefitted by The Son of Man's glide path. Behind the power of the state and the rankness of oppressive religion was/is Lucifer and his fallen demonic messengers. Pretty much everywhere Jesus strolled He jettisoned the devils that possessed and oppressed people. As you can imagine, The Prince of Darkness wasn't thrilled giving ground to The Son of God. In addition, Satan really didn't like it when Christ eternally crushed him via his resurrection and ascension, thus defeating the one who had power over death, namely ... The Devil.

So, we kinda know that Jesus (Hello!), was on the right side of history; and this not just by the sinners who loved Him but equally, maybe more importantly, by the demonic louts who loathed Him.

Which brings us to President Trump.

Now granted, Trump is no Jesus. He's definitely not sinless. He doesn't have the Ted Nugent hairdo and I can't imagine (and don't want to imagine) him in a robe, wearing sandals. That said, Trump's enemies are very ... very ... how shall I say it ... *interesting*. However, most of his current foes were friendlies not so long ago. For instance, prior to becoming President, when Trump used to wine and dine the Hollywood glitterati and parasitical politicians, everyone and their Liberal and/or NeverTrumpkin dog used to just *"love"* Mr. Trump. Oh, yes. They L-O-V-E-D ... *loved* ... The Donald. The Libs courted his favor and the politicians courted his cash.

They slobbered over him.

DJT was the shiznay, y'all.

Between 2004-2015, Trump's show, *The Apprentice*, was killing it. Celebrities just couldn't get enough of his show, his parties, his resorts, and his country clubs. Yep, if it had Trump's name on it you'd find those who dig the finer things fawning over that which Trump was spawning.

Everyone praised The Donald.

Everyone needed The Donald.

Everyone toady me-monkey truckled with oodles and oodles of flattery for The Donald principally because he had the wherewithal to propel them into stardom or power if Trump saw them as legit talent, who were hard and smart workers with a commitment to excellence.

Indeed, peeps, he was sliced bread and Christmas to the Hollywood hotties and the political establishment.

Yes, pretty much everyone swooned over Mr. Trump right up until June 16th, 2015. That's the day he declared he was sick of lame-ass politicians and Hollywood dorks driving this great nation into a debt-addled ignoble ditch beholden to foreign powers and taking its cue from the UN and he was going to fix this crapsicle by running for President ... as a Republican.

His vision was simple: he wanted to Make America Great Again by re-establishing America as an economic powerhouse, a military monster, a nation with borders that embraced its original intent and traditional values and that, my friends, went over like hot and runny low-fat yogurt at Rosie O'Donnell's plus-sized pool party.

In other words, according to The Big Government Church Of The Poisoned Mind, Trump's verbalized, 2015 MAGA vision, was heresy and he had committed the unpardonable sin. He deviated from their wet-dream of deconstructing our great land of opportunity and morphing it into something resembling Venezuela.

Immediately they tried to toss Donald into the 24/7/365 "Destroy-Trump-At-All-Costs" woodchipper. Those who "loved" him straight away ceased with their affections when he declared his afflatus for a rich, vibrant, free, traditional, safe, militarily powerful, and conservative America. This was no mild disdain, ladies and gents. This was and is a *syndrome*. A Trump Derangement Syndrome ... on steroids.

Once elected, rage-filled pandemonium ensued against President Trump. The NeverTrumpkins, on The Left and Right, couldn't believe Hillary didn't get the national nod. They couldn't believe that all the skewed, pro-Hillary, CNN and MSNBC polls were more off-kilter than Yoko Ono trying to hit the high notes in Mariah Carey's song, *Emotions*. They couldn't imagine Rachel Maddow and National Reviews', Gang of 22, were wronger in their 2016 election forecasts than the Crystal Pepsi R&D team was back in 1992. The crap was hitting the fan, folks.

Anti-Trump college students needed cry rooms. Tests were cancelled at several colleges because the snowflakes were so upset.

A through D grade actors and unfunny comedians had anti-Trump public meltdowns on Twitter. And they're still having them.

The sight of MAGA hats at Starbucks, Sam's Club, and March For Life rallies caused caustic Trump loathers to go MACH 2 with their hair on fire with violence and/or threats of violence.

ANTIFA protesters, who accused Trump of violent rhetoric, actually spawned violence by attacking and harassing blue-haired old ladies who carried an American flag or sported a MAGA hat. ANTIFA also commenced, in liberal cities across the country, to vandalize cities and businesses. I know. Go figure, eh?

The word "Nazi" and "Trump" got tossed around more than a drunken midget at a Molly Hatchet concert via "The Most Trusted Name In News."

Speaking of CNN, they have officially turned into one big, 24/7/365, anti-Trump forlorn festival. They're now predictable, embarrassing, pathetic, and boring with their Trump Derangement Syndrome.

Those on The Right, that were so wrong about Trump winning, are now rooting for our Nation to actually suffer and Trump not succeed with his MAGA agenda simply because they look like myopic morons with their anti-Trump predictions and maledictions.

It's really pretty sad. It's especially sad watching so-called Christians wish him ill and try to justify their hatred with the scripture. Good luck with that when you die and go toe-to-toe at The Bema Seat with Jehovah.

It was and has been quite the hissy fit The NeverTrumpkins have been throwing.

They hate Trump with a perfect hatred.

They don't like Trump's supporters either.

They perceive Trump as their enemy.

So, let's look who hates Trump and who's warring against him. I'll say it at the outset, it's a veritable and unwholesome rogue's gallery.

I think a good group to highlight in this opening salvo of malevolent monosyllabics that hate Trump would be ... drumroll, please ... Witches!

Now, correct me if I'm wrong, but if witches are against you, generally and historically speaking, you're probably doing something right, correct?

According to BBC.com, a month after Trump took office, witches organized a global campaign to try to voodoo hex The Donald.

Check it out ...

The BBC article titled, "Witches cast 'mass spell' against Donald Trump" 25 February 2017:

> At the stroke of midnight on Friday, followers of witchcraft across the US performed a mass spell designed to stop the president doing harm. A spell to bind Donald Trump and all those who abet him. A Facebook group devoted to the ritual has attracted over 10,500 likes, and coined the hashtag #magicresistance.[11]

Well, isn't that special? I wonder who could've inspired that curse against President Trump? Hmmm. Maybe ... Satan?!

Look, I'm not the coldest beer in the 'fridge, but I'm a-guessin' if witches and warlocks don't like you and they're tossing tarot cards, lighting candles, praying to Satan and breaking their Ouija Board over your public policies then you're probably kind of close to being in proximity to that which is holy, just, and good, eh?

Who else isn't mondo jovial Mr. Trump has taken his seat behind the same desk where Bill boinked Monica? Well, it's people and organizations like the following fifty pouters ...

Satanists.
Communists.
Socialists.

Venezuelan Dictators.

Occasional-Cortex.

ANTIFA.

Abortion Advocates (Especially the late-term enthusiasts.)

The DNC (Who, by the way, booed God during their 2012 convention. Google it if you think I'm lying. Enjoy.)

Mr. Compromise, Mitt Romney.

TransBathroom Devotees.

Misandrists.

Anti-Theists.

Anti-Christian Groups.

The Anti-White Men Cabal.

Those Who Are Envious of Our Prosperity.

Open Border Droogies.

Peeps Who Hate ICE.

Anti-Cop Morons.

Jussie Smollett.

Colin Kaepernick.

Cher.

George Clooney.

Chelsea Handler.

Lena Dunham.

Robert DeNiro.

Stephen Colbert.

Seth Meyers.

Arianna Huffington.

Louis Farrakhan.

Al Sharpton.

Sarah Silverman.

Alyssa Milano.

Jimmy Kimmel.

Jeb Bush.

George W. Bush.

Barack Obama.

Michelle Obama.
Hillary.
Rosie.
Kathy Griffin.
Hollywood.
Jihadists.
CNN.
MSNBC.
Morning Joe.
Bill Kristol.
Miley Virus.
Katy Perry.
Madonna.
Ashley Judd.

Most of the aforementioned folks and organizations ain't coming from a Christian Worldview.

Most of 'em's love for the Constitution and our founding docs is *muy poquito.*

A lot of these clowns have zero problem with the likes of Fidel & Che, Hugo, and Osama, and most have no problemo with our nation being wide-open to either MS-13 or ISIS.

The whole lot of them are not known for biblical righteousness, peace and joy in the Holy Ghost, correct?

Therefore, if, *IF,* if I'm right in regards to the aforementioned's antipathy towards the scripture, traditional values, America's founding documents, and our original intent and they hate Trump then I would say Trump's on the right path. Call me crazy.

Trump's doing to them what Jesus did to His first-century opposition, namely ... eradicating their credibility and careers.
Indeed, Trump's crushing their control, their authority and
their precious cash with his pro-America, very Bible-friendly
policies and that, my friends, is why they hate him.

CHAPTER SIX

Would Jesus Agree With Trump's Stance On Abortion?

Brandon Vallorani

Verily, verily, I say unto you, Before Abraham was, I am.
John 8:58, KJV

W hat would Jesus have done in 2016? If He were looking at His options through the lens of the abortion
issue, what were His choices?

One: He could go with the Democrat Option. Two: He could
go with the Billionaire Playboy who once called himself "pro-
choice," but now said he's pro-life. Or would He have supported
a third option, perhaps a "more reasonable" Republican?

What about Kasich? (And by the way, did you know his dad
was a mailman?) People tried to frame Kasich as a "moderate."
Likeable. A unifier. How was Kasich on this issue? During the
primaries, he did pretty well. In early 2016, he passed legisla-

tion that kept the state from signing contracts with anyone performing non-therapeutic abortions. Maybe he would be the guy who could be trusted to carry the torch for the life issue?

Not so fast.

Kasich did sign that bill, sure. But what else did he do? In the closing days of his Governorship, Ohio put another bill in front of him, all wrapped up and ready to go. It only needed his signature to put it into law. It was dubbed the Heartbeat Bill. The reason it was called the heartbeat bill is that it outlawed abortion if the baby's heartbeat could be detected. The heart starts beating at about 6 weeks. But you can't really hear it unit week 10 or 12. This law would have effectively capped out abortion at no later than 12 weeks. Would it have outlawed abortion? No, but it sure would have saved a lot of babies' lives. When the moment of truth came, the mailman's son folded like a cheap tent. He vetoed the bill, and it died there, without a signature as he left office. He had a smooth transition from the Governor's mansion to CNN as a "Senior Political Commentator." That's code for a pseudo-conservative they keep around to pretend they're not in the tank for the Democrats. Kasich will be joining the bullpen with such bold conservative voices as Ana Navarro.

The new Governor of Ohio, Mike DeWine, has pledged to sign the heartbeat bill into law if they can get it back up to him. Would Jesus have pushed Kasich as the guy to carry the banner in a pro-life fight? Hardly.

That leaves Hillary Clinton or the billionaire Playboy that was pro-choice before he joined the Republicans. Would Hillary maintain the status quo? Would Trump give up ground?

Hillary spent the last 20 years repeating the now-obsolete mantra "Safe, Legal, and Rare." Bill coined the phrase, after all. Or at least he's credited with it. But it has been a while since we've heard anyone talking that way, hasn't it? Now that slogan has given way to others. "On demand and without apology" – which claims to be a 1970's retread – is one example. "Shout Your Abortion" is another.

We were learning some new things about abortion, too, weren't we? For example, those undercover baby parts films that were hidden by the 9th Circuit until they were proven to be valid in the courts of Texas. The films were not deceptively edited. Baby parts really were for sale. Eyes. Brains. Arms. Skin. The whole deal. And for what? Profit. One Planned Parent exec even talked about the Lamborghini she was hoping to buy. That's pretty ghoulish by any measurement.

Horrified, the Republican Senate put forward a bill that would obligate every medical practitioner to provide proper medical care to every fully-born, living baby. It should have been a slam dunk, right? Nope. The Democrats -- who have become the Infanticide Party -- straight-up blocked the bill, defeating it. Democrats have slid so far into the pockets of the abortion lobby that they can't even take steps to protect an unwanted baby's life even after it's left the womb.

If you were paying attention, this shouldn't come as a surprise. It wasn't so very long ago that it came to light that a certain presidential candidate in 2008 opposed a very similar Born Alive bill. According to Politico, Obama completely lied about his role in that legislation in an interview with *Purpose Driven Life* author and Saddleback Church pastor, Rick Warren, in legislation designed to protect babies who survived abortion. They added in their piece, *Obama The Abortion Ex-*

tremist12, that it was not redundant legislation because abortion providers were, in fact, leaving infants to die without any care.

Mario Cuomo famously made distinctions between his private faith (in which he says he opposed abortion) and his public policy (which allowed for it). Cuomo made his central argument: a Catholic politician can, in good conscience, personally oppose abortion while politically fighting to protect it — including even subsidies for abortion. However dubious the claim, at least it gives a pretense of acknowledging the moral horrors implicit in the act of willfully ending an innocent human life. Compare that to the new laws Andrew Cuomo announced (with Hillary at his side) in January 2019.

In a direct response to Trump's second SCOTUS appointee, several Governors feared that abortion law would be once again examined, and perhaps laws would change.

Abracadabra, several deep-blue states suddenly became rock-ribbed believers in States' Rights. Not that this means they're now arguing against any decisions they find helpful – say, Obergefell. But States like New York and Vermont were getting ahead of any potential legal changes by passing new state laws on abortion.

These new changes were aggressive.

So far as homicide law is concerned, it now applies only to those who have been born alive. This definition is convenient for pro-abortion advocates but one necessary consequence of this change is to the legal status of an unborn child in other contexts.

If a pregnant woman is injured or killed, harm to a kid – even if that kid is loved and wanted – does not fall under the legal status of "alive." Therefore, in a legal sense, that baby cannot be considered "murdered" if his or her life is cut short by violence ... not even deliberate violence. The only laws on the books governing charges available for use against coercive violence bringing a pregnancy to an unwanted conclusion were struck down in Penal Law Sections 125.05, 125.40 and 125.45. No replacement legislation governing such a situation was put in its place.

This change has already had real-life consequences. One man physically assaulted a pregnant woman with his fists with the intention of causing a miscarriage. When the laws changed, the felony charge of abortion in the second degree against a man from Gansevoort was no longer on the books and had to be dropped. But we are assured these laws are enacted to "protect" women's rights.

The legislation invokes the language of a "'fundamental right'... with which the State cannot discriminate, deny or interfere..." This language could potentially legally obligate people to provide abortion services against their will.

There's another big change in the scope of who and when. There is no longer an upper limit in terms of date, age, or size beyond which abortion is no longer a viable medical option. That's only part of the problem. The rationale for an abortion has been made far more elastic.

No longer is it administered for the protection of the mother's life ... now they can invoke the mother's health. Health is a junk-drawer term that can – and has – encapsulated anything from age, social, economic, and emotional factors. This legislation – which was announced so proudly by lighting up New York's major monuments with pink lights – has another curious feature.

Far more people can legally administer an abortion now than could have in times past. You need to look no further than Kermit Gosnell to imagine why abortion laws have restricted the lawful performing of abortions to specifically trained medical professionals. No federal law has ever extended authority to perform an abortion to anyone apart from an M.D. But now, in New York, you don't need to be a doctor to provide an abortion anymore. Practitioners certified under Title Eight include nurse practitioners, physician assistants, midwives, as well as other non-physicians. Critics worry that other Title Eight practitioners could be granted this authority, potentially putting lives in danger.

This aggressive third-trimester abortion is no longer a minority position in the Democratic party. Among those hoping to get the Democratic nomination, there is strong support for abortion. Bernie Sanders opposes abortion restrictions – full stop. Robert "Beto" O'Rourke was asked a point-blank, carefully worded question about his support for late-term abortion. It's not a medical emergency procedure because physically, third-trimester abortions take up to three days to have, so ... in that sense, if there was an emergency the doctors would just do a C-section and you don't have to kill the baby in that instance. What was his answer? "So, the question is about abortion and reproductive rights. And my answer to you is that that should be a decision that the woman makes. I trust her." For anyone keeping score at home, that was a coward's "yes." He hid behind the skirts of the women in the crowd rather than give a definitive answer. At least Bernie had the cojones to say it.

Booker voted to keep abortions legal until birth. Kamala Harris supports abortion until birth. Elizabeth "Pocahontas" Warren said about abortion, "I think the role of government here is to back out." Can you imagine a Democrat saying that about any other issue? Say, for example, free speech or gun ownership?

It's gotten to the point that even Hillary's *bona fides* on this issue have been described by the uber-liberal site *Mother Jones* as "murky"[13] compared to the really committed people like Bernie Sanders. Yes, indeed. We've now gone so far down the rabbit-hole that Hillary Clinton is seen as "too moderate" by the Left's purists.

But they saved the most extreme for last. When everyone else was still reeling from the changes to NY law, Governor Northam shocked us all. It started in Virginia when Democrat Kathy Tran was being questioned on her proposed legislation, after establishing that there was no upper limit in the bill, the blunt question was asked: "Where it is obvious that a woman is about to give birth, she has physical signs that she's about to give birth, would that still be a point at which she could request an abortion if she were so certified? – She's dilating." When pressed for an answer after dancing around it, and clarifying that she is not a physician, she replied, "My bill would allow that, yes."[14]

Days after that the Virginia Governor (who, incidentally, received something like $2 Million in support from Planned Parenthood) went on a radio show and applied his medical expertise to the question.

> If a mother is in labor ... the infant would be delivered. The infant would be kept comfortable.

> The infant would be resuscitated if that's what the mother and the family desired, and then a discussion would ensue between the physicians & mother. [15]

Suddenly, the question of whether a baby should live or die was now taking place after that baby was born, and that changed the conversation completely. In the scenario he suggested, there was some kind of a deformity in the infant, but that was not at all a requirement of the proposed bill itself. An unnamed aspect of the hypothetical mother's mental health would be sufficient to trigger her right to abort under the proposed legislation. Just days later, Northam's yearbook photos with someone wearing blackface and someone else wearing a KKK hood came out. We're still not sure which one was him (he denies that he was either of the individuals), although he has since admitted to wearing blackface while pretending to be Michael Jackson and doing the moonwalk. It's a sad reflection of our nation today when a blackface photo is more shocking to public sensibilities than a casual conversation about infanticide.

The CDC reports that America performs about 13,000 late-term abortions a year. But we are supposed to accept that they're all medical emergencies, right? Not so much. The largest study done on the topic found that fetal abnormalities "make up a small minority" of late-term abortions.16 Even fewer are done to save the mother's life.

How prevalent have abortions become? Jason L. Riley reported a devastating fact: more black babies in New York are now aborted than born. It's more than a little dishonest for alleged "Progressives" to claim "bigots" on the Right are afraid of the "browning of America" when those same supposed bigots are the only voices yelling stop as we watch an entire generation of black babies snuffed out before they even see the light of day.

> According to a city Health Department report released in May, between 2012 and 2016 black mothers terminated 136,426 pregnancies and gave birth to 118,127 babies. By contrast, births far surpassed abortions among whites, Asians and Hispanics. [17]

Blackface Governor Northam casually discussing infanticide, black babies ripped from the womb more than any other – Margaret Sanger would be pleased indeed. Oh, you didn't think we had all forgotten Margaret Sanger's dirty little secret, did you? If the Left ever had to face a hostile press, they would have some serious questions to answer about their associations. Not just the historical connections between themselves and the KKK, or Jim Crowe, or Japanese Internment. All of those are bad enough. But their hero-worship of Margaret Sanger is at least as big a black eye as any of those. In light of how bad the other things are, you may be wondering "how is that possible?" – unless you know her history.

Are you familiar with the term eugenics? It was a particularly nasty little ideology resulting when you take the Evolutionary Theory and you apply it to political philosophy. You wind up with superior and inferior races.

Read that again, slowly.

One little Austrian politician with a distinctive Charlie Chaplin mustache is remembered for his application of eugenics theories into something called the "Final Solution" during the Second World War. (Come to think of it, that war itself was his idea, too.)

Sanger wrote this piece in defense of her eugenics – note her use of the phrase "race regeneration."

> Seemingly every new approach to the great problem of the human race must manifest its vitality by running the gauntlet of prejudice, ridicule and misinterpretation. Eugenists may remember that not many years ago this program for race regeneration was subjected to the cruel ridicule of stupidity and ignorance. Today Eugenics is suggested by the most diverse minds as the most adequate and thorough avenue to the solution of racial, political and social problems. The most intransigent and daring teachers and scientists have lent their support to this great biological interpretation of the human race. The war has emphasized its necessity. [18]

She was just solving "racial problems." This is the left's champion of women's rights, in her own words. There's more. In *My Way To Peace* Sanger wrote:

> MY WAY TO PEACE would be First, to put into action the fourteen points of President Wilson's, upon which Germany and Austria surrendered to the Allies. Second, to have Congress set up a special department for the study of population problems, and appoint a Parliament of Population Directors representing the various branches of science.
> This body to direct and control the population

through Birth rates and immigration, and direct its distribution over the country according to national needs consistent with the taste, fitness and interest of the individuals.

(a) to raise the level and increase the general intelligence of our population.

... (c) keep the doors of Immigration closed to the entrance of certain aliens whose condition is known to be detrimental to the stamina of the race, such as feeble-minded, idiots, morons, insane, syphiletic, epileptic, criminal, professional prostitutes, and others in this class barred from entrance by the Immigration Laws of 1924.

(d) apply a stern and rigid policy of sterilization, and segregation to that grade of population whose progeny is already tainted or whose inheritance is such that objectionable traits may be transmitted to offspring.

(e) to insure the country against future burdens of maintenance for numerous offspring as may be born of feeble-minded parents, the government would pension all persons with transmissible disease who voluntarily consent to sterilization.

(f) the whole dysgenic population would have its choice of segregation or sterilization.

(g) there would be farm lands and homesteads where these segregated persons would be taught to work under competent instructors for the period of their entire lives.[19]

Any "unfit" person was supposed to be rounded up and put to work doing agricultural work ... against their will. Didn't Americans fight a civil war to put a stop to just that sort of policy?

From a Washington Times piece:

> She even presented at a Ku Klux Klan rally in 1926
> in Silver Lake, N.J. She recounted this event in her
> autobiography, "I accepted an invitation to talk
> to the women's branch of the Ku Klux Klan ... I
> saw through the door dim figures parading with
> banners and illuminated crosses ... I was escort-
> ed to the platform, was introduced, and began
> to speak ... In the end, through simple illustrations
> I believed I had accomplished my purpose. A
> dozen invitations to speak to similar groups were
> proffered."[20]

And in 1947, she even advocated that in "developing countries," no babies should be born for ten years. Some continue
to claim she wasn't actually racist, but the black pastors that
were protesting her exhibit at the Smithsonian do not share
that view. Whether she was personally motivated by racism
or not, the end result is the same, the majority of those who
never see the light of day are black babies.

With this left's newfound rabid dedication to ever-more extreme abortion practices, let's step back and see what their
beloved "international community" has to say about it. Surely
their abortion practices are far more liberal than the "oppressive" American "patriarchy" right?

The Left wants to present abortion-until-birth as a fairly
commonplace and ordinary attitude toward abortion. But is
it? Not at all. Did you know that, apart from the USA only six
countries in the world even permit abortions after 22 weeks?
These countries are the Netherlands, Singapore, Canada, Vietnam, China, and North Korea.

Of that list, Netherlands and Singapore restrict abortions after 24 weeks except in cases of rape, incest or risk to the mother's life. That means only four countries besides America allow abortion after 24 weeks. China, North Korea, Vietnam, and Canada. Canada's status on this is a little misleading. Here's why: their Supreme Court struck down existing abortion law in the 1980s and every politician since has been too gutless to debate or even discuss where the line should be drawn, so they've got no law on the books at all. There are laws about what color (actually, it's "colour" to them) their margarine has to be (I'm not even kidding,) but no laws governing the practice of abortion.[21]

This means American politicians are taking their political cues on the abortion issue from such human rights leaders as China, Vietnam, and North Korea – as well as the political gutless wonders of the Great White North. Now that's some kind of leadership!

Meanwhile, in Africa, there's serious push back against the Western insistence that so-called developing nations adopt liberal attitudes toward abortion. Obianuju Ekeocha, an African pro-life activist, wrote *Target Africa* which shone a light on "the ideological neo-colonial masters of the 21st century who aggressively push into Africa their views on contraception, population control, sexualisation of children, feminism, homosexuality and abortion."[22]

Hit with their own accusation – Leftists have their own "white man's burden" project in remaking Africa in their own image. With or without the consent of the locals. The Left's arguments are in direct conflict with the scriptural references to pregnancy, where life in the womb is the furthest thing from being "a mere cluster of cells."

Jeremiah was told, "Before I formed you in the womb I knew you, and before you were born I consecrated you; I appointed you a prophet to the nations." (Je. 1:5)

Jesus said, "Before Abraham was, I am." Yes, that speaks of His particular Divinity, but it also reminds us of something else ... humanity has more complexity than just as a flesh-and-blood physical being.

What was Jesus' first recorded interaction with the outside world after His Incarnation? When Mary (then pregnant with Jesus) met with Elizabeth (then pregnant with John the Baptist): "And when Elizabeth heard the greeting of Mary, the baby leaped in her womb." (Lk. 1:41) This is the same baby of whom it was said earlier in that chapter "He will be filled with the Holy Spirit, even from His mother's womb." If He can be filled with the Spirit, it would logically follow that He must have true personhood, otherwise, there is no "He" for the Spirit of God to fill.

While the Democrats were busy lining up to sing their support for third-trimester abortion, and refusing to pass a Born Alive Law that protects babies that survive an abortion, Trump went the other direction.

Trump jumped into the pro-life effort with both feet.

His Vice President, Mike Pence, directly participated in the March for Life marches. Trump, for his own part, passed an expanded Mexico City policy forbidding taxpayer funds to be applied to organizations who might use those funds for abortion. He did this on Day One of his presidency.

Trump highlighted his defense of the unborn in his SOTU speech:

> There could be no greater contrast to the beautiful image of a mother holding her infant child than the chilling displays our nation saw in recent days. Lawmakers in New York cheered with delight upon the passage of legislation that would allow a baby to be ripped from the mother's womb moments before birth. These are living, feeling, beautiful babies who will never get the chance to share their love and dreams with the world. And then, we had the case of the governor of Virginia where he stated he would execute a baby after birth. To defend the dignity of every person, I am asking Congress to pass legislation to prohibit the late-term abortion of children who can feel pain in the mother's womb.
>
> Let us work together to build a culture that cherishes innocent life. And let us reaffirm a fundamental truth — all children — born and unborn — are made in the holy image of God.[23]

Supposing His deciding issue was abortion, what would Jesus, Who spoke pointedly of the drowning of anyone whose actions lead little children to sin, vote for? Is there even a *shadow* of doubt about the answer to this question?

CHAPTER SEVEN

Is Jesus Cool With Self-Defense?

Doug Giles

If you love the God-given, common sense, Constitutional right to keep and bear arms, then you gotta love Number 45 because Trump doesn't soft-pedal his support for the Second Amendment, he shoves it up The Left's tailpipe. Like in, sideways.

Indeed, I'll venture to say that in my fifty-six years of sucking oxygen he has to be the most vociferous advocate for the Second Amendment to ever sit behind the same august desk as Bill and Dubya.

Trump not only defends your right to armed self-defense but when he was a New York City businessman, he too was packed, stacked and ready to whack. Yep, he had a hard-to-obtain NYC concealed carry permit. Ergo, he is *muy simpatico* with 2A advocates because he also has been viewing life through the iron sights of an armed man for many moons.

In addition, Trump doesn't just say he loves guns. Oh, hizzle to the nizzay. Trump goes the second mile, as Jesus commanded us, and appointed Neil Gorsuch and Brett Kavanaugh to the Supreme Court.

I have one word for that move and it's ... #Boom.

I guess that's two words if you count the hashtag.

Anyway, the point is Trump's not just blathering about our Second Amendment, he's making sure that it's protected after he leaves 1600 Pennsylvania Avenue and he did that via the addition of two Originalist Supreme Court Justices that he appointed. Oh, by the way, with Ginsburg gettin' up there in age, he'll probably appoint another Justice to the Supreme Court before his epic presidency comes to an end.

For the few Trump-hating, NeverTrumpkins, who like the Second Amendment, can you imagine if The Hildebeast would've been elected as you had predicted? Thank God you were wrong because our gun and ammo rights just got blessed with long-lasting, consequential, protection thanks to President Trump's appointment of Neil and Brett.

So, does Trump's stumping for Americans' right to armed self-defense square with Christ's teachings? Or is he out of sync with The Son of God? Here's my two cents for what it's worth.

I was on a talk show the other day defending the Second Amendment and discussing with my host The Left's incessant yarbling about banning guns. I made it clear to the listeners that I am a Christian and I am extremely cool with our right to keep and bear arms.

After we trounced the anti-gun lobby for their goofy, doe-eyed, John Lennon-like *Imagine* solutions to violent crime, we opened up the phone lines for folks to weigh in with questions and opinions. The first caller was a woman who asked if I thought Jesus would carry a weapon if He were here today, to which I quickly replied, "yes, of course, He would—especially if He lived in Miami and was driving down I-95 at four o'clock in the morning."

The female caller, being far more spiritual than I am, didn't think that was funny and went on to make it personal by asking if someone were attacking one of my daughters and I had a gun if I thought Christ would be cool with me killing the felonious punk. I informed the caller that both my daughters have black belts in jiu-jitsu and carry weapons so they probably wouldn't need my help. That said, if I were to let the air out of an attacker, I sure hope Jesus would understand otherwise He'd be terribly disappointed in me and would just have to forgive me. Common sense and primal instinct tell me that the bad guy should die and the good girl should live. Call me carnal.

Of course, the holier-than-me caller was aghast that as a Christian I would have no problem whatsoever defending my friends, family, and person with deadly force. Her reason being was that she couldn't picture Jesus doing it and concluded that because she couldn't wrap her mind around Him green-lighting the destruction of a demented perp that He certainly wouldn't and thus I shouldn't.

When discussing what Christ would do in a given situation, it's usually good to actually go to the gospel accounts, read them and then draw conclusions. Here's what I've gotten after scouring scripture a few times:

1. Jesus in His earthly ministry didn't carry a weapon, except the time when He took a whip and did the Tomb Raider on the televangelists in the Temple. Please note: He didn't chide them or write them a strong but tasteful email asking them to please not do that kind of stuff in church.

What did the meek and mild Messiah do? He made a whip and cleared the punks. Dear Lord, I hope You have that on video for me to watch when I get to heaven. I wonder if the "Christ-is-a-pacifist" lady can picture sweet Jesus laying the leather to the backs of the marketers who were making His Father's house a place of merchandise.

If Christ were to do that today He'd be thrown in prison, and 99.9% of churches in the USA wouldn't have Him speak at their annual *Hallelujah Aren't We Fabulous Conference* because Jesus wouldn't be behaving very Christ-like.

2. It's clear from scripture that Jesus didn't need weapons because He had at His disposal an angelic host that could flatten armies. I, unfortunately, don't have that capability. Nor can I walk through walls or split oceans. Christ had supernatural protection, and His disciples carried swords. I, too, believe that God supernaturally protects me, to a great degree, because I should have been dead a long time ago. However, should my guardian angel be napping or busy doing something else other than trying to keep up with me, I'll be okay because Smith & Wesson art with me as well.

3. Lastly, in Luke 22:36-38, Christ told His disciples, even though He personally did not pack a weapon, that they, in light of His departure, should get a deadly weapon—namely a sword. Check it out ...

And He [Jesus] said to them [His disciples], "But now, whoever has a money belt is to take it along, likewise also a bag, and whoever has no sword is to sell his coat and buy one. For I tell you that this which is written must be fulfilled in Me, 'And he was numbered with transgressors'; for that which refers to Me has its fulfillment." They said, "Lord, look, here are two swords." And He said to them, "It is enough."

Jesus told them—didn't ask or mildly suggest—but told His buddies to sell their jacket if need be and buy a sword. The sword which Christ told His compadres to purchase was not a QVC decorative Claymore to hang on their walls to commemorate the good times they had when Jesus was around. The original word used for sword in this text was a large knife used for killing animals and cutting flesh. It was particularly fashioned for short, deadly thrusts in hand-to-hand combat.

Jesus didn't tell them to carry a whistle, a shofar horn, or a bag of sand to blow in bad guys' eyes, but a dagger-like sword. A vicious, nasty and deadly weapon not used for cutting vegetables, spreading butter or splitting a bagel but for violently tapping a lung or heart in case of an attack.

Now, in a 21st century WWJD context, even though He didn't personally carry a weapon, what do you think He thinks about His followers defending themselves with deadly force, huh, pacifists?

Here's how I've heard that verse explained away ...

Jesus didn't mean a "literal" sword. Yep, according to some sweeties He was speaking metaphorically about the Bible because, you know, Paul called it the "sword of the Spirit" in

Ephesians 6. So, Jesus was telling His boys to buy a Bible? If so, what color? Teal? That would be tough for His first-century amigos to purchase one seeing that the canon hadn't been cobbled together yet for Johannes Gutenberg to roll press on. That's so mean of Jesus to frustrate His disciples with an impossible task upon His departure. Also, if the word "sword" doesn't mean sword in the literal sense of the word, do the words "money belt and bag" literally mean money belt and bag? And if none of these words mean what we think them to mean then who has the decoder ring to help us poor plebeians rightly interpret their meaning? Help me, sage scholars! Help me!

The other way I've seen this text tortured is by Bible wizards mangling this bit from Lk.22:38, "They said, 'Lord, look, here are two swords.' And He said to them, 'It is enough.'" The anti-self defense Christians try to make His "enough" response to mean Jesus was tired of their sword talk and He was shutting them down like my mom used to do to me and my brother when we would go at it ... "That's enough, you little devils!" I can hear and see her now. Sitting in her La-Z-Boy, smoking Winstons', watching The Young & The Restless and telling us little demoniacs, "Enough! Dammit!" Eugene Peterson's The Message translation is particularly odious with his eisegesis of this passage. Check it out.

"But He (Jesus) said, 'Enough of that; no more sword talk.'" Wow. No wonder Bono was such a fan of The Message. Now, I'm not a Greek scholar, but I have stayed at a Holiday Inn Express, but from what I hear, the Greek word used in Dr. Luke's text means "adequate" ... "sufficient" ... "satisfactory" and does not and cannot mean, in the Greek, "stop" or "no mas senorita!" It. Has. No. Such. Meaning. In. The. Greek. Google it if you don't believe me. I dare you.

Could it be that Jesus actually greenlit the getting of a weapon for self-defense seeing that things were about to change drastically for His boys upon His departure? From a no-duh, *prima facie,* standpoint it sure does to this simpleton.

I can hear my naysayers queueing up with Jesus' admonition to "turn the other cheek" from Matthew 5:39 right now as a proof text against self-defense and to some extent, I would agree with them.

As a provocateur, I get insulted all the time. Mostly by liberals and they often call me gay which is weird because they use that term as a bad thing when all the while they tell us it's a great thing. Go figure. By the way, I'm not gay, but I do like Kate Hudson flicks.

Anyway, I get insulted often. Some of it's over my conservatism. Some of it's over my brutal writing style. Some of it is because some people perceive me as a living heart donor and some of it is over my faith in God.

When these digs come in, I don't sweat it. It's par for the course in my field. *C'est la vie.* I don't get offended. I don't defend myself. I don't go on social media and have vanity wars with some online hashtagger. I don't hire some company to try to scrub the internet of all untoward stuff folks say about me. I plow on and I turn the other cheek. And that's pretty much how every Bible commentator and their dog sees Jesus' exhortation in Mt.5:39 as ignoring the radical feminist who mocks you for your Jesus-fish on your minivan. What it does not mean is passively standing by and watching one daughter getting raped while offering to the rapist your other daughter as well.

And here's another thing to note: Jesus doesn't ban us from fleeing violent persecution (Lk. 4:29-30; Jn. 8:59, 10:39; 2 Cor. 11:32-33). Sometimes a good run is better than a bad stand.

For all the pacifists out there, that believe Christians should be this doormat for the powers of darkness and the people they control, and that we're not to defend ourselves in any form or fashion, what do you do with Jesus, the apostles and other Christians defending themselves when confronted by evil priests and politicians (Mt. 23:1-36, Lk. 12:11-12, Acts 22:1, 24:10)? They didn't just let people talk mad smack about them and God. When "slapped" with some bogus charges of blasphemy, or called to account for their beliefs, they didn't curl up in the fetal position, wet their big Christian diaper and just "turn the other cheek." They defended themselves and rebuked their enemies to their faces as they fought earnestly for the faith (Jd. 3,4).

No doubt, some are thinking right now, "Yeah, Jesus & The Boys argued their points but they didn't cut their persecutors' heads off with a sword." I agree. That, they did not. Which brings me to Christ's advice to believers when being persecuted for their faith. Clearly, He said you're blessed when you're persecuted (Mt. 5:10) and He said to boldly declare your faith in the midst of opposition (Mk. 8:38) and if people hated and killed Him, well, we shouldn't expect better treatment (Jn. 15:18-25). That's clear and undeniable. What scripture does *not* say is that all violence is persecution.

Here's what I mean: if you want to punch me in the nose for telling you, "God loves you and he's got a wonderful plan for your life" then I'll take that and not hold it against you. I, too, was once lost and didn't like annoying Christians when they ruined my buzz by telling me I was a sinner when I was getting high with my girlfriend. I also wanted to punch some of them.

In addition, if someone drags me to the gallows and tells me to deny Jesus or they're going to lop off my noggin. Well, goodbye my noggin. I'll see you soon in the world-to-come right after my head gets severed.

However, if you want to harm my loved ones and innocent people, and it has zilch to do with persecution for one's faith and has everything to do with you're just an evil jackass, well … that's a whole 'nother ball game.

"Well, Christians still shouldn't arm themselves. That's what cops are for." Hey man, I think the world of police officers who truly serve and protect us. God bless 'em. However, when a violent altercation goes down it usually happens at three feet, in three seconds and you have three shots to drop the perp. In other words, when seconds count … the police are minutes away. If you want to wait for the average twenty-two minutes for a cop to rock up while you're being robbed, raped, or beaten to a pulp then go for it. That's your right. For me, I prefer having my .357 magnum at my side because it answers the call at about eleven hundred feet per second.

"Yeah, but Paul says in Romans 13:1-7 that only the government has the authority to use the sword to protect citizens." I saw a movie once where only the government had guns. I didn't end that well. I can't remember the title though. What was it? Dang it, I'm getting old. C'mon on Doug, think! Oh, I remember now. The movie was called *Schindler's List.*

Again, pardon my redundancy but I'm very grateful for police protection and our epic military might. That said, thankfully, our government, here in The United States of America, has also given us the right to keep and bear arms. That's what makes us different than godless Iran. So, as Americans, we have Jesus Who said, "buy a sword" and our country that says you have the right to defend yourself. Seems pretty plain to me but then again I'm just an ol' 2.1 grad from Texas Tech.

Also, and I never ever hear this being part of the holy, "buy a sword" exhortation Jesus gave to the guys but, I don't know if you know this or not: The Apostles didn't stay at The Ritz Carlton or some snazzy AirBnB while they were upsetting the world. They also didn't drive around in some armored limousine when they schlepped from town to town. They walked through the frickin' woods folks and that part of the planet, in ancient times, held lions and bears. Paul even spoke of being in "perils in the wilderness." (2 Co. 11:26).

Finally, when it comes to Jesus and Trump on self-defense, as you can tell, I think the twain are on the same page in light of Lk. 22:36. I can tell you right now who loves the anti-self-defense bent of the effeminized branches of Christendom. Here's a short-list of twenty folks living and dead, who don't/ didn't want Christians armed:

Dictators in socialist countries.
Rapists.
Murderers.
Burglars.
Michael Jackson.
Hitler.
Stalin.
Lenin.
Eric Holder.
ISIS.

Al Qaeda.
Rosie O'Donnell.
Chairman Mao.
Carjackers.
Sheila Jackson Lee.
Fidel Castro.
The DNC.
Catholic priests who squat hump altar boys.
Alexandria Occasional-Cortex.
Satan.

CHAPTER EIGHT

Trump Loves Nationalism. The Left Says It's Evil. What Saith Jesus?

Brandon Vallorani

My Italian grandfather, Big D, turned 90 in July of 2013. To celebrate, we flew him from his home outside of Pittsburgh to Atlanta for an epic birthday party that turned into a huge family reunion.

Before the relatives arrived, I got some quiet moments with my grandfather. We sipped Italian wine together while he told me stories of his childhood in Italy — some I'd heard many times, and others were completely new.

During one of those stories, Big D started singing the chorus of an Italian song called, *Giovinezza*. I immediately pulled out my iPhone to film it and share it on social media. The likes, comments, and shares from everyone began pouring in. I was so proud.

A few years later, after my grandfather had passed away, I decided to look up the words to this song. Here's the chorus:

Giovinezza, giovinezza,
Primavera di bellezza
Per la vita, nell'asprezza
Il tuo canto squilla e va!

When translated, it reads:

Youth, Youth,
Spring of beauty,
In the hardship of life
Your song rings and goes!

Continue through the verses and you will discover some eye-opening statements, that lead the researcher into finding out that Italy, Germany, and Japan all united on their own versions of the same song, proudly bowing at the altar of fascism.

I was shocked to discover that this song was composed and commissioned under Mussolini's government at the height of his regime. Why would my grandfather remember this song from his childhood?

The words of the song are stirring and were meant to rally Italian citizens to something bigger than themselves – pride in the Fatherland of Italy. *Giovinezza* was sung before sporting events, films, and other public gatherings. Those who did not join in were often roughed up by bystanders if they did not remove their hats. The song was banned in post-war Italy and remains so to this day.

When he was only 13 years of age, my grandfather was forced to march down the streets of Rome with the other schoolchildren and sing *Giovinezza* while Mussolini and Hitler looked on with pride. The chorus of the song was burned into his young mind.

My great-grandfather, Luigi Vallorani, wanted nothing to do with fascism, Hitler, or Mussolini. This was the breaking point for Luigi, so that very day he made arrangements to send my grandfather across the Atlantic to live with his relatives in America. My great-grandfather had lived in America for several years before returning to Italy, and he loved America and what it represented. Luigi wanted a better life for his son than to follow the footsteps of tyrannical leaders, of whom he didn't even know the depths of evil and terror to come.

Big D overcame many challenges of an immigrant's life in the USA, even being placed with children half his age in school because he couldn't speak English. But he grew up to become an American Hero, serving in the Army-Airforce during WWII to defeat the very Axis Powers he had been coerced to march for in his youth. I know that my grandfather was too young to know what the song meant when he sang it. The tune was catchy, and anything sung in Italian sounds beautiful!

I agree that the song *Giovinezza* should be banned in Italy. But what about our own national anthem, *The Star-Spangled Banner*? It is a source of immense pride for most Americans who willingly stand, remove their hats, and place their hand over their heart when it is sung. As a sign of protest, however, many NFL players are choosing to kneel rather than stand for our national anthem.

The Star-Spangled Banner has come under heavy fire in recent years because the Left claims it was written during America's "racist" colonial period. This attack on our national anthem is the latest chapter in the anti-American movement that manifested itself during the 1960s.

It's no wonder that the recent surge of patriotism and nationalism under the presidency of Donald J. Trump has infuriated The Left. They equate patriotism and nationalism with fascism. What is the difference between these three ideologies?

Patriotism simply describes the feelings of love and devotion that citizens feel for their country as well as its historical, ethnic, and cultural distinctives. While Patriotism and Nationalism are not the same, they are not mutually exclusive.

Nationalists believe that their nation should be sovereign, self-governing, and unified around a common language, belief, and history. They also believe the interests of their nation come first and foremost over and above any other nation. On the surface, the Left despises nationalism because they believe it excludes other languages, cultures, and faiths.

More importantly, Liberals fundamentally disagree with the historical fact that America was founded as a Christian nation. They claim that America's founding fathers were white supremacists in an attempt to discredit them and undermine the Constitution. Why?

The Left has been working behind the scenes in Hollywood and University campuses for decades to radically change America into an entirely new nation — leaving no vestige of Christianity or the conservative values that made us great. Their tactic is to equate patriotism and nationalism with fascism and

> Nationalists believe that their nation should be sovereign, self-governing, and unified around a common language, belief, and history.

eliminate patriotism as we would all wish to eliminate Nazi pamphlets from the streets had we lived in the 1930s and '40s.

When we think of fascism today, we think of Hitler and Mussolini and the great atrocities of the Holocaust. We think of the millions of people who died, who had their belongings and homes – and family members – ripped from them. It was a horrible time in humanity's history.

Wikipedia describes fascism as a "far-right, ultranationalist ideology." But the truth is, Hitler and Mussolini were much closer to the socialist Left than the conservative Right. After all, the Nazi Party was officially the *National Socialist German Workers' Party.*

It is widely agreed that Fascists coerce their citizens to subordinate their personal interests to the "common good." Conservatives promote individual freedom and free-market competition while socialists limit individual freedom and increase government regulation for the benefit of the people. The "common good" becomes the first line of reasoning to promote socialist extremism.

The dirty little secret is that members of the Democratic party are the real fascists. Their God is the State and their religion is Atheism. Unwanted children are aborted. Dissenting conservatives and Christians are discriminated against. The First Amendment is gone, and the Second Amendment is in grave danger, just like it was in Nazi Germany.

The Left equating our patriotic and nationalist pride with fascism is a case of "the pot calling the kettle black." Freedom to hold a different opinion is censored. As one writer put it: 2019 is the New "1984."[24]

At a rally in Houston on October 22, 2018, President Trump openly claimed to be a nationalist.

> "A globalist is a person that wants the globe to do well, frankly, not caring about our country so much. And you know what? We can't have that," Trump said.
> "You know, they have a word – it's sort of became old-fashioned – it's called a nationalist. And I say, really, we're not supposed to use that word. You know what I am? I'm a nationalist, okay? I'm a nationalist. Nationalist. Nothing wrong. Use that word. Use that word."[25]

President Trump wants to put America First. He believes that globalism is a threat to American security and prosperity. To modern globalist ears, this may sound archaic and selfish. However, it's the Left's attempt to undermine America's position as a global power that will adversely affect the economies and safety of many other nations.

There's nothing intrinsically wrong with being proud of one's country and putting its interests first, as long as the country is moral and just. The ancient nation of Israel is an example of a nationalist movement that was ordained by God Himself. Read the Torah to follow their journey from Egypt to the Promised Land and you will see that God was a nationalist. The Zionist movement that led to the founding of the Jewish State of Israel in 1948, was also a nationalist movement. Only anti-Semites would be opposed the Jewish people returning to the land which God gave to them.

Fast-forward four thousand years. Was the Pilgrims' journey to the New World in 1620 any different? Look at how richly God has blessed America because our founding fathers built a government based on the Word of God. Look at the many churches dotting our countryside. They are a symbol that America was meant to be the "shining city on a hill" that President Reagan envisioned frequently during his addresses.

> These visitors ... do not come as white or black, red or yellow; they are not Jews or Christians; conservatives or liberals; or Democrats or Republicans. They are Americans awed by what has gone before, proud of what for them is still... a shining city on a hill. [26]

> I've spoken of the shining city all my political life, but I don't know if I ever quite communicated what I saw when I said it. But in my mind it was a tall, proud city built on rocks stronger than oceans, wind-swept, God-blessed, and teeming with people of all kinds living in harmony and peace; a city with free ports that hummed with commerce and creativity. And if there had to be city walls, the walls had doors and the doors were open to anyone with the will and the heart to get here. That's how I saw it, and see it still. [27]

An honest reading of the scripture proves that God believes in national sovereignty. This does not mean that all nations are good. In Romans 13, the Apostle Paul tells us that the government is ordained by God to punish evil-doers and should be obeyed. In the Gospel of Mark 12:17, Jesus tells us to "Give back to Caesar what is Caesar's and to God what is God's."

Just a few chapters later, a Gentile woman comes to Jesus begging for healing for her daughter who was tormented with demons. What was His response? "I was not sent except to the lost sheep of the house of Israel."

> And behold, a woman of Canaan came from that region and cried out to Him, saying, "Have mercy on me, O Lord, Son of David! My daughter is severely demon-possessed." But He answered her not a word. And His disciples came and urged Him, saying, "Send her away, for she cries out after us." But He answered and said, "I was not sent except to the lost sheep of the house of Israel." Then she came and worshiped Him, saying, "Lord, help me!" But He answered and said, "It is not good to take the children's bread and throw it to the little dogs." And she said, "Yes, Lord, yet even the little dogs eat the crumbs which fall from their masters' table." Then Jesus answered and said to her, "O woman, great is your faith! Let it be to you as you desire." And her daughter was healed from that very hour. (Mt. 15:22-28, NKJV)

Jesus is clear that He has been sent *first* to redeem the lost in Israel, *then* to the rest of the world.

Clearly, the concept of a sovereign nation is ordained by God himself. Jesus' Kingdom is not of this world. But He expects us to obey the earthly powers — so long as their laws do not contradict His Law.

President Trump wants to Make America Great Again and that's why I voted for him in 2016 and I will again in 2020.

This can only happen if we obey 2 Chronicles 7:14: "If My people, who are called by My name, will humble themselves and pray and seek My face and turn from their wicked ways, then I will hear from heaven, and I will forgive their sin and will heal their land."

CHAPTER NINE

The Judge of All And Trump's Judicial Appointments

Doug Giles

"In a certain city there was a judge who neither feared God nor respected man. And there was a widow in that city who kept coming to him and saying, 'Give me justice against my adversary.' For a while he refused, but afterward he said to himself, 'Though I neither fear God nor respect man, yet because this widow keeps bothering me, I will give her justice, so that she will not beat me down by her continual coming.'"
And the Lord said, "Hear what the unrighteous judge says. And will not God give justice to His elect, who cry to Him day and night? Will He delay long over them? I tell you, He will give justice to them speedily. Nevertheless, when the Son of Man comes, will He find faith on earth?
Luke 18:2-8, NASB

How jacked up is the 9th Circuit?

It boasts an 84% reversal rate, second only to the Federal Circuit. Now close your eyes and imagine ... a Supreme Court that takes its cues from the 9th Circus.

Don't laugh. It nearly happened.

Think back to February 13, 2016 – the date that changed everything. What makes that Saturday so special? I'm glad you asked, you inquiring mind.

That's the day Antonin Scalia punched his ticket for the Great Hereafter. That made it the day we also realized our knife-edge balanced Supreme Court was *this* close being stacked by nuttier than a squirrel turd activists on the Left.

It's the stuff of nightmares.

This close to seeing SCOTUS stacked with judges ready to start some serious legislating, deciding once and for all which of our inalienable rights could really use some spicing up with a fresh coat of fine print and alienating.

On that day the 2016 election stopped being just about the Presidency. The Courts were on the ballot too. It was Go-Time.

Garsh. Who would have expected voters to notice that judicial decisions are only as good as the judges making them, and it may *ipso facto* matter what sort of fish we stock our judicial pond with?

Lemme think back ... I know I just went to public school and all, but wasn't it a SCOTUS decision that said prayer is *verbo-*

ten in school? Why yes, Spanky, I believe it was. And was it a SCOTUS decision that a Ten Commandments display was taken down in Kentucky because it was too "Christian"?

Looking at those examples, do you have the sneaking suspicion that Jesus might have an opinion or two about why the courts might matter just a little bit?

What about our rights?

Do you think the tribe of tinkerpots that thrilled to news of our semi-socialist northern neighbors' duplicitous decision making "hurtful" language offensive to Islam and the Pronoun Police illegal should be the ones stacking the American Supreme Court?

Occasional-Cortex got excited and got a little *too* honest about her political intentions.

She was asked in a town hall meeting what should be done about the courts. She showed her true colors and thirst for political power. "We take back the House, we take back the Senate, we take back the Presidency, we pack the Supreme Court of the United States of America... Next. (giggle)"

Not so long ago, even Democrats slapped down FDR for trying to play that card. Why should the courts suddenly need "packing" now?

For the first time in many, many moons, the courts are tipping toward Originalism again.

She can't allow that. She wants control of the courts. It's the bread and butter of pushing their agenda. She knows courts hold the key to cultural change they couldn't get any other way. You already know this. You've seen it happen.

The Courts are the enforcement arm of legislation and policies the Regressive Left could never force down the throats of We The People or Congress. So they put Progressives in the Courts, and litigate their will onto the rest of us.

Are Christians still praying in schools? Take it to court.[28]

Can't get the abortions you want, when and where you want them? Take it to court.[29]

Did those pesky citizens (even in California!) vote against your same-sex marriage laws? Take it to court.[30]

The ink wasn't even dry on the paperwork when the pastry artist, Jack Phillips, at Masterpiece Cakeshop won his case in front of the Supreme Court[31] before they went after him again. Another lawsuit-happy activist set a trap for him on the same day of the ruling. They knew what lines he wouldn't cross, and went looking to pick a fight. A transgender woman ordered a pink birthday cake with blue icing as a sort of "gender transition" cake.32 This violated the Christian baker's personal moral convictions that gender is based on biology. She simply couldn't stand that his religious rights had been protected. It's not about justice or fairness, it's about moving the agenda forward, by whatever means necessary.

But judges aren't supposed to twist the law, you say? Go ahead ... take them to court. Oh, wait ... you already did, and were shocked to find out what kind of judges were running the show. Or have you forgotten the Obama administration already?

Are you running into problems with passing Obamacare? No problemo, take it to court, and let Judge Roberts rewrite the law to push it through.[33]

Are you mad that Trump is using his Article II powers? Take him to court.[34]

We've seen judges make sketchy decisions before, haven't we? Decisions are only as good as the judges who are making them, and their ideas.

Bad ideas breed bad policy, and as bad ideas go, it's hard to beat the left for they're a veritable cornucopia of crappy content.

Would support of that "Forced Sterilization" Law[35] in 1927's era of eugenics and Margaret Sanger fly with today's feckless feminists? No? How about the Japanese Internment?[36] Would that be yummy to voters today, or would the ACLU be all over them like white on rice?

What gave us trainwrecks like Plessy vs. Ferguson[37], or Dred Scott[38]? Wasn't it because the jackass justices that handed them down were chock-full of bad ideas.

And we know exactly what kind of people Ocasio-Cortez and Team Transform America would love to pack the court with, don't we?

They'd fill it with justices who seethe at the sight of the (5-4) Heller decision[39]. Justices who would gladly get with the gun grabbers, and outlaw the scary "fully semi-automatic" guns[40] that CNN bravely warned us about.

They'd fill it with justices who would tell Trump and his exclusion of transsexuals in the military to go pound sand… and by the way, you can't block the border, either!

They'd fill it with justices who think free speech is *muy bueno*, at least so long as it isn't "offensive" to anyone.

But we never woke up to that nightmare, did we, my little kiddies?

Their little, progressive choo-choo train never left the station. While visions of sugarplum appointments danced through Hillary's head, Mitch blocked Obama's lame-duck appointment of old what's-his-name. Oh, right. Merrick Garland.

Whatever happened to Merrick? I'm glad you asked. We looked back in history to Biden's plan to block a judicial appointment in an election year and we fish-slapped them with their own strategy. #Boom. Liberals were angrier than Rosie O'Donnell after a three-day juice fast.

Then Trump went ahead and spoiled their victory party by announcing a list of judges he'd be choosing from. A list of names assembled by the Heritage Foundation and the Federalist Society.

Suddenly, The Donald wasn't a laughing matter anymore.

The louder the Democrats whined and moaned about the Republican Senate blocking Obama's court pick, the more it reminded voters how much that mattered … and the Supreme Court appointment quickly became one of Trump's key promises.

Trump – when he got elected – picked a real fine judge in Neil Gorsuch. Just how good was the Gorsuch pick?

He was such a good pick that whenever NeverTrumpkins hit fever-pitch with their whining, they could always find their Zen again with the magical mantra ... "but Gorsuch." They can criticize his Twitter use, the blasting of his political opponents, his brinkmanship with North Korea, the Paris Accord, holding NATO's feet to the fire, Iran, moving the Embassy to Jerusalem, whatever he might do to make NeverTrumpkins wet their collectivist diapers, they could usually talk themselves back to pseudo-sanity with the mantra, "But Gorsuch."

The Democrats, on the other hand, cranked the crazy up to eleven and broke off the knob.

Bernie Sanders complained about women's rights, corporations, and campaign finance reform. Pelosi called Gorsuch a "very hostile appointment," a "very bad decision," and "well outside the mainstream of American legal thought." Warren and Schumer didn't like him either – which was another good sign.

But we're not asking about Democrats, Patriots, or RINOs are we? The big question is ... who would Jesus nominate?

Let's crack open His book and see what the Lord of All Creation has to say Himself.

The Son of God once told a parable about an "unjust judge" who doesn't fear God or men. The parable wasn't really teaching us about judges, it was talking about persistence in prayer. But He made the point that there is such a thing as an unjust judge ... and then He went further – He defined it.

If we want to know what a good judge looks like, maybe we should know what a bad one looks like, first, eh?

How about the kind that has personal agendas? The kind that uses his office dishonestly? Would that be *verboten* to the Judge of All Men's Souls? Why yes. Yes, it would. And what about the kind of judge that rejects both faith and tradition, the kind that would rather Fundamentally Transform his country than uphold the sound foundations upon which it rests? Might that be the kind of judge that would give him an urge to flip some tables? Isn't that a good picture of the kind of judge who "Doesn't fear God or men"?

In America, we call them "Activist Judges."

Now, they weren't really happy when Gorsuch got slotted in to replace Scalia. But they weren't too worried, either, after all, he's replacing one Originalist with another.

The real test came when Justice Kennedy announced he was retiring. Suddenly, all Hell broke loose. When Scalia was replaced by Gorsuch, it was no big deal. One conservative judge replaced another ... and who knows? Maybe this guy would be a little softer than Antonin Scalia, so despised by the Regressive Left. After all – Kennedy was a Republican appointee, but a "swing" judge on some "transformational cases" where it really mattered to the Liberals' long game. Sure, they'd rather have the win, but nobody really goes nuclear over a draw. It's a whole other ballgame with Donald J. Trump picking a replacement for Kennedy. The Left saw Kennedy as an ally – or at least a swing vote that supported some of their favorite causes. When Kennedy hung up the robes for the last time the Activist Left went to DEFCON 2 ... and they were itching to ramp it up even higher.

Justice Kennedy had been considering retirement for about a year before he finally hung up his robes. The fact that Kennedy retired when he did indicated that he could trust Trump with his legacy.

For his part, Trump was playing chess when his resistance rivals were playing checkers. Even Vanity Fair gave a tip of the cap to how Trump convinced Kennedy to retire before the midterm election in 2018. Trump went out of his way to give deference to Justice Kennedy. By picking Gorsuch, Trump picked someone that clerked for Kennedy himself. That was no accident. Kennedy was part of the swearing-in ceremony.

Ivanka had lunch with Kennedy after the Inauguration, and she even brought her daughter to the Supreme Court to hear oral arguments – as a special guest of Justice Kennedy.

After Kennedy was glowing with father-like pride over Gorsuch's confirmation, the White House floated two names that were on the shortlist for the next SCOTUS vacancy -- Judge Brett Kavanaugh of the U.S. Court of Appeals for the District of Columbia Circuit and Judge Raymond Kethledge. Coincidentally, both *also* had clerked for Kennedy. What a small world!

When Chuck Grassley went on radio in March 2018, the topic of aging judges came up. Grassley said, "If you're thinking about quitting this year, do it yesterday."

Kennedy heard him loud and clear. He resigned in June. Boom!

But why, little kiddies, was he willing to resign in the first place?

Hearken to the words of Constitutional Law Prof., Jonathan Turley:

> I think the Gorsuch nomination was reassuring, I think it gained him a level of trust with Trump that he could discern a quality nominee [...] I think the Gorsuch nomination had a huge impact on Kennedy and if I was to point to anything explaining the timing, I would probably have to say it was the Gorsuch Nomination.[41]

Say what? Did that oafish rube with the golden comb-over manage to parlay one Supreme Court appointment into two? That's some real *Art of The Deal* stuff right there.

But the fight didn't stop there. The light touch he used to gain Kennedy's confidence wouldn't mean Jack Squat if his candidate stalled out in the confirmation process. And the Left was bringing out every dirty trick in the book to try and stop Trump's Kavanaugh appointment. They may play dirty, but at least they play to win. That's the process where our kick-butt and take names Billionaire Real Estate Developer President showed exactly why Trump could do what no "War Hero" or "Boy Scout" could in the previous two election cycles ... unlike most Republicans, he *also* plays to win. He had to. The stakes were higher than a starlet's skirt in her private meeting with Harvey Weinstein.

The Left played dirty from day one. They had their astroturf protesters ready from the get-go. On the day Trump's nominee was announced – protesters were ready with their slogans and placards. They weren't taking any chances. They had their signs and emails ready protesting all four of the short-listed candidates. One protester was shown filling in the name in the pre-written poster board complaining about Trump's "horrible" pick. Others didn't even bother to throw away the professionally made protest sign with a different short-listed name on it.

There were some dead giveaways in the mistakes the resist crowd made. Women's March got busted with their press release: "In response to Donald Trump's nomination of XX to the Supreme Court of the United States ..." They went on to describe how the candidate would be a "death sentence" for "thousands" of women across the United States.

The nomination of "XX"?

Oops. Somebody forgot to fill the name in the form letter before they sent it. It's almost like it didn't matter who was nominated, isn't it?

The next huge gaffe was by Democracy For America: "...she represents an assault on justice, freedom, and core democratic values."

"She" ... ? Did those tools just assume Judge Kavanaugh's gender? Is "mis-pronouning" people totes kewl now?

Right out of the gate, it was obvious Trump's second Supreme Court nomination was going to be a slugfest.[42] Skittish little tinkerpot Republicans were ready to melt like a snow-cone on South Beach at the first sign of a fight. They had learned nothing from the "Borking" of a good judge. Not Trump. He rolled up his sleeves and got ready for a fight. He lives for this.

Trump didn't play by prissy establishment rules. He didn't blink. He didn't cower. He didn't withdraw the name under intense pressure to do so. He didn't flinch. He didn't give one single inch of ground. He went pedal-to-the-metal to back his nominee. And – astonishingly – he even rallied the gutless wonders in his party to do the same.

Let's back up to the pick itself for a second.

Kavanaugh was not the only choice he could have made. He wasn't the perfect choice, or even the best choice of the names on his list. Some were stronger on issues. But this isn't Trump's first rodeo. He had to size up his friends and his foes and pick the best choice for the fight at hand. He's a negotiator by nature, and the best deal is always one you can actually close.

He had to make the right pick to balance his choice – it had to be a good one – keeping both his allies and his opposition in mind. He threaded the needle with Kavanaugh. Here's how it happened:

He had a couple of choices for nominee he could have gone with, but he knew his Senate support was shaky. There were a couple of spineless lumps he knew he couldn't depend on ... and McCain wasn't just unreliable, he was unavailable because he held onto his seat long after he was able to fulfill its function.

Trump picked Kavanaugh – a comparatively safe nominee. That was a slick move because he was a Bush appointment, which united otherwise warring factions on the Right.

Then we saw the full fury of the Left's bag of dirty tricks. We thought Spartacus was going to be the high-water mark for big, stupid dramatic moments. Not even close. Feinstein ran out the clock and then she played the "Ford" card pushing the hearing into unscheduled overtime while the Democrats tried to run out the clock before the midterms.

If they could just hold on long enough to get the midterms and maybe take the Senate, that nomination committee would be under *their* control. They swung for the fences.

Any other Republican Politician might have caved at this point. But Trump and Kavanaugh stood strong. It took all of that strength to stand against the coming storm.

Dems threw the most insane stories up against the wall looking for something – anything – that would stick. We heard stories about keggers, drugged punch, and rape gangs trotted through the Senate chamber, with the doe-eyed Media(D) hanging on every word and liberally spicing their reporting with the words "credibly accused."

In a shocking display of Republican masculinity, "Cocaine Mitch" McConnell and Lindsey "Grahambo" Graham stepped up in defense of Kavanaugh and the presumption of innocence, savaging the Democrats for how they were hammering him, and Kavanaugh himself gave an impassioned plea for his innocence.

It was a bar fight and the truth got knocked around like a midget in a mosh pit. But eventually, Kavanaugh got confirmed.

And, just like magic, as soon as he was confirmed what happened next? Those allegations against Kavanaugh suddenly dried up. Some – like the one Creepy Porn Lawyer Michael Avenatti was hawking – even got referred for potential criminal investigations. But would any of this have happened unless Trump was willing to put his own credibility on the line, roll up his sleeves and jump into a high-stakes political knife-fight? Of course not.

He broke from a long-standing Republican tradition of wilting under media and political pressure. He stood his ground, fought for what he believed in, and won.

The reason Republicans held onto the Senate – and got stronger, even – was at least partly because Republicans showed up in support of what they've been doing with appointments, despite Team Resistance's dogged slow-walking of every single appointment.

Trump has appointed two Justices ... so far. Can you imagine what happens if Ruth Bader Ginsburg rides off into the sunset? The only thing keeping her going right now is spite and a clenched-fist rejection of everything Trump stands for. I remember when RBG called Trump a "faker" who "should resign." Even CNN's Chris Cillizza called her "the face of Trump's resistance"[43] ... this is the same guy that called the first two years of Trump's Presidency a "Hellscape for Democrats."[44] Nope, no bias there.

Wouldn't it be a kick in the crotch to poor Cillizza if his precious face of the resistance packed it in and RGB was replaced by another Trump pick? How about a lovely pro-life Catholic woman like Amy Coney Barrett? Why not? She clerked under Scalia, and is a proud mother to her seven children (two of whom were adopted from Haiti) and the youngest of her biological children has special needs? It would hit them like holy water on a vampire, wouldn't it? And just in time for all these national changes to abortion law, too.

Roe v. Wade. Isn't that why having the President matters so much? He's the one picking the appointments. Where would we be today if Hillary had made those two picks – three if you count Ginsburg stepping down to be replaced by a strong Democrat. That "living" Constitution would be stretched thinner than the elastic on Michael Moore's sweatpants.

When he took office, Trump worked a kind of magic nobody expected: Democrats are so worried about the newly rebalanced SCOTUS they're getting desperate. They're even rediscovering ... Federalism![45]

And we haven't even gotten to the good news about his other court appointments yet. Like the vacancies that Trump will be filling in the Ninth Circus.

Even as I sit writing this, SCOTUS is hearing a case demanding that a cross built after WWI be taken down because the government took over the Legion land it was built on.[46] It's no secret that the courts know the Establishment Clause test formulas are more jacked than Jason Momoa. Would you rather have Trump's appointees hearing that case, or Hillary's?

Exactly.

The Democrats have been dreaming up every trick they can try to jam a stick in the spokes of these Judicial appointments. They have been stalling every single nomination, dragging it out as long as they possibly can. And then they got a huge assist by a NeverTrumper RINO with an axe to grind.

Jeff Flake decided it was important to let those nominations die on the vine unless the Senate passed legislation (absent any Constitutional authority to do so) blocking the President from exercising Article II powers with respect to ending the Mueller investigation. And so, just because he wanted to be an obnoxious tool, a stack of good judicial candidates were not confirmed, and their benches remained empty.

Oh, and did you know that Trump has appointed more female judges than any GOP President so far? The dorks at CNN missed that little gem, didn't they? Not bad for a Racist-Sexist-Homophobe.

Let's see – we've got a stack of judges who respect the rule of law, who aren't looking to burn down every traditional institution in the country, and who give due deference to the role of religious liberty in the country?

Do you see anything at all in that list that Jesus would find objectionable?

Yeah, me neither.

CHAPTER TEN

Sorry Hipsters, Jesus Was Not The Original Socialist

Brandon Vallorani

*When they came to Capernaum, the collectors of the
two-drachma tax went up to Peter and said, "Does your teacher not pay the tax?" He said, "Yes." And when he came into
the house, Jesus spoke to him first, saying, "What do you think,
Simon? From whom do kings of the earth take toll or tax?
From their sons or from others?"
And when he said, "From others," Jesus said to him, "Then the
sons are free. However, not to give offense to them, go to the
sea and cast a hook and take the first fish that comes up, and
when you open its mouth you will find a shekel. Take that and
give it to them for Me and for yourself."*
Matthew 17:24-27, ESV

Have you ever asked yourself what the Lord's philosophy toward taxation is? The easy and obvious answer might be to flip directly to Matthew 22, where He was asked a direct question about taxes to Caesar. It's a familiar text, and often quoted:

> *Then the Pharisees went and plotted how to entangle Him in His words. And they sent their disciples to Him, along with the Herodians, saying, "Teacher, we know that You are true and teach the way of God truthfully, and You do not care about anyone's opinion, for You are not swayed by appearances. Tell us, then, what You think. Is it lawful to pay taxes to Caesar, or not?" But Jesus, aware of their malice, said, "Why put Me to the test, you hypocrites? Show Me the coin for the tax." And they brought Him a denarius. And Jesus said to them, "Whose likeness and inscription is this?" They said, "Caesar's." Then He said to them, "Therefore render to Caesar the things that are Caesar's, and to God the things that are God's." When they heard it, they marveled. And they left Him and went away.* (Mt. 22:15-22, ESV)

But does that example really shine any light on His thoughts about taxes? He was answering a Catch-22 question while flipping the question on its head and making it a question about personal devotion to God. It was hardly a free and frank discussion about His political thoughts about taxes. Not that Jesus was first and foremost political in anything He was doing. His life and legacy was a fulcrum of political change throughout history, of that there can be no doubt. But unlike so many of the political philosophers from Plato on down, this was never His focus. Don't take that to mean He was entirely silent on the issue. That's why we opened this chapter with the story about the fish.

Peter assumed Jesus would always do the right thing, which, naturally He does. But sometimes what we think our obligations are and what *Jesus* thinks our obligations are don't exactly line up. Peter asked Him about the Temple tax. Jesus, playfully riffing off how the Pharisees are the easily-offended snowflakes of His day, said He didn't want to offend them. But He took this conversation in a different direction. It was a Temple Tax, finding its justification in Exodus 30. But do the sons of kings pay taxes? Jesus as much as said He was free from having to pay taxes (being, in effect, the Son of the King). He paid them not out of any *moral* duty, but so as not to give them any seemingly just cause to denounce Him. That shows us that taxes to Him are not the innate moral good the Left thinks taxes to be.

Paying taxes, while necessary for the proper financial running of things, is a civil obligation, but it is not a moral one. That's a far cry from the Left's cries of "paying your fair share" isn't it?

Let's look back at the moment Israel demanded a king for themselves, and the warnings God's prophet Samuel gave them about exactly what that would look like. He gave a pretty clear description of what bloated government waste would look like through the eyes of the people he would tax to keep it going.

> *So Samuel told all the words of the Lord to the people who asked him for a king. And he said, "This will be the behavior of the king who will reign over you: He will take your sons and appoint them for his own chariots and to be his horsemen, and some will run before his chariots. He will appoint captains over his thousands and captains over his fifties, will set some to plow his ground*

and reap his harvest, and some to make his weapons of war and equipment for his chariots. He will take your daughters to be perfumers, cooks, and bakers. And he will take the best of your fields, your vineyards, and your olive groves, and give them to his servants. He will take a tenth of your grain and your vintage, and give it to his officers and servants. And he will take your male servants, your female servants, your finest young men, and your donkeys, and put them to his work. He will take a tenth of your sheep. And you will be his servants. And you will cry out in that day because of your king whom you have chosen for yourselves, and the Lord will not hear you in that day." (2 Sm. 8:10-18, NKJV)

Did you notice the recurring phrase "he will take" running through that text? The Lord's prophet didn't take any time extolling the virtues of setting up a Big Daddy Government. He told his people that this thing they had asked for would come at a very heavy price.

Let's go even deeper into history, all the way back to the book of Genesis where Joseph was serving as Pharaoh's Right-hand Man. In their extreme need, the people of Egypt agreed to some very harsh terms.

And when that year was ended, they came to him the following year and said to him, "We will not hide from my lord that our money is all spent. The herds of livestock are my lord's. There is nothing left in the sight of my lord but our bodies and our land. Why should we die before your eyes, both we and our land? Buy us and our land for food, and we with our land will be servants to Pharaoh. And give us seed that we may live and not die, and that the land may not be desolate." So Joseph bought all the land of Egypt for Pharaoh, for all the Egyptians sold their fields, because the famine was severe on them. The land became Pharaoh's. (Gn. 47:18-22, ESV)

Now that desperation during the famine had turned the Egyptians into literal slaves, what was expected of them by their new master? "And at the harvests you shall give a fifth to Pharaoh, and four fifths shall be your own, as seed for the field and as food for yourselves and your households, and as food for your little ones." And they said, "You have saved our lives; may it please my lord, we will be servants to Pharaoh." (Gn. 47: 24-25) They owed the lord of the land 20% of everything it produced.

What was that "reasonable" tax rate Alexandria Ocasio-Cortez was proposing again? Seventy percent of every dollar past $10 Million, wasn't it? What do you suppose the ancient people of Egypt would have called that arrangement?

So, throughout scripture, paying taxes has been obligatory, but has been a kind of "necessary evil," not the engine or proof of a nation's morality, like the "pay your fair share" crowd might claim. But what about charity and people in need? Great question.

Can you point to the verse in scripture where Jesus encourages the rabble to demand Caesar raise the taxes on the rich (presumably, "that guy over there") to help the poor? Take as much time as you want. You won't find it. Because He never said that. The government has responsibilities ... but they are more the "convict the guilty and acquit the innocent" kind of responsibilities than the "feed and care for individuals in need" type. It was never supposed to fall to big government programs to identify and meet the needs of the poor. The charitable model was always going to be *people* helping people, Good Samaritan kind of stuff. When Jesus talked about the widow and her offering -- "the widow's mite" -- she was giving it as a free will donation to charity, the Temple, not as a service fee owed to the government at the tip of a Roman sword.

One editor over at ClashDaily.com covers charity in more detail in his slim little book, *A Blueprint for Government that Doesn't Suck*, but here's the short version: charity should be prioritized – first it should be offered by family; second it should be offered by extended community, ie. the religious or some other social network, and finally – only after both of those are exhausted – should the government step in. (See 1 Ti. 5:16) The first two options are more personal, responsive, and less subject to waste while also being far more redemptive since the receiver can have gratitude to a person in a way that he can't to some faceless government institution.

You may be noticing by now that scripture broadly, and Jesus personally, had a lot to say about money. In fact, He spoke more about it than He spoke about faith or even Hell. Why? Well, who we are in our daily lives and what we do with our money are intimately wrapped up together. Which is why you can't just gut a financial a system without touching some of the deepest aspects of our humanity. Even two of the Ten Commandments are directly involved in this conversation about financial systems, while others are also implied. The questions of personal property, and envy.

Does the government get to decide that there is a "greater good" that justifies taking a citizen's personal property? And should one interest group be pitted against another one with "fair share" language just because one group has more wealth than another?

Should we accept the modern attitude that being rich is some kind of a sin? Abraham, Issac, Jacob and of course, Kings David and Solomon are examples of significant wealth where they were never condemned for having a wage gap from the common day-laborer. Even Job, after all his testing, had his wealth restored and then some. There is no special virtue in being rich or poor.

As for the money we do have, Moses sets us straight on that count, too, in Deuteronomy 8:18, "But you shall remember the Lord your God, for it is He who is giving you power to make wealth, that He may confirm His covenant which He swore to your fathers, as it is this day."

Such wealth as we have, we only have because God gave us the ability to acquire it. Work is a good thing, and goes right back to the Garden of Eden, before their act of rebellion. The punishment was only found in the increased toil of that labor.

The Bible has harsh words for people who have wealth and are unwilling to do good with it. Certainly. But nowhere does it view wealth *itself* as wicked or unjust. It is more concerned with the attitudes of the person who *owns* the wealth so that the wealth doesn't begin to own them and give them an illegitimate sense of superiority.

As for the giving under compulsion, even Peter and Paul agree that isn't how giving is supposed to work.

Paul taught "Each one must give as he has decided in his heart, not reluctantly or under compulsion, for God loves a cheerful giver." (2 Co. 9:7)

Peter's thoughts on this were far more dramatic. It was in the context of a married couple who had seen early Christians sell their property, sharing the proceeds among all who had need. One couple wanted the praise that came with doing that while misrepresenting the amount they got for the sale, and keeping some back for themselves. (Acts 5) Short version: they got called out for it and it went badly for them.

But in the midst of that story, we hear this:

> Ananias, why has Satan filled your heart to lie to the Holy Spirit and to keep back some of the price of the land? While it remained unsold, did it not remain your own? And after it was sold, was it not under your control? Why is it that you have conceived this deed in your heart? You have not lied to men but to God. (Acts 5:3-4, NASB)

There was never any obligation to sell the land. Nor was there even an obligation to give the full amount. It was their property. The problem was in the deception.

Notice how, through the words of Peter and Paul, even God himself respects the property rights and free will of the person who owns it.

Moral obligations of a certain degree are necessary – but even the tithe is only 10% – everything else you give is guided entirely by conscience. Big Government has no such scruples. As Reagan put it, "Government is like a baby. An alimentary canal with a big appetite at one end and no sense of responsibility at the other."

The account in Acts opens up the communism question. Weren't Christians really proto socialists? Look at that verse

144

where they sold and shared what they had! You'll notice this model wasn't repeated in every New Testament city. Early believers were warned by Jesus' own words, and elsewhere, that Jerusalem would be facing a devastating conflict and Christians were to be ready to flee at a moment's notice. Such flight is far less difficult when your wealth is no longer tied up in the land.

This sharing wasn't the solution to all their financial problems either. You read in Paul's letters how Christians in other cities had to take up an offering to help feed them during a famine.

Skipping ahead to our modern day, we have two competing financial models to choose from. We have the Big Government Socialist model pushed by people like the Bernie Bros and Alexandria Ocasio-Cortez, and we have the more traditional American models where the best thing a government can do for an individual is to get out of his way and let him prosper.

We weren't always a society that trained its youth to land a job in somebody else's company. A large percentage of us were farmers and shopkeepers, (like my great-grandfather, Luigi Vallorani,) -- independent businessmen and women, who understood that wise allocation of resources, and the ability to recognize timely opportunities worked together to make a huge difference in your family's standard of living.

There was no need to pit labor against management, a big percentage of us had no distinctions between those categories. It was, in many cases, a family business. The Industrial Revolution changed that equation. Now we have gravitated to the cities and are largely a nation of employees.

Post-Obama, suddenly the two economic models are up for debate. On one hand, we have Socialism (which basically re-hashes Lenin's empty promise of "Peace, Land, Bread") follow me and we will have a system where uncertainty and risk are done away with. Everyone will have food, everyone will have a home, and everyone will have peace. The Soviet (like the Venezuelan) record on each of those promises stands as a stark reminder of just how much easier those promises are to make than they are to keep. In order for the State to give all those things – which it never actually did – the "benevolent" State required greater and greater control of everyday life and business. It led to breadlines, chronic shortages, and a virtual end to innovation since nobody was working for himself, but for the State. Why bother working hard, you get nothing to show for it anyway? It became *necessary* for the State to shut down any rival to State authority, anything that might endanger their rule by criticizing their actions – especially religious groups – Churches, Temples, etc.

America, on the other hand, made no such promises of security. Its model was established on freedom rather than security. Life, Liberty, and the Pursuit of Happiness, to be precise. In America, can you risk big and lose it all? Absolutely. You can also hit the big-time. It's up to you – not some government bureaucrat – to decide your place in society. In that model, the government doesn't pick a magic number of how much money you're allowed to keep before it confiscates the rest.

How many of our nation's successful businesses were set up by "Angel Investors" – successful businessmen and businesswomen who had already cashed out some of their projects and were ready to roll the dice on helping some other entrepreneurs build their dreams into a reality? It's a lot. But the envy-driven class-warfare types can't see it that way.

All wealth is somehow "stolen" from the sweat of some poor working stiff.

Socialists insist the workers "deserve" a cut of the success, but where are the workers when a business goes under? Aside from their jobs, what do the employees lose? Unless they, too, sunk money into the start-up, they lose nothing.

Bill Whittle once gave the perfect illustration for the difference between these two systems. We already know of two places where you can see the socialist utopia they are describing in action. Places right here in our midst. These are places where everyone really does have enough to eat, a place to sleep, and nobody ever worries about either of those realities changing. Those places are the Prison and the Zoo. But strangely enough, nobody is trying to break into either.
Freedom is risky, sure. Things can go wrong. But giving up your freedom for security is far, far worse. It's hard to believe, after defeating the Soviets that this debate has come into America's political discourse, but it has. Now that it has, we've got two political parties, each going a different direction.

One is championing the socialist model of envy and confiscation, while the other is championing the one that slingshotted America from being a modest colony on the back-half of nowhere to the leading economic and innovation engine of the entire world.

Even leaving aside the specific jobs and economic accomplishments Donald J. Trump has delivered on (they'll be covered in another chapter), the President stood up in his State of the Union to declare "America will never be a socialist country — ever."

Based on everything we've seen in this chapter so far: how Government largess is *not* to be confused with compassion; how envy is specifically denounced in scripture; how the burdens of big government were specifically predicted by the prophet Samuel; how wealth is *not* innately evil or gained at the expense of others - and is, in fact, something granted by God himself; how even God doesn't confiscate wealth by force to help the needy, but asks that it be granted freely – is there really any question which of these two models Jesus Christ would favor?

Is there any doubt that – at least on this economic issue – He'd be more likely to pull the lever for Trump?

CHAPTER ELEVEN

The Earth Is The Lord's, It's Not The Left's

Doug Giles

They are like children sitting in the marketplace and calling to one another, "We played the flute for you, and you did not dance; we sang a dirge, and you did not weep."
Luke 7:32, ESV

T he party that booed God at their national convention claims that they're not religious. That's hilarious. If you buy that line, then you've probably got a time-share in the Everglades, too. Of course, they are – they're extremely religious. *Politics* is their religion.

They don't ask questions about ideas and policies or problems and solutions. For them every issue is an epic struggle of "good versus evil" and, guess what, little Christian? *You* are the ones wearing the black hats in their little morality tale. Every. Single. Time. Want me to prove it, Skippy? No *problemo*.

Try having an out-dated opinion on gender or sexuality and see what happens. Mention someone by their pre-transitioning "dead name," or ask whether women in sports are at a disadvantage when competing against biological males, or bring up a scientific study about gender differences in brain development in utero and watch some heads explode.

The life issue, as another example, is not something they see as a conflict of visions between a positive value of pro-aborts wanting full autonomy for a woman over her body in tension with another positive value of life being sacred and requiring protection. Not at all. We've got famous-for-being-famous activists like Alyssa Milano agreeing wholeheartedly with tweets that the Life Movement wants "to control you, to impose their religious beliefs on you, to dominate you. They want your obedience and they want you to show gratitude."[47]

No wonder we can't have a conversation with these people. They want to understand us about as much as Jussie Smollett wants to find the "real" attackers. It's easier that way; if we're unreasonable and monstrous, it's enough to denounce us. Debating becomes unnecessary.

You don't debate with the Nazis -- you just crush them. If you can slap a swastika on your enemy or make a MAGA hat into a KKK hood, the debate is over. Nobody asks "evil" people about their ideas. That's good news for the Liberals, because they win by default, and nobody will know that their ideas suck worse than an airplane toilet until long after they've been implemented. Yahtzee!

But if you *really* want to see Leftists turn the shrill up to eleven, try breaking ranks with "accepted wisdom" on the Environment. You see, Mama Gaia is a jealous god, and she does not suffer heretics gladly.

Alexandria Ocasio-Cortez coming down Mount Sinai with her Green New Deal is just the latest of the heroic prophets of Mother Earth to pronounce certain doom upon us all.

Do you remember Al "Pregnant Chad" Gore? He must be Old Mama Nature's least favorite prophet because she always seems to be upstaging his Global Warming speeches with ill-timed blizzards.

Remember all those warnings about the polar bears? How they're supposedly facing grave danger because of global warming and it's all our fault? Maybe you saw the National Geographic photo with a skinny polar bear captioned, *"This is what climate change looks like."* But did you see the retraction that came after?

National Geographic went too far in drawing a definitive connection between climate change and a particular starving polar bear in the opening caption of our December 2017 video about the animal. We said, "This is what climate change looks like." While science has established that there is a strong connection between melting sea ice and polar bears dying off, there is no way to know for certain why this bear was on the verge of death. [48]

The 2018 *State of the Polar Bear Report49* came out with news in early 2019. The report's author, zoologist, Dr. Susan Crockford, says that there is now very little evidence to support the idea that the polar bear is threatened with extinction by climate change.

But such "serious" sources as the New York Times and a bevy of blogs call anyone asking questions about polar bear populations "denialist." That's their dogma talking again. They demonize heretics to the faith, with a fresh, updated lexicon, because "pagans" and "witches" are *sooo* 17th Century. Goodbye "pagans" and "witches", hello "Climate Change Deniers!" That punchy title conveniently leverages the emotional force and repugnance of the words "Holocaust Denial" while demonizing people for the crime of being skeptical. These are the same people that un-ironically celebrate Galileo for his famous historical statement ... "and yet it moves."

The world is coming to an end, people! Just ask Occasional-Cortex. If we don't address climate change right now, "the world is going to end in 12 years."[50] The rest of us must implement radically drastic changes ... or else! Changes that will cost trillions of dollars, will require that we kill all cows, ditch air travel, and end our reliance on fossil fuels. And that's just for starters.

Or else, what? Ah, nothing much, it's just that the world is going to end, and boy are your grandkids going to be mad at you!

Didn't she get the memo? The Eco-Messiah already came in 2008. He even said so when he announced after winning the Primary, "this was the moment when the rise of the oceans began to slow and our planet began to heal."[51] He was President for 8 years. Didn't he fix all the world's problems while he was in office? Or was he a complete fraud?

Let's check the record:

Right out of the gate, Obama was very excited that he would be offering incentives for "green jobs" which he assured us were the future of energy. Billions in taxpayer dollars was dumped into these programs. Did they flourish and become the great companies of the future, like we were told?

Let's put it this way... how much stock do you have in Solyndra? Betcha haven't heard that name in a while, eh? They were the politically-connected outfit that went belly up after soaking the taxpayers for a cool half-billion dollars. Obama's Green Agenda would have seen more bang for the buck if he'd used that money to buy a crap-ton of Priuses for Oprah to give away to strangers. At least that would have supported manufacturing jobs.

Flint Michigan's water nightmare happened during his watch, too, didn't it? Why, yes, it did. People even died. Oh, and his EPA got sued over it.[52]

Remember "Gold King"? Under Obama, in 2015, the EPA federalized all waters covered under the Clean Water Act, and less than a month later, was directly responsible for poisoning the Colorado River. Whoopsie.

At least one whistleblower saw the catastrophe coming and tried to warn us about it in a letter to the editor of *The Silverton Standard* on July 30th[53]. Scott Pruitt spoke about Obama's environmental record this way while being interviewed by Hugh Hewitt: Forty percent of the country has failed to hit Ozone targets. About 140 Million people live in areas that haven't hit air quality targets. There are more Superfund sites than there were before Obama came into office. He brought up Gold King and Flint Michigan and the regulations that failed on carbon ... twice. Then he asks the million-dollar question: "So when you look at their record, what exactly did they accomplish for the environment that folks are so excited about?"

Don't just take the Right's word for it. Here's how the somewhere left-of-Lenin online rag *Vox* described Obama's environmental legacy: "Despite vigorous recent attempts to greenwash his legacy, President Obama's climate policy in his first term was largely indistinguishable from George W. Bush's."[54]

Ouch! Shots fired! But ... but ... but ... don't forget the Paris Accord! Oh, don't worry, Spanky, we're getting there.

Obama was very pleased to announce, along with so many other globalists, like Trudeau, Merkel, and Peña Nieto, that he was signing the Paris Accord. If it were truly a treaty, it would have required ratification by two-thirds of the Senate ... which was never going to happen. So it was an "accord." This accord was, we were assured, "non-binding."

If it was so meaningless and harmless, why can't America officially walk away from it until 2020? And why did everyone lose their minds when Trump announced he wanted nothing to do with it?

Could there be a turd in the punchbowl nobody's talking about? Keep that Paris accord in mind. We'll come back to those targets. But first, let's dig into that Green New Deal. We've got twelve years left of schlepping this pebble before we turn the planet into a self-cleaning oven and our blue-green cosmic speck becomes Dante's Easy-Bake.

Well, shucks. If things are really that urgent, then all the true believers are leading by example and living an energy-austere life, right? Guess again.

Al Gore, in a quest to become the "World's First Carbon Billionaire,"[55] got fat and happy from selling a new kind of indulgences to the self-flagellating eco-sinners. You've probably heard of "carbon credits" or "carbon offsets." That little scheme was a get out of hell free card for those who had sinned against Mother Gaia. It let them pay someone to (maybe) plant a tree (somewhere) to atone for the sin of using fossil fuel. Great swindle if you can pull it off, I guess.

True convert to the cause that he is, Gore must be doing all of his conferences over video so that he doesn't have to needlessly jet set around the globe, right? He must have a single relatively modest house, far from the ocean that threatens to swallow us all, right? Nope. None of those are true.

Being a Democrat means having quadruple standards. He's a prophet for the cause, so he isn't expected to constrain his carbon use like the rest of us.

He's a lot like Bernie Sanders – the "socialist" and climate alarmist – who has not two but *three* homes ... and a stack of frequent flyer miles. In the month of October 2018, he spent $297K on private jet travel[56] ... and $5.2 Million in private jet services over 6 months during the primaries Hillary rigged against him. Isn't travel by private jet just about the biggest sin in the carbon values scale? And he's spent five million on private flights in six months? That's gotta be right up there with firebombing a tire warehouse, isn't it?

How can he look us in the eye and tell us the world is going to burn in 12 short years while he's crisscrossing the country in private planes? You just can't have it both ways.

Twelve years. That's how long we have left. Not a moment to spare. But you can't really expect Bernie to plan his campaigning around commercial flights, do you? There's always some reason *you* are the exception to the rule, isn't there?

The eco-zealots are buying into the hysteria – or at least, they're assenting to it in public. So, why aren't those "deplorables" on board with our regularly scheduled panic?

There are a few reasons. For one, crackpots screaming into the wind, announcing "the end is nigh" is not a new idea. People like that crop up all the time, only to find that the end wasn't all *that* nigh after all, and the crackpot's followers slink away, hopefully wiser from the experience.

We don't really care what cult your end times prophet belongs to, if he's worshipping comets, drinking Kool-Aid, or just some over-caffeinated huckster selling books on late-night TV. We don't care.

We've got plenty of reasons from scripture and from science to not buy into the hype.

Genesis gives a pretty solid basis of declaring that whatever power we may have to mess up our planet has limits. Any handwringing about an "extinction event" is nuttier than a squirrel turd. Verse 8:22 – "While the earth remains, seedtime and harvest, cold and heat, summer and winter, day and night, shall not cease."

While the Earth remains ...

Now, I know I went to public school and all, but "as long as the Earth remains" sounds like a pretty long time. So long as this dirt clod we're riding around the sun keeps turning, and isn't smashed into cosmic dust or sucked into a black hole, a few trillion years from now, as long as *that* doesn't happen, we're still going to get summer and winter, right on time.

I hate to break it to you, but this means you probably need to cancel those tickets to the apocalypse party and maybe stop ringing up the credit card debt.

If you thought that we had a parade of *religious* crackpots telling us that the "end is nigh" just take a gander at the environmental ones – it's like a freaking game of *Whack-a-Mole*.

Let's see, just to name a few ecological disasters we've seen come and go:

We had "The population bomb" in 1968 promising we'd all starve in the 70s when our population would climb all the way up to 3.5 or even *gasp* 4 billion people![57]

There was an oil crisis. [58]

There was a scare with DDT destroying the entire food chain. [59]

Then there was global cooling – no that's not a misprint – "The Cooling World." *Newsweek* April 28, 1975.[60]

We heard all about Acid Rain[61] and Nuclear Winter[62], and giant holes in the Ozone layer caused by the hairspray from 80s Glam Rock and Styrofoam containers for McDLTs that could keep the hot side hot and the cold side cold. That was going to kill us all.

The weather came back into the news, it was Global warming with Al Gore promising that Arctic sea ice would be gone by 2013[63], (It's still there) and then losing in court over bogus ecological claims in a movie so bad that it made *The Rocky Horror Picture Show* look like *Citizen Kane*.

Finally, they hedged their bets by calling *everything* climate change.

Refugee Crisis in 2015? That was because of climate change. [64]

Forest fires in California where the flammable eucalyptus trees and the accumulation on the forest floor create a worst-case scenario? Climate change.[65]

Four hurricanes hit Florida in a single month? That's climate change. [66]

When we go a long time with very few major hurricanes making landfall? Climate change.[67]

The Guardian even ran a story with the insane title, *How climate change triggers earthquakes, tsunamis and volcanoes.*[68]

Jesus Himself said don't sweat it.

> *As He sat on the Mount of Olives, the disciples came to Him privately, saying, "Tell us, when will these things be, and what will be the sign of Your coming and of the end of the age?" And Jesus answered them, "See that no one leads you astray. For many will come in My name, say-*

ing, 'I am the Christ,' and they will lead many astray. And you will hear of wars and rumors of wars. See that you are not alarmed, for this must take place, but the end is not yet. For nation will rise against nation, and kingdom against kingdom, and there will be famines and earthquakes in various places." (Mt. 24:3-7, ESV)

If you skip down a little further, He dropped a big clue in verse 14. "And this gospel of the kingdom will be proclaimed throughout the whole world as a testimony to all nations, and then the end will come."

The final buzzer won't sound for our time here on *Terra Firma* until God is good and ready for it. And that won't happen until *after* all the key pieces fall into place ... like the gospel work.

But let's get back to the Green New Deal where the world ends in 12 years. Let's pretend we actually believed that. What would we do?

If you're Alexandria Ocasio-Cortez, that's simple. Her New York office is one minute away from a subway stop. The only right thing for a true believer to do is take mass transit to save the planet – right? Well, you'd *think* so. But no. Her office spent $29K on Uber and Lyft[69] instead of having to commute with the unwashed masses. She's compared the war against global warming to WWII in its urgency. But for her, that "sacrifice" comes without the inconvenience of a war rations policy.

How we answer this climate question is (supposedly) of the utmost importance. She called herself the boss "how 'bout dat" because nobody else "had a solution."[70] She got most if not all of the Democrats running for 2020 to endorse her Green New Deal.

It doesn't really matter if anyone endorses it or not. The whole Green New Deal has been called out as a fraud. By who? By none other than a Co-Founder of Greenpeace.[71] Unlike their general and vague ideas, his criticisms are very specific and detailed.

After calling her a pompous little twit[72], Patrick Albert Moore explained on Twitter why she deserved that title.

> This is a key point, unintended consequences of rash actions based on flawed analysis. @AOC probably never thought about basic food production as it is always there for her in the supermarket. She didn't know she was prescribing mass death but at least now she has been advised. [73]

> Isn't @AOC a bit young to talk about WW2? It was Hell & more than 60 million died. It's her @ GND that would be worse than WW2. Imagine no fuel for cars, trucks, tractors, combines, harvesters, power plants, ships, aircraft, etc. Transport of people & goods would grind to a halt.[74]

He was interviewed on a radio show and he kept pounding away at her ignorant ideas.

> And then you've got the green politicians who are buying scientists with government money to produce fear for them in the form of scientific-looking materials. And then you've got the green businesses, the rent-seekers, and the crony

capitalists who are taking advantage of massive subsidies, huge tax write-offs, and government mandates requiring their technologies to make a fortune on this. And then, of course, you've got the scientists who are willingly, they're basically hooked on government grants.[75]

Did the Libs line up like lemmings? The GOP put it to a Senate vote. How many Democrats stood up for the If You Don't Support It The World Will End legislation? Crickets. Not even the Presidential hopefuls that are co-signers on the Green New Deal voted "Yea." It lost 57-0. Not a single vote was cast in favor of it ... and 4 Democrats voted *against* it.[76] AOC then claimed voting "present" was her idea. I guess she learned a little something from Barry's stint in the Senate, eh? There's some real courage of your convictions.

That shouldn't really surprise anyone, though. Remember "Standing Rock" where environmentalists protested about pipelines? AOC proudly claims she was part of that protest. What do we know about that "environmental" protest? When everyone left, there was enough trash left behind to fill 480 dumpsters. With friends like that, does the environment really need enemies?

All the world lost their minds that Trump was walking away from the Paris Accord! What changed because of it? Not much. With everyone, except for Trump, still playing along did they manage to save the world?

Here's a headline and subhead from Scientific American: *Global CO2 Emissions Rise after Paris Climate Agreement Signed -- Emissions climbed in Asia and Europe, but declined in the U.S.*[77]

America walked away and *still* had the best reductions? This all happened when America was achieving energy independence and recovering manufacturing capacity? Can you say "MAGA"?

The Gaia groupies will hate this Western Journal headline almost as much as Michael Moore hates salad: *After Dumping Paris Accords, US Leads World in Reduction of Carbon Emissions*

> According to the data compiled last month, the carbon emissions in the U.S. during 2017 represented a drop of more than 42 million tons over the previous year. By comparison, Ukraine showed a reduction of roughly 20 million tons.
>
> Among several nations still committed to the terms of the Paris accords, the results are much less impressive. In Spain, Canada, China and the European Union, 2017 actually saw a spike in the amount of carbon dioxide released into the atmosphere.[78]

We even got some insights into what helped America take that leadership role in curbing emissions. This is juicy. (from the same WJ article):

> The American Enterprise Institute has analyzed the recent data and believes America's unique energy production capabilities have helped keep the nation on the right environmental track. The conservative think tank specifically cited the process of hydraulic fracturing as well as increased drilling for natural gas as practices that have helped combat carbon emissions.[79]

Environmentalists can thank American frackers.

Read that sentence again. Slowly.

Yep. That's pretty much what Conservatives have said all along. There are real environmental issues – like Flint and Gold King that need to be cleaned up. But the *real* strength of American ingenuity is how it gets unleashed to solve a problem in ways the "government experts" might never imagine.

Not so long ago, there was a movement to outlaw incandescent lights and require people to use the spiral lights to force us to change – even though the spiral lights had real disposal problems of their own. The Free Market provided an alternative – the LED bulb.

In the same way, environmentalists insist that we accept their solutions including wind and solar, and using lithium batteries in electric cars. But these technologies have problems in their own right – not just reliability, but land use, life cycle, environmental impact on wildlife, a whole host of real issues. And let's not even talk about where the lithium for our batteries comes from!

Why should we lock into "green" solutions that haven't panned out very well, and have a maximum upside when there might be some other idea we've not looked at? Reports are suggesting we might be 20 years out from commercially viable fusion power plants. Clean, safe and stable power generation. That's a game-changer that makes these other ideas instantly obsolete.

What other ideas are being neglected because we're locked in this stupid world-is-going-to-end debate?

All of these "green" ideas have one thing in common. The solutions – always – require a big-government high-tax solution, one that makes bureaucracy bigger, and increases the power of the politicians pitching them – or the companies standing in line to exploit these "new policies" for market share.

God never once told us to worship the Earth, He told us to look after it, make use of it and be responsible in how we did that.

And then He did something interesting ... right in the second chapter of Genesis, He told us about deposits of gold and precious stones. Do you really think He'd tell us about gold and gems if He had a problem with us digging them out of the earth? Yep. God is pro-mining. If He's cool with gold, do you think He's upset about coal? After all, He put it there.

The same Jesus Who had to straighten His Jewish listeners out by explaining that "The Sabbath was made for man, not man for the Sabbath," would probably say something similar to us. The world was made for humanity, not the other way around.

We are not some virus infecting the world and ruining its beauty, nor vermin or an enemy to be destroyed. We are caretakers who can use it, enjoy it, and in doing so, glorify the God who gave it in the first place.

Jesus wouldn't applaud the left for their nature-worship. He'd sit them down and tell them they've lost the plot.

CHAPTER TWELVE

How Would The Great Physician Diagnose Our Heathcare System?

Brandon Vallorani

Now a certain man was there who had an infirmity thirty-eight
years. When Jesus saw him lying there, and knew that he
already had been in that condition a long time,
He said to him, "Do you want to be made well?"
The sick man answered Him, "Sir, I have no man to put me
into the pool when the water is stirred up; but while I am
coming, another steps down before me."
Jesus said to him, "Rise, take up your bed and walk."
And immediately the man was made well, took up
his bed, and walked.
John 5:5-8, NKJV

Jesus cares about the complete person. When people came from miles away to hear Him speak, He fed them rather than send them away hungry. When the wine ran out at the wedding, He cared about the newlyweds and the public humiliation that running out of wine in that culture would have caused. He cared about a paralytic lowered through the roof, and about Jairus's daughter. He cared about a woman who'd spent all her wealth trying to cure her "issue of blood," and He cared about a blind beggar on the street.

Some people see Jesus' compassion and care and they reduce the gospel to a "social justice" message that focuses only on feeding the poor, helping the sick, and clothing the needy. Jesus cared about all those things, but He never lost sight of those things being the lesser part of His mission, as we see right in the beginning of Mark's gospel:

> At evening, when the sun had set, they brought to Him all who were sick and those who were demon-possessed. And the whole city was gathered together at the door. Then He healed many who were sick with various diseases, and cast out many demons; and He did not allow the demons to speak, because they knew Him. Now in the morning, having risen a long while before daylight, He went out and departed to a solitary place; and there He prayed. And Simon and those who were with Him searched for Him. When they found Him, they said to Him, "Everyone is looking for You." But He said to them, "Let us go into the next towns, that I may preach there also, because for this purpose I have come forth." And He was preaching in their synagogues throughout all Galilee, and casting out demons. (Mk. 1:32-39, NKJV)

Jesus understood that His kindness and compassion to those in need was important – and something He also expected of His disciples – but His mission was not swallowed up by that need. Jesus even acknowledges that He didn't rush off to save his friend Lazarus from dying – although He could have – but

He raised him from the dead. In AD 890, a tomb was discovered saying "Lazarus, four days dead, friend of Christ". Yes, Jesus raised His friend from the dead, but he still died again, just like the rest of us. Resurrection was only a temporary solution to Lazarus' bigger problem. The real reason Jesus came was for something deeper and more enduring.

That's why the cross and His message of the Kingdom of God matter so much. The true hope He points to is the forgiveness of sin, the new birth, and an everlasting life. That's why it was important that Jesus move to the next town rather than stick around until everyone who had been sick was well again. He was aiming for a higher goal. But He was still compassionate. In and among the other things He was doing, within the scope of His larger project, He still helped those in need.

Does anyone remember that verse where He accomplished those things by organizing grassroots protesters to petition Rome for better hospitals and care for the poor? Go ahead and look for a verse that says any of those things. I'll wait.

What's that? It never happened?

Of course not. Jesus wasn't a community organizer bent on shifting our personal responsibilities onto the government's shoulders. A family needs to care for family members in need. That's where charity really starts. Or did you miss the verse where Jesus jackhammered people who masked their greed and hardened hearts with super-spiritual language that might easily fit in at far too many Christian gatherings? Flip open to Mark 7: 9-13 and you'll see it right there:

> *He said to them, "All too well you reject the commandment of God, that you may keep your tradition. For Mo-*

ses said, 'Honor your father and your mother'; and, 'He who curses father or mother, let him be put to death.' But you say, 'If a man says to his father or mother, "Whatever profit you might have received from me is Corban"—' (that is, a gift to God), then you no longer let him do anything for his father or his mother, making the word of God of no effect through your tradition which you have handed down. And many such things you do."

That's right. Jesus got right in the face of religious types who thought they were too "spiritual" to look after their own family members. What's that got to do with health care? Simple – there were no hospitals or nursing homes in those days. If someone got sick, you didn't just shuffle them off to an "expert" to look after. You brought them home and cared for them there. Is it expensive? Is it inconvenient? Sure. But when we were infants, were we any less work or expense? The point is, if you're looking for the government to solve your problems, then maybe, just maybe, you might be looking in the wrong place.

Of course, since we don't live in First Century Rome anymore, how do these scenarios and lessons translate into our modern day circumstances? Depending on your politics, and party you are looking at, we've got some very different ideas about what health care is, what it does, and how it is supposed to work.

The more traditional American option is some type of private health insurance – with a *voluntary* participation component – balancing the sort of risk you are likely to have with the premiums and coverage you are willing to pay for. It's a private agreement between two willing parties where the price is set by market forces just like any other insurance instrument. Insurance companies compete for market share by tailoring the plans and services to best suit the needs/price the customers are willing to absorb. Fairness is established for the customer, in part, the same way all other business models protect the customer: through competition maximizing customer choice.

A second model was established by Obamacare. It brought in changes that the American model had never seen before – things like compulsory participation and government-mandated plans. It was a complete re-boot of the Insurance system, with some far-reaching unpleasant effects. Simple, inexpensive plans that only covered catastrophic needs were now off the menu. We were promised you could keep your plan and your doctor – if you liked them – but that soon proved to be a lie. The left-leaning site Politifact counted no less than thirty-seven times that Obama gave an *unqualified* promise that customers could keep their plan and their doctor.[80] We all saw how that worked out. Did you get to keep your plan? Didn't think so.

What else happened? The expectation was that everyone would get coverage, and the price of the plans would not go up. Is that how it worked in practice? Not even close. They messed with the funding formula, and who could be charged how much. That changed everything.

The reasons why are pretty clear. But to see why, you need to think about something less emotionally charged – like car insurance. Bean-counters have very detailed and complex tables that know how much it will cost in payouts for different demographics. A 20-year-old with a high-end sports car is a very different risk than a soccer mom with a minivan. What it would cost the insurance company to keep both of these customers on the books (based on the likelihood of future insurance payouts) will be part of the pricing model for their premiums.

Life insurance works the same way. A thirty-five year old non-smoker in good health with a ten-year term policy will not have the same life insurance premiums as a thirty-five-year-old morbidly obese chain-smoker locked into a whole life policy. The chances of the policy cashing out for the first guy are a lot less than the second guy. Lower risks mean lower costs. Savings get passed along to the non-smoker.

How do you suppose the picture changes if they're not allowed to charge the chain-smoker more than the healthy guy? Or if they're not allowed to charge the hotshot in the sports car more than the soccer mom? Would the insurance company magically save money just because they're not allowed to charge a bigger premium? Of course not. Statistics and actuarial tables don't care what some pencil-pusher in Washington decides the law is going to look like tomorrow. The stats are the stats whether they're convenient or not.

So what happens to the car insurance and the life insurance in these examples? Simple – if the high-risk users can't pay a higher premium to pay for their higher risk, low-risk users ends up paying more. The same risk has to be spread among more people.

But Obamacare went further than that, didn't it? It didn't just spread the risk among people who were already covered, it made participation mandatory ... and that included people with pre-existing conditions. That "little detail" is a game-changer. Why is that important? Simple – instead of just spreading the risk between hotshot new drivers and soccer moms, you're now adding people with a few dozen speeding tickets. Drivers who have totaled three or four cars. People convicted of Auto Insurance fraud. Drunk drivers whose licences have been suspended. It doesn't matter. By law, *all* "pre-existing conditions" now *have* to be covered, no matter what they are.

Does that expose insurance companies to a little more risk? You better believe it!

Here's a clue: a McKinsey & Co. report from 2015 said that health insurance companies lost $2.1 billion – partly because payouts were more than the expected.

What happens to the soccer mom with the clean driving record when all these other high-risk drivers enter the pool? Poor Aunt Mildred suddenly has to shoulder the insurance company's projected costs of her risk *and* the shared risk of all these other drivers who are almost guaranteed to wreck their car. Her rates will spike. Big-time. Sound familiar?

Are you starting to see where Obamacare went off the rails? It was doomed to failure right from the beginning. But that's only part of the story. It gets worse.

What happens if our soccer mom gets sticker shock and realizes she can't afford these new prices? Does she need to sell her van? Not at all. For one thing, they *want* to keep her business. She's helping carry the foreseen costs of all these risky drivers, after all.

They want to keep her around; more specifically, paying that premium every month or year. They've got a little accounting trick that can bring her monthly costs down ... it's called a deductible. It's simple, really. If you take, say, a five-hundred, or a thousand-dollar deductible on the van, you save a chunk of change on your monthly payments. Monthly costs don't seem to go up very much; that sounds great, right? Sure it does – until you get in a fender-bender. That first five hundred or thousand dollars is coming straight out of Minivan Mom's pocketbook, not the Insurance company. If the total damage is less than the deductible, it costs them nothing. The bill lands entirely on the shoulders of the 'insured'. That sucks, right? That's what is happening with health insurance. Higher premiums are only half the story.

Bloomberg reported that from 2009-2018 employer-paid plans saw a big change. Employers who offered only high deductible plans jumped from 7% of the total in 2009, to 39% in 2018. An article called, *Sky-High Deductibles Broke the U.S. Health Insurance System* details some horror stories about how crippling deductibles have destroyed the personal finances of ordinary families[81] ... and isn't that the problem insurance was supposed to solve?

MarketWatch pointed out another little problem with Obamacare. It was a jobs killer. In a 2017 article entitled, *Businesses eliminated hundreds of thousands of full-time jobs to avoid Obamacare mandate* it gave some harsh numbers to back up that claim.

> Up to 250,000 positions may have been eliminated by small businesses seeking to avoid Obamacare's employer mandate, according to estimates in a new working paper distributed by the National Bureau of Economic Research. Altogether between 28,000 and 50,000 businesses appear to have reduced their number of full-time employees from 2014 to 2016 because of the mandate.[82]

It gets worse still. *Money* ran this story in 2017. *One-Third of Counties Will Have Just One Obamacare Insurer by 2017*:

> According to a new analysis from the nonpartisan Kaiser Family Foundation, almost a third of counties will have just one insurer participating in the exchanges by 2017, significantly more than the 7% of counties who had one option this year. That equates to 19% of all enrollees facing just one insurance option.[83]

And what happens if the one insurance option you have is not one accepted by the doctor you want to see because that insurance plan won't pay doctors enough to cover their costs? That "coverage" you think you have is literally meaningless.

Obamacare – the "Patient Protection and Affordable Care Act" – is broken, obviously. It doesn't protect patients nor does it provide affordable care. Even the Democrats have stopped trying to save it. They've latched onto a different idea.

What are the Democrats offering in its place? It's the "holy grail" the Left wanted since the beginning – Single-Payer Healthcare. "Single-payer" sounds harmless enough, doesn't it? Sure, until you look under the hood.

What's so bad about it? For one thing, it's been tried on a smaller scale had had no end of problems. You've heard of the VA, haven't you? The problems of access and service got to be so bad in the VA system that the government is now opening access to regular health care, hoping to rescue it. Under the previous system, there had been a VA Wait-Time Scandal with administrators who had been "doctoring" appointment schedules to paper over problems with delivering care.

Back in the spring of 2014, several members of the Media(D) were loathe to report that as many as 40 veterans had died waiting for treatment at one Phoenix facility because of these secret "waiting lists."[84] You wouldn't want to slander the idea of single-payer or their savior, Obama, right?

It's too soon to know how effective the proposed solution is because it still runs into the problem of being funded by the government. This means a finite budgeted amount has to be spread among a large number of people looking to bene-fit from this service. After literally putting their own life and limb on the line for their country, there is a strong argument for the government's moral obligation to pick up the tab for health care. Moral obligation or not, this is not a cheap en-deavor. The $55 Billion set aside by Congress to implement this Choice program is already under strain of running out of money.

That $55 Billion is for one aspect of the VA, which serves 9 Million patients a year. Sure the medical issues relating to veterans can sometimes be complex and expensive – but so can issues relating to civilian medical conditions.

Just how expensive do you think it would be if we were looking after the health care needs of more than 300 million patients?

Just like the deductible was an accounting trick for managing the costs of premiums, there are accounting tricks a govern-ment can use in managing health care costs. Like providing care to fewer people. Maybe because they don't meet their criteria for care, or because they are unwilling to pay for cer-tain treatments. They could even limit access so that they pay for fewer procedures in a given year.

The next time some Bernie Bro pitches Socialized single-payer health care, be sure to ask them about wait times. Be ready for their blank stare. You can explain it's like bread lines, only for hospitals. In Canada, for instance, the Frasier Institute expects the following wait times for diagnostic procedures: 4.3 weeks for a CT scan; 10.6 weeks for an MRI; and 3.9 weeks for an ultrasound. Unless you're a cat or a dog, of course. Fido doesn't need to wait:

> "We're catching up to human medicine, and there's no wait list," clinic veterinarian and animal neurology specialist Dr. Andrea Finnen said. "We mostly do imaging for cats and dogs and sometimes horses, but if you send me a sheep, I'll do that, too."[85]

Why can Canadian dogs get MRIs without a wait list, but human patients in hospitals don't? It's the magic of the Free Market: veterinarians are subject to market forces, not government decisions. That's the entirely predictable result of 'single payer Healthcare' in action.

Do you remember when Sarah Palin was mocked for talking about 'Death Panels'? Sure, the language she used was provocative, but the principle was accurate. Health care is expensive. The people footing the bill run a cost-benefit analysis of who they think *needs* the care and who doesn't need it, or isn't worth spending the money on. Since the government is footing the bill, there is no appetite for anything like the 'right to try' legislation signed by Trump.

If you want an extreme example, think back to the British cases of Charlie Gard and Alfie Evans. Their socialized health care means the government has authority over your health care. It isn't even your decision anymore. Charlie Gard and Alfie Evans were two babies with critical illnesses.

The Gard family managed to raise 1.6 Million dollars so they could seek experimental treatment in the US to try and save their baby's life, but the British Government, with the court's help, literally refused to let the baby leave the hospital. In the end, Charlie's condition had deteriorated so badly while the case worked through the courts that he was past saving. Did the hospital let the doomed baby go home and spend his final days in a crib in his own home? Nope. Did they allow family members time to say their goodbyes to little Charlie before the hospital pulled the plug? Nope. The State has spoken, it was time for Charlie to die. There was no reprieve.[86]

The story of little Alfie Evans was even more horrific. Alfie was a sick toddler who the British health care system claimed was beyond treatment. Parents, desperate to save his life, sought other options. They found some. Alfie was offered honorary Italian citizenship, and an Italian hospital stood by offering treatment. Not only did the British government oppose this offer, they placed a line of police officers shoulder-to-shoulder across the front of the hospital to prevent Alfie from being taken from the hospital to receive medical care somewhere else. The government literally decides who gets treated and who shouldn't. In other words ... Death Panels.[87] Would they have said "no" if Alfie's dad was a Royal? Of course not.

It gets worse. Look up the phrase "Liverpool Care Pathway" the next time you're online, an Orwellian term if ever there was one. The NHS banned something called the Liverpool Care Pathway, a practice of denying food and water to end-of-life hospice patients to hasten their deaths. A year later, it was reported that some parts of the country were *still* withholding food and water.[88]

Writing off some patients as a lost cause is part of how they save money. Another part is by limiting what kind of care the "universal" health care actually covers. For example, did you know that Canada's "universal health care" does not cover: dental care, vision, physiotherapy, cosmetic surgery, or "non-essential" services like chiropractic care, massage therapy etc. They also restrict which treatments are available. For example, in 2015, a Canadian with a form of cancer was recommended by his regular doctor to have a PET scan, which was unavailable in Canada. He went to the US, where that scan detected his cancer. Canadian doctors successfully treated him. That was the good news. The bad news was that the Provincial health care called the scan "experimental" and refused to cover it. After appeals and significant public outcry, the cost was eventually covered.[89] All of that is at the discretion of some panel of experts somewhere. Can you imagine what Canadian care would look like if the "pressure valve" of cash-pay no-waiting services American health care was suddenly taken out of the equation? Canadians would be out of luck.

But what about health care being a "right"?

Hey Bernie Bros – how, exactly, would that work? Not all rights are the same. The right, say, to free speech is easy. You can say what you want without fear of punishment for saying something that offends a powerful person or institution. How would a "right" to health care work? They actually have that "right" in Venezuela. But there are no medicines or supplies in the hospitals. At the time of this writing, the cities don't even have electricity or running water. What kind of medical care are you going to get for "free"? Cuba is no better. An Argentinian was given a discrete tour of a Cuban hospital in which student doctors were working the ER in the night shift, three of the hospital's 4 stories were closed (with only the ER still open) and there was only a single functional toilet to be found anywhere.

> I left the hospital after a couple hours. Once outside, puzzled by the large bags the people entering the hospital were carrying, I asked my friend to explain. "Well, they have to bring everything with them, because the hospital provides nothing. Pillows, sheets, medicine: everything," he said. – *'Inside the Cuban Hospitals That Castro Doesn't Want Tourists to See'* [90]

You have the "right" to shoddy care, badly delivered. Socialized health care is truly an empty promise.

Meanwhile, Trump's proposed health care solutions involve:

1. Scrapping the Obamacare mandate that makes a citizen sign up ... "or else."

2. Inviting greater access to and competition between various insurers across state lines.

3. Seeking ways to reduce costs of prescription medication.

The conservative approaches, you will notice, are entirely voluntary. They do not compel either the individual or the corporation. They leave room for creative innovations and ideas like health care savings accounts or voluntary associations like Medi-share.

Which brings us full circle to the beginning.

Do you think the sweet Jesus Who fish-slapped someone for being so "spiritual" that he wouldn't care for his own aging parents would have something to say about health care? Of course, He would.

Do you think He would insist that Caesar care for your relatives, or that believers find some better way to truly care for the needs of one another?

If Jesus had a bumper sticker on His car, would it be for the empty Bernie-bro health care promises that don't actually deliver the promised care? Or would it be for the sort of health care that led to many of the world's greatest medical innovations? The sort of innovations, for example, that let neurosurgeon Dr. Carson separate conjoined twins. Or that made John's Hopkins, The Mayo Clinic, and St. Jude Children's Research Hospital possible.

You can look all you want for any verse that says, "by this all men will know you are my disciples, by your love for nanny state government" – but you'll never find it.

CHAPTER THIRTEEN

That Which God Hath Joined Together

Doug Giles

He said to her, "Go, call your husband and come here." The woman answered and said, "I have no husband." Jesus said to her, "You have correctly said, 'I have no husband'; for you have had five husbands, and the one whom you now have is not your husband; this you have said truly." The woman said to Him, "Sir, I perceive that You are a prophet."
John 4:16-19, NASB

When Stormy Daniels blew into town with her Creepy Porn lawyer, CNN and Team NeverTrump were putting the champagne on ice. They finally had the goods they needed to nail the New York billionaire to the wall.

News of his marital infidelity would finally send evangelicals crying home to mama. Except, to their great surprise, that never happened. It's almost like Christians already knew he was a man with a past, eh? Like maybe that was already baked into the cake on election day?

You see, Christians understand morality, but it's more nuanced than the mere ledger-book rule-keeping outsiders suppose it to be. They understand it's about something bigger than "mother may I?" and "Father forgive me." They learned that little Truth Bomb from the Lamb of God Himself. And Christians have read this story before. Nobody's blind to society's convenient double-standard.

Sure, it's ok for a typical Hollywood billionaire to traipse around with half-nekkid starlets on his arm – just make sure you drop your drachmas in support of the right progressive causes and ... *abracadabra* ... all is forgiven.

But a Republican? That's what leftist quadruple standards are for. Let any hint of a scandal besmirch a Republican's honor, and suddenly the critics find that old-time religion and start preaching fiery sermons about damnation that might have made Jonathan Edwards break a sweat.

That's Edwards the *Sinners In the Hands Of An Angry God* guy, not John Edwards, the Democrat whose donors paid the mistress he knocked up during the campaign to disappear. He's the one where HuffPo, Slate, and his other leftist droogs told us they didn't share the story "because it wasn't news." Those are exactly the quadruple standards we're talking about. Maybe you could explain that logic to Herman Cain, who was thrown to the wolves even without any "love children" – or campaign donor money – being involved.

Anywho ...

182

It's no secret: DJT had been around the block a couple of times and the media was itching for a way to exploit it to break off support from his base.

Imagine the shocked look on Anderson Cooper's face when he found out his Stormy "bombshell" was a dud. Evangelicals never threw the President overboard. So the left tried to do it for them.

"Did you know that Donald Trump was *(gasp)* divorced and remarried?"

Yeah. We already knew that, media flunkies. Thanks for coming out.

They pulled out their square-buckled shoes and sharpened their pointing fingers in the "defense of the institution of marriage." Christians ought to know that Jesus would never put up with a horn-dog like that!

RINOs got in on it, too.

Remember Bob Corker? Maybe not. If you Google him, you'll find out that he was a "Republican" Senator (just like Flake was a "Republican") who went on record telling us all how Trump had "debased the nation." Just wait until Corker hears about what Bill Clinton can do with a cigar and an intern!

You really think Trump's critics are the first people to ever leverage marriage as a political weapon? Have you never cracked open the Good Book?

The Sadducees were First-Century thought leaders, you see. They'd be having their own TED talks if someone had invented them back then. They really thought they could make Jesus look like some dumb punk from the back-half of nowhere, Who really hadn't thought through the complexities of these knotty moral issues.

The Carpenter's Son hit them like a 20 lb sledge hammer.

Jesus showed them that these "wise men" hadn't even figured out how to ask the right questions yet.

Ouch.

That wasn't the first time they tried to spring the marriage question on Jesus, either.

Remember that chick they wanted Jesus to condemn to death? She got interrupted getting down and dirty with some guy, so they dragged her out of bed for Jesus to lead the crowd in a good old-fashioned stoning. Use the Law of Moses to trap Him and put Him in a no-win situation.

Ignoring them, Jesus took His finger and started drawing in the dirt.

I can assure you, that is not the reaction they were expecting.

They asked whether she should die by stoning, like the Law says she should. He said whoever was without sin should throw the first stone, and went back to drawing in the dirt. What was He writing in the dirt? Names of their ex-girlfriends? Websites from their browser history? It doesn't say. But the accusers left. And when everyone had gone but the woman and Jesus, He said, simply: "Neither do I condemn you."

Wow, we know it'll be a cold day in Hell before any Pharisee then or now wraps his lips around that sentence. You can say the same for any NeverTrumpkin for that matter. "He's on his *third* marriage!"

If you were paying attention, something was a little – off – with that whole stoning incident. Did you catch it?

Notice anything ... missing?

They did say the woman was caught *in flagrante delicto*, right? OK ... so, where's Waldo? Shouldn't there be someone else right with her, expecting scattered showers ... of heavy stones and packets of gravel? A second person, perhaps? Last I checked, the charge of adultery takes two to tango, doesn't it, little kiddies?

The accusers weren't interested in justice -- not really. Sound familiar? If they were, the bro she'd been busily boinking would be right there with her, naked, embarrassed, and afraid for his life. But somehow, the guy was a no-show at this shindig. What, didn't he get the invitation to his own stoning? Lost in the mail, was it?

So what if this chick really was the village bicycle? Even those wizards should be bright enough to figure out ... a bicycle doesn't ride itself. To them, this woman was a disposable casualty. But not to the Lord of Life. The restoration of a wayward soul -- that was Jesus' meat and drink. The Nazarene cared about redemption. His enemies were just out to settle scores.

And the modern Never-Trumpers, are they playing the same game as those accusers who left – afraid to throw the first stone knowing they had guilt of their own? Have any of to-day's legalists taken a ride or two on their own village bicycles? Or, if not, have they secretly wished they had?

If we're talking about sexual sin, let's go all-in.

Jesus didn't wimp out. Keeping your package in your pants is the easy part. Let's talk about lust. Jesus didn't just say sleeping around is bad. He made it personal. Lusting after someone in your heart is no better than doing the dirty deed. But that's not any of us, right? Before you answer, stop and think about your browser history. The history you thought was "private" isn't as private as you thought.

Anyone remember that Kurt Eichenwald, guy? Ok, maybe not. He's a fully credentialed member of the Media(D). He's a devout Trump critic whose head is firmly lodged somewhere in Obama's lower intestine. He's the guy, while trying to "own" Tucker Carlson on Twitter, accidentally posted a screenshot that included his own tentacle porn search on social media. Alright, that's just nasty. It's strictly "research" purposes, eh Kurt? Just like the guy who insists he reads Playboy "for the articles."

Of course, no other person who enjoys bashing Trump would fail to live up to his own high moral standards, right? #PlankEye

What about Ashley Madison? Anyone remember that garbage site? It was supposed to be a super-secret adultery site aimed at helping men and women hook up on the down-low. Just one problem: when their security measures failed, someone looked at the member lists, and the news reported that it was mostly just full of creepy old men talking to each other. Gross.

Keep that in mind next time you go online. That "friendly face" online isn't quite what you thought 'she' was. "She" could be some 300 lb Crisco-sweating chain-smoker named Louie.

How many straight-laced Puritianical NeverTrumpkins were shotgunning Pepto when they heard that the Ashley Madison user names were leaked to the public in the security breach? Santa had himself some new additions to his Naughty List that year!

I can't help but notice that the Son of God's "Neither do I condemn you" line was only said after the accusers all walked away. Every last one of them. Those words weren't said for their sake, He said them for hers. Jesus knew the game against that woman was rigged as a trap for Him. He wasn't interested in playing along. The only one who could have thrown that first stone spared her life, and called her to a new way of living. That's what a good God looks like.

"Sure, He let her go, but my sweet Jesus would never trust a sinner with anything important. That's for the super-saints."

You're sure about that, are you, Spanky?

What about that time Jesus schlepped his way through Samaria?

There in those beastly badlands where respectable Jews never showed their faces, Christ did the unthinkable, and stopped for a chat with a sinful woman. This was a Ron Burgundy-sized Big Deal.

Samaritans had a bastardized form of Abraham's religion and they'd married foreigners. That's not a really great combination to win the trust of the Jews next door, who were under Roman rule and desperately trying to hold fast to both their tradition and way of life. To "respectable" Jewish people, Samaritans were sellouts. Compromised. They were hopeless, no good and rotten, too.

You don't have to read very much of the Bible to figure out that most first-century Jews and Samaritans weren't inviting each other to weddings and bar mitzvahs.

That's why the woman at the well was surprised when Jesus asked her for water.

Why's she here in the heat of the day slogging water back in the hot sun in the first place? She's an outcast. Some other women Jesus talked to might have been shady. But to be really blunt, this one was loose. Did "Seeker-sensitive" Jesus tiptoe around her sin, afraid to offend her? Nope, He hit her with it right between the eyes.

> *He said to her, "Go, call your husband and come here." The woman answered and said, "I have no husband." Jesus said to her, "You have correctly said, 'I have no husband'; for you have had five husbands, and the one whom you now have is not your husband; this you have said truly." The woman said to Him, "Sir, I perceive that You are a prophet." (Jn. 4:16-19)*

Normally, telling someone how jacked up their sex life is won't get you very far. But it's exactly what she needed to hear.

What happened next? He was gracious to her. He shared His secret, without any metaphors or hidden meaning. After she said that the Messiah would come and declare all things to us, He answered, "I who speak to you am He."

So she brought half the village there to see Him. This same outcast woman who'd been knocking sandals with more men than she cared to admit suddenly had purpose and was – literally – leading people to Christ. Not too shabby.

But for Super-Saints who have leisure to list and name every sin the President has ever made, leading a whole community to Christ on a sunny afternoon is probably a typical Tuesday, right? Or maybe our attitude toward people "with a past" needs some serious rethinking. Sure, you might say, that's the woman at the well. But really, Jesus did all the work there.

Let's go one better. Ever hear the name Mary Magdalene?

She's the one that Holy Writ introduced as the chick who used to be a happy home for seven demons.

Read that again.

Slowly.

A troop of *El Diablo*'s tribe had taken up residence in that woman. In the scale of messed-up, it's not quite up to the "naked and living among the tombs" tier, but you can bet this chick wasn't on anyone's short list when they went looking for babysitters. This lady had more baggage than Octo-mom.

Was she the pirate-hooker pop-culture has turned her into? I couldn't tell ya. But that "seven demons" thing was important enough that it kept getting mentioned in scripture when her name came up.

Imagine this was your story:

"Hey, James – which Mary are we talking about here? Do, you mean the one that used to have seven demons?"

"Yeah, Mark, that one."

"Gotcha. Thanks."

How would you like to have *that* on your CV? Of course, it beats still having seven demons tormenting you. Could someone that broken be trusted with anything truly important? See for yourself:

> *Now after He had risen early on the first day of the week, He first appeared to Mary Magdalene, from whom He had cast out seven demons. She went and reported to those who had been with Him, while they were mourning and weeping.* (Mk. 16:9,10, NASB)

First witness to the Resurrection. Is that important enough for you?

Maybe Jesus isn't looking for the Precious Moments Figures our typical Christian TV series tell us He's looking for.

The first words out of the Apostle Peter's mouth when he realized just who he was dealing with were "Go away from me, I am a sinful man!" (Lk. 5:8) And he denied Jesus three times. But he was still the right man for the job God had in mind.

And have you ever really looked at the Son of God's family tree? It's a train wreck. Rahab's a harlot, right? Not only did she save the Jewish spies, survive the Jewish conquest, and gain acceptance into Israel, but she got married! That's a pretty good plot twist, right? It gets better. You might have heard of her great-great grandson ... David. Not too shabby for a foreign-born harlot from a city doomed to destruction.

Salmon was the father of Boaz by Rahab, Boaz was the father of Obed by Ruth, and Obed the father of Jesse. Jesse was the father of David the king. (Mt. 1:5,6, NASB)

That David guy was another hot mess. How many wives and sons did he already have on the night he should have been at the battle front, but instead stayed back at the palace and caught that fateful glimpse of bathing Bathsheba? David summoned her to the palace and got busy with her. When Bathsheba told David he'd knocked her up, he knew he was the one who was now royally screwed.

David tried to hide his sin by calling the husband home from the front. If Uriah takes his hot wife to bed, then the math works, and the king's adultery stays a secret.

No dice.

The soldier had more honor than his king, and refused to get laid while the troops were in battle. Long story short, David arranges that the husband, Uriah, should die by the hand of the other nation's army.

How could Jesus ever tolerate such a lusty leader?

David paid a personal price for his sins, but that didn't mean Jesus wrote him off as king. Those are different issues. And that's kinda the point.

"Son of David" was even one of the Lord's chosen titles, despite David's many personal moral failings. Remind me ... has Trump had anyone murdered to cover for his sins?

Crickets?

Take all the time you need. Still nothing?

That's what I thought.

Last we looked, non-disclosure statements – with a payout – are a lot gentler than anything David dished out. But somehow David still got to be described as "a man after God's own heart." Could it be that our own moral checklist is just a little bit jacked up?

Oh, but those nondisclosure agreements!

Ok, while we're talking about those non-disclosure statements ... here are a few fun facts to noodle over. It's not yet been shown whether Stormy Daniels *actually* bumped uglies with Donald Trump, or just claimed to have done so. All we know for sure is that Trump paid her not to drag his name through the mud over something that either did, or did not happen a decade before the election. Remember, Trump's name is *literally* his brand. Daniels took the non-disclosure money, and wrote a tell-all anyway, including an unflattering description of the President's junk. Any money Trump paid her (or anyone else) came out of his own personal fortune, not campaign money or donors.

Notice the year Trump is alleged to have knocked boots with these chicks? Was it this year? Last year? Or are these claims a decade or more old?

Congress, meanwhile, has spent $17 Million dollars on paying to keep allegations of sexual wrongdoing quiet. Where are the questions about taxpayer money being used for that? Taxpayers don't have a hot clue who any of the accused in Congress are, if they're still in office, or even whether any have been accused more than once.

Some of the loudest whiners about Trump's "hush money" didn't care when it was Bill Clinton's hush money buying women's silence. Journalist Nina D. Burleigh just wrote a scathing book about Trump and women, even though Nina admitted she would have gladly strapped on the Presidential Kneepads to thank Slick Willy for his service. Paying a woman not to kiss and tell is far more civil than threatening to destroy an intern for going public with Clintonian indiscretions.

There's a book from the Old Testament that will not only blow these Church Ladies' pink hair straight back, but knock their dusty old Thomas Kinkade paintings right off their walls, too.

Ever hear of a guy named Hosea, fair reader? No, not that hipster who teaches Spanish classes at the community college. Hosea, the Old Testament Prophet. When the Lord first spoke through Hosea, the Lord said to Hosea, "Go, take to yourself a wife of harlotry and have children of harlotry; for the land commits flagrant harlotry, forsaking the Lord." (Ho. 1:2)

Yes, Skippy it's true. The Good Lord Himself told His prophet Hosea to marry a whore. Right off the start, in verse 2. That's one heckuva how-do-ya-do, isn't it?

In the beginning of Hosea, the prophet takes an unfaithful wife who promptly gets herself knocked up with some other people's kids. They get slapped with some really cheerful and edifying names like "she has not received mercy" and "not my people." But even after living with the personal hell of being married to a prostitute – he finds out this wife is still worth keeping, and (would you believe?) worth pursuing, too. And if you're paying attention, guess what? That's a story about God's own attitude, not just to Israel, but the motley crew that came along after, too.

How does Christianity's circular firing squad compare to the example God Himself set for us? Too often, Christians show "grace" with a one-strike-you're-out-rule.

How often should I forgive my brother, up to seven times?

What was Jesus' answer?

"That depends – is he a politician?" It's, uh, right there in Second Hezekiah or something, right? Nope, it was "seventy times seven" or, to paraphrase it: keep forgiving the person as many times as you expect God to forgive you when you mess up.

One strike you're out? What would that even look like?

Imagine taking that measuring stick to the really jacked-up people we already call "saints" in the Old Testament. We'd have to start knocking a lot of familiar faces out of our stained-glass windows.

Samson. You've heard of him, right? He was the randy lad who ran with Philistine whores. (Jg. 16:1) In fact, the very same night he spent with a hooker was the one he ripped the city gates of their hinges and carried them up a hill. (To the glory of God.) Probably didn't even shower first, either.

Not exactly a detail of the story you'd bring up in Sunday School, now is it?

What about Judah? He was one of Jacob's twelve sons. Unlike his older two brothers, his dad had nothing bad to say about him. Both David and Jesus were among this guy's descendants. But Judah had a "whore" in his life who wasn't a whore (Gn. 38), and when he went to punish her for her sin, he realized it was actually his own sin. That kid, too, showed up in the Messianic family tree.

If it were up to the Ned Flanders-type Christians, stories like these would never have found their way into the Bible. And let's not forget about the drama with Jacob, or Abraham.

Relationship status: "It's complicated" could describe half of the Old Testament. Surely God could never use such untidy, imperfect people to further His greater purposes, eh? Actually, those are exactly the people He's chosen to use. Sure, but since we're talking politics, what about marriage as a political issue?

Could sweet Jesus vote for someone like Trump? Are church-going Democrats right when they say that marriage might be the issue that would have made YHWH pull a lever for Hillary?

Hillary? Defender of Marriage?

That's rich.

She took a strong stand in support of traditional marriage. For about seven seconds. Then, standing on newly-revised principles, she "evolved" to take a "strong stand" in favor of same-sex marriage. Just like Jesus would have, according to

Christians(?) who say Jesus would call same-sex marriage just peachy. And Obama was giddy when he lit up the White House with a ... rainbow. Funny how God had a very different message in mind with the rainbow. Maybe Barack missed it. (Gn. 9:11-17)

The real Jesus? He's no political weathervane. He sounded more like this:

> And He answered and said, "Have you not read that He who created them from the beginning made them male and female, and said, 'For this reason a man shall leave his father and mother and be joined to his wife, and the two shall become one flesh'? So they are no longer two, but one flesh. What therefore God has joined together, let no man separate." They said to Him, "Why then did Moses command to give her a certificate of divorce and send her away?" He said to them, "Because of your hardness of heart Moses permitted you to divorce your wives; but from the beginning it has not been this way. And I say to you, whoever divorces his wife, except for immorality, and marries another woman commits adultery."
> (Mt. 19:4-9, NASB)

The "respected leaders" of Jesus' day kept saying things like "if He knew what kind of a person that was, He'd have nothing to do with her (or him)." And yet, those are exactly the sort of people Jesus kept calling to His side. "Neither do I condemn you. Go and sin no more." (Jn. 8:11, NKJV) The second part of that sentence is the part the Left likes to leave out, isn't it? They do so while pretending there's no such thing as sin ... especially sexual sin. Even though dealing with sin was the very reason Jesus came in the first place.

When it comes to marriage, the Son of God isn't buying what Hillary's selling. And He'd probably tell you that while chomping down a delicious Chick-fil-A sandwich.

CHAPTER FOURTEEN

Who Would Jesus Censor?

Brandon Vallorani

For no good tree bears bad fruit, nor again does a bad tree bear good fruit, for each tree is known by its own fruit. For figs are not gathered from thornbushes, nor are grapes picked from a bramble bush. The good person out of the good treasure of his heart produces good, and the evil person out of his evil treasure produces evil, for out of the abundance of the heart his mouth speaks.
Luke 6:43-45, ESV

From the very beginning, Christians have had an interest in speech. That makes sense. Christ Himself, after all, is honored as the incarnate Word of God.

Unguarded speech provides a useful window into who we are really dealing with in our daily lives. For example, someone who complains endlessly that "life's not fair" is really announcing his problem with taking responsibility for his own life choices. But the Bible goes further than just being interested in our words. It carefully anchors freedom of speech in something grander and more transcendent than mere human law. It elevates human speech beyond the reach of human institutions, making it a function of conscience.

We see this from the very earliest days of Church history. In Jerusalem, the Apostle Peter, after healing a crippled man by the Temple, (Acts 3) made it clear that it was the name of Jesus, not Peter's own piety that was responsible for the man's healing. Since Jesus had been crucified and buried in that same city's recent history, that was a big deal. An obvious and undeniable miracle like a man – crippled from birth – standing up to walk is an even bigger deal, especially when so many recognized the (formerly) crippled man walking around in their midst.

Peter and John began preaching Christ, to the frustration of the same religious leaders who thought they had taken Jesus out of the picture in the first place. Peter preached a not-very-seeker-sensitive sermon about Jesus. You delivered Him to Pilate. You denied the Righteous One and asked that a murderer be granted to you, instead. You killed the Author of Life, whom God raised from the dead. But you acted in ignorance ... He moved from that starting point to the Christian message of hope, reconciliation to God, repentance and redemption.

Then the religious leaders sent out the captain of the guard to arrest them, being "greatly annoyed" that they were teaching the people and proclaiming in Jesus the resurrection from the dead. At this point, thousands now believed in Jesus as the Messiah. The rulers made the mistake of questioning them the following day ... giving them another opportunity to speak boldy. (Acts 4)

The religious leaders were now stuck in a bind. They couldn't deny the miracle. But they didn't want them spreading this dangerous new claim about Jesus, either. So they called the Apostles and sternly warned them not to speak or teach about Jesus to anybody else. Their reply? But Peter and John answered them, "Whether it is right in the sight of God to listen to you rather than to God, you must judge, for we cannot but speak of what we have seen and heard." (Acts 4:19, ESV)

Jesus himself set the example of speaking honestly without concern about just how upsetting it might be to His audience. If you find that surprising, just wait until you read how He slapped the religious leaders of His day around in Matthew 23.

The Lord had set for us a new moral standard where you didn't do whatever a king told you to do – your voice is captive to your conscience and the truth, not to the dictates of family, culture or even a King (like Caesar) who held in his hand the power to end your life at a whim.

And when they bring you to trial and deliver you over, do not be anxious beforehand what you are to say, but say whatever is given you in that hour, for it is not you who speak, but the Holy Spirit. (Mk. 13:11, ESV)

This moral standard was quickly put to the test. Tradition tells us that eleven of the twelve disciples (Judas had a replacement) faced gruesome deaths ... and even the remaining disciple – John – faced torture that only just stopped short of killing him.

That wasn't enough to silence any of them. Their commitment to the idea of Christ rising from the dead in a real and meaningful way was greater than anything that could be forced under fear of imprisonment, violence or even death.

Even within church history, that courage paved the way for examples like Athanasius *Contra Mundum* (Against The World), the Egyptian Christian who singlehandedly defended Christian Orthodoxy against a heresy that was accepted even by most church leadership of his day.

What does that religious devotion have to do with politics or freedom of speech today? Absolutely everything. This provided a moral roadmap for how, two thousand years later, a single bold man or woman could stand up in defiance of what the entire world holds as true. As often as not, it was the Christians who did the standing up, too.

For the sake of conscience, they have stood up to the most powerful social-political institutions on the planet. For example, when one devout German monk objected to certain clerical abuses and wanted to push for reform within the church, he, Martin Luther, unknowingly triggered the Reformation. When mounting his defense at the Diet of Worms, early written accounts spread the tale of his daring reply when told to retract:

"I cannot and will not recant anything, for to go against conscience is neither right nor safe. Here I stand, I can do no other, so help me God. Amen." That trial, and his elevation of personal conscience about human authority was a significant hinge point of history.

We see an echo of that courage on the Catholic side in the last words of Thomas More while he was executed for standing opposed to Henry VIII. "If honor were profitable, everybody would be honorable. I die the king's faithful servant, but God's first."

Courageous and free speech does far more than just vindicate you before an accuser. It can change the world in other ways, too. What might normally be taken for one man's ignorant, pigheaded stubbornness can be noted by historians as "visionary courage" if the dissenter's gamble pays off. Case in point: Christopher Columbus. Don't buy the "flat earth" myth. Nobody really believed the world was flat in Columbus's day -- the Greeks had mathematically inferred the curvature long before. The problem he really faced was much more pragmatic. There were dangerous uncertainties associated with attempting to cross the Atlantic. What if the trackless ocean is so vast that food and water ran out long before you can cross it? Despite all the risks, Columbus somehow convinced financial backers and sailors to risk it all on one ship captain's certainty. What he discovered in that voyage changed the course of the world forever.

Not only was bold, vocal opposition to conventional wisdom and authority figures key to discovering America, but to our Founding as well. The events of 1776 obviously required a willingness to stand against authority – and more, take action against it. If the pamphleteers and the early patriots had no means to speak a dissenter's opinion, our Great Experiment would never have seen the light of day.

That great revolutionary generation understood the true nature of universal principles. Aspects of their arguments for freedom were deeply anchored in arguments from natural law and that shall be applied to both sides equally. That idea required real consequences in policy and practice.

In one of the truly magnificent moments in American history, no less an American patriot than John Adams stood in the defense of British Soldiers accused at the Boston Massacre. It became clear that the demands of the mob – however loudly they might cry – shall not, in America, overrule the due process of law. It took courage to stand before the angry mob and tell them that these hated Redcoats would see a fair trial.

It was the great life's work of Christians like William Wilberforce and former slave-ship captain turned abolitionist and author of hymns, John Newton, who stood against powerful political and financial interests in the Transatlantic Slave Trade.

It was the work of Elizabeth Cochran Seaman, better known to history as Nellie Bly, who set the standard for investigative journalism when she managed to get herself checked into an asylum and did an expose on Blackwell Island called *Ten Days in a Mad-House*. The medical "experts" of the day did not see an institution that needed reforming, they didn't even see a problem that needed solving – that required one citizen whistleblower to stand up and tell the world how dehumanizing and corrupt their system was.

Rev. Dr. Martin Luther King Jr. knew a thing or two about standing strong with an unpopular cause. Even more amazing was his method. Unlike some of his contemporaries, who counseled rage, MLK counseled peace. He called for black and white to be reconciled as brothers, not to be locked in an endless war of attrition. So many decades later, his *I Have a Dream* speech continues to inspire in America and around the world. And can we really mention MLK's role in history without also mentioning the plucky courage of one Rosa Parks?

Gandhi is an example of this same idea taking root abroad, of one man risking everything to stand for a cause he believes is just. The jaw-dropping photos at Tiananmen Square is another. Who can forget the images of one student, by himself, facing down a column of tanks - and it wasn't some token protest. After all, this had been a protest where some 10,000 Chinese students are believed to have died at the hand of their own government.

> Courageous and free speech does far more than just vindicate you before an accuser. It can change the world ...

Free speech isn't just good to have, it is a necessary ingredient to propel every important change in society. Free speech for merely positive or popular opinions is of little use. For speech to be truly free, the most dangerous and offensive opinions are the ones that need the most protecting. The reason should be obvious – society doesn't know in advance which of its' strongly-held ideas are unjust and need to be overthrown – until after they get challenged. More importantly, the people with the power to enforce the status quo are the ones most motivated to protect it from being challenged.

Aleksandr Solzhenitsyn and his scathing criticisms of the Soviet model was a voice the Soviet Union would gladly have silenced if it could ... but both he and his words became internationally famous. He gave the world insights which – if they were read – might make the new crop of cheerleaders of Socialism seriously rethink their emotional infatuation with it.

The true test of commitment to Free Speech comes only when those who clamored for it when they were outsiders become the new insiders and gatekeepers, who don't really like it when someone comes along, rocking the boat. This brings us to the problems we have been seeing in the modern day. The gatekeepers have certainly changed. And with it, any pretense at caring about free speech being "granted" to the ideologically impure.

Somewhere along the way, the West began to forget why Free Speech was so important and shifted our priorities. We stopped protecting speech and started policing language to protect people from hurt feelings. We started telling people what could not be said, and where they could not say it. You could even say the censorship began with the best of intentions – in a nation that is trying to put a history of racial division behind us, for example, there are certain derogatory terms that don't really belong in what we used to call "polite society."

Now, because of that trend, we find ourselves in a bizarro-world cultural blend of libertines and legalists. We have a culture that no longer thinks twice about blaspheming God or dropping the "f-bomb" in casual conversation. But let some poor newscaster report on the West African country of *Niger* and he'll break into a sweat for fear of being fired for accidentally mispronouncing it.

In the years that followed 9/11, the West was trying to grapple with how to understand the newly-redefined relationship with Islam. Some radical activists wanted to kill our civilians in the streets with the most craven kinds of attacks one might imagine, but there were still many thousands of Muslims in our midst that just wanted to be left alone to live and work and worship in relative peace. It didn't help to set the West at ease when people shouting, "Allahu Akbar" had this annoying habit of exploding in public places. This tension led to an international incident over – of all things – a political cartoon. Political cartoons have long been a place where politically incorrect opinions have been able to find safe harbor. Because of the unique ability of images to convey ideas, some of the most powerfully subversive criticisms of governments have leaped from the drafting board of a gifted cartoonist.

Imagine the Danish cartoonist's surprise when his image criticizing radical Islam's more, ahem, "explosive" tendencies triggered events that set the world on fire – in some cases literally! Maybe you remember it, that was September 2005. It was the cartoon of Mohammed with a bomb as his turban.

The Islamic world and the West freaked out for different reasons. Islam – which has no objection to using their catchphrase *Allahu Akbar* which translates roughly to "our god is better" – found themselves deeply offended that someone would dare to blaspheme their prophet. If you're keeping score at home, that's called a "double standard."

The Secular West was upset for other reasons. For shame! We were so insensitive to a minority. Minority? Really? Have they done a global headcount of religions lately? Islam ought to be big enough to look after itself by now, thanks!

What did the cartoonist, Flemming Rose, say in his own defense? He gave the only rational answer in the bunch:

Modern, secular society is rejected by some Muslims. They demand a special position, insisting on special consideration of their own religious feelings. It is incompatible with contemporary democracy and freedom of speech, where one must be ready to put up with insults, mockery and ridicule. It is certainly not always attractive and nice to look at, and it does not mean that religious feelings should be made fun of at any price, but that is of minor importance in the present context. ... we are on our way to a slippery slope where no-one can tell how the self-censorship will end. That is why Morgenavisen Jyllands-Posten has invited members of the Danish editorial cartoonists union to draw Muhammad as they see him.[91]

And what about those so-called "firefighter" heroes of ours in the press? Those great defenders of our freedoms, without whom *Democracy Dies in Darkness*, the same ones who promise us 'all the news that's fit to print'? Where were they with respect to a story where religion and free speech collide?

They had been quick to defend as art and free speech *The Last Temptation of Christ,* or one artist who made a name for himself dropping a plastic crucifix into a jar of his own urine and photographing it.

Obviously, they have no scruples against being profane or offensive to religious belief. But for some strange reason, they scattered like roaches when The Danish Cartoon came up.

If an English speaker wanted to see what all the fuss was about, and why a cartoon had spurred mobs setting fire to embassies, you wouldn't find it in any American newspaper or website. You had to look North to a country that doesn't even *have* the luxury of a First Amendment. Ezra Levant – who later co-founded the right-wing outlet *Rebel Media* – was one of only two publishers with the cojones to run the cartoon as reporting a relevant news story.[92] The lawsuits and Human Rights complaints that were later launched against him accomplished their objective of destroying the publication. Telling the story even when doing so means risking your entire publication? Somebody, please let Jim Acosta know -- *that* is what journalistic courage really looks like.

Honest intent like reporting the news or mispronouncing a word without malice is now no defense at all. The mob will pounce and devour offenders alive. That's not quite true either, is it? Only *some* offenders get devoured. If you happen to be considered an "ally" to the Left, you get a pass. Madonna, for example, as a Leftist icon made the mistake of calling her white son Rocco a "ni–a," was scolded for a while, but she wasn't destroyed entirely. The truly harsh treatment is reserved for people who oppose them politically.

With the rise of digital technology, and more control resting in fewer hands, we find ourselves seeing censorship take new forms we had never imagined possible. Roseanne Barr, Trump supporter, made a single tweet, mocking the Chosen One's close friend, Valerie Jarrett, and her punishment was swift and certain. She was systematically "erased." The *Roseanne* reboot was immediately dropped. Syndicated reruns of the original show from the '90s were pulled. Eventually it came back as *The Connors* -- conspicuously *sans* the title character, Roseanne.

And that is the new tactic in a nutshell. They took it for a spin with Alex Jones. You may remember him as an overheated crackpot who was a little like the late-night radio guys who liked to talk about things like aliens, werewolves and time travel while he peddled "miracle" supplements. He had a huge following, more because he was an entertaining persona than a serious political figure. But he was ruthless in his criticism of the Left and of CNN. Officially, he was taken out because he pushed the Pizzagate story. But there's a good chance that CNN didn't like that he used his platform to mock them by launching a "Meme War" when CNN got their panties in a twist over that WWE parody video in 2017. Videos mocking CNN came pouring in as a result of it.

So, what happened? Jones got squeezed out of digital and economic platforms one by one. He was suppressed and demonetized in social media. He had accounts suspended and then closed. Mail programs refused to send his mailers out. On and on it went – a coordinated attempt to shut out a dissenting voice.

Why does this matter? Because we're already seeing this being used to rig elections and tilt public debate in the favor of one or two people. ClashDaily wrote a piece called *Leftists Want A 'New Civil War' - This Post Is Disturbing*[93] in which Tech Giants told us in their own words how they wanted to force their politics down Red America's throats – whether we wanted it or not. Like all tyranny, it is being done for the proverbial "Greater Good" of course. If any groups can be so powerful as to silence the unpopular or dissenting voices we no longer have any real free speech.

They're already cutting off people and businesses on social media for the crime of Orwellian Wrongthink. We're not allowed to ask, for example, whether there's any downside to biological males competing against biological females for athletic scholarships or in full-contact sports.

The digital world has become the Public Square where we meet and share ideas, but we are seeing massive companies like Twitter and Facebook deliberately squeezing right-of-center ideas out of the conversation. We aren't all really supposed to believe that it's a coincidence that on opening weekend the pro-life story of Abby Johnson, the movie called *Unplanned*, had its Twitter account go dark, are we? Or that the people complained that Twitter wouldn't let them click "Follow" on that account?

Like it was "just a coincidence" that Facebook pulled the plug on a boatload of right-of-center websites in the Great Purge of 2018, which just happened to perfectly match a strategy the Clinton hacks from Media Matters had been demanding since Hillary and her Chardonnay disappeared into the woods to mope about losing in 2016.

Top that all off with the Fake News media slant we've mentioned elsewhere and we are robbed of the two things a citizen in a democracy should have every right to. One: access to the full range of different facts and opinions on the topics of the day – not just a curated list of the acceptable ones – so they can exercise their own good judgment on what truly matters. And Two: a voice with which to engage other citizens in the Public Square of his day.

For example, it's one thing for the Acostas and Maddows of the media to solemnly tell us that there is no border emergency. It's quite another to tell us what the actual numbers are and how well Border Patrol is coping with the surge of foreigners that have been rushing our border. Telling us what opinion we should have is *not* journalism. This might indoctrinate the public, but it does not inform it.

You might expect countries like China, Russia or Pakistan to forbid the discussing of certain taboo political or social topics – or only permit the "correct" side of a debate. Silicon Valley doesn't really seem to object to such censorship policies at all.

It's here in the One Nation where Free Speech is supposed to be culturally sacrosanct that they are happy to appoint themselves to the role of societal censors. That raises an obvious objection – who are they to wield such power? And to whom do they give an account when they are on (to use the phrase) "the wrong side of history"?

This is why conscience – and not human institutions – must guide the limits of our speech. It is also why Reagan famously warned us how fragile our freedom really is:

> Freedom is never more than one generation away from extinction. We didn't pass it to our children in the bloodstream. It must be fought for, protected, and handed on for them to do the same.[94]

CHAPTER FIFTEEN

WWJD About The
LGBTQ Movement?

Doug Giles

"It is done! I am the Alpha and the Omega, the beginning and the end. To the thirsty I will give from the spring of the water of life without payment. The one who conquers will have this heritage, and I will be his God and he will be My son. But as for the cowardly, the faithless, the detestable, as for murderers, the sexually immoral, sorcerers, idolaters, and all liars, their portion will be in the lake that burns with fire and sulfur, which is the second death."
Revelation 21:6-8, ESV

T he same sweet Jesus who – in the Book of Revelation takes such a hard line on not just sexual sin, but the whole range of sin, including such "minor" offenses as cowardice, also dealt with individual sinners with what was, to the zealots of His day – a shockingly light touch. He was much more interested in the restoring of a broken soul than He was in the crushing of a rebel who had lived a life that cursed his maker.

That list of rebels Jesus wanted to restore included hookers and extortionists -- you might know them as "tax collectors." (Some things never change, eh?) It was so radical that it even extended to pompous and sanctimonious religious types.

He is a Lord of Grace, but He also preached repentance, a message of *"go and sin no more."* So, in a world that has suddenly become as complicated – sexually – as ours has in the last generation or two, what kind of a leader would Jesus raise up for our nation?

Is the goal an iron-fisted top-down theocracy? Or is His method of "being the change you want to see in the world" something that works on a more subtle level? He's more of a "change the hearts and the rules will follow" kind of a guy. That's the method that He used to overthrow slavery that was so prevalent in His day. He granted value to everyone. Not just one class or gender or race ... but everyone made in God's image. It took time for that idea to take root, but when it did, it changed a culture, not just a law.

He even said as much in His own words in the closing chapter of The Book:

> *Let the evildoer still do evil, and the filthy still be filthy, and the righteous still do right, and the holy still be holy. Behold, I am coming soon, bringing My recompense with Me, to repay each one for what he has done. I am the Alpha and the Omega, the first and the last, the beginning and the end. Blessed are those who wash their robes, so*

that they may have the right to the tree of life and that they may enter the city by the gates. Outside are the dogs and sorcerers and the sexually immoral and murderers and idolaters, and everyone who loves and practices falsehood. (Rev. 22:10-14, ESV)

This certainly is not the sort of picture that firebrand preachers on either side might paint of the Lord of Hosts, is it? It lands somewhere between the two extremes of either (a) the 'progressive' message that Jesus would be A-OK with a couple of dudes riding off to Brokeback Mountain and (b) the angry Westboro Baptist placard-wavers.

With so many people swapping ideas out of Divine Writ like it was a game of Mad Libs, how are we supposed to figure out which political stance Jesus would really agree with? With so much up for grabs about what Adam and Steve, or Janet and Eve, or even two guys, three girls and one Billy goat Gruff might do with their wedding tackle, what's a politician to do?

What political position would Jesus give a hearty thumbs-up to?

Let's roll the clock back a few years to the last guy in office. Remember him? President 44 waltzed into town mouthing all the acceptable words about not rocking the boat, and solemnly swore he'd uphold traditional marriage. And like suckers, people believed him. When he was still just a Senator, Obama assured us that he was so Very Traditional in his views on the legal definition of marriage that he'd make Andy Griffith's Mayberry look Like *RuPaul's Drag Race*. Hillary and the rest of the Democrat lemmings sang traditionalists the same siren song. But once he was elected, before you could say "preferred pronoun" Obama started some transitioning of his own … into an activist for the cause.

Funny how *that* little nugget was left off the menu when he came a-campaignin'. That's something that the electorate – on either side of the issue – ought to have had the opportunity to think through and vote accordingly.

In March 2009, Obama laid claim to the historic act of inviting the first trans person to the White House to *explicitly* celebrate their sexuality. In 2011, he stopped defending the DOMA act. By 2015, the White House was lit up in activist Rainbow colors.

He gave Americans the old bait-and-switch. Big time. That precedent made people wonder: What kind of President would Trump be? Would his views (and checkered personal history) make him a *verboten* option to the Precious Moments believers? Will he, too, dance to the tune of the activists? Would he advance their agenda? Would he walk it back? Nobody could say for sure.

Right and left, everyone had their own Worst-Case Scenarios. Pearl-clutching Uber-Conservative NeverTrumpkins were certain they saw a Democrat in disguise. One solid push from the Left, and he'll cave to their every whim.

"He's not one of us," they said. "He's a New York Elitist. He doesn't even give a rat's *tuchus* which bathroom in Trump Tower Bruce/Caitlyn Jenner drops a deuce in. The whole world is going to burn if Trump takes the Presidency."

In their worst-case scenario, it was only a matter of time before Trump drops his fake-Republican mask and starts implementing the same rainbow agenda that Obama was praised for championing. You can't trust this native New Yorker... don't you even know the man has got a ... *gasp* **past**???

216

OMG. Stop the presses. Trump had a checkered past. It sure is a good thing nobody in scripture ever had one of those. It's a good thing that Samson, for instance, didn't wake up sweaty after a busy visit with a Philistine hooker, walk out of the city in the middle of the night and rip the city gates off its hinges with some God-inspired strength, as a foreshadowing of the Lord's victory on Calvary, eh? It's a good thing that God didn't raise up a nation from morally messed up people who, in a fit of jealousy, kidnapped their kid brother and sold him to slavers, huh?

But Bruce/Caitlyn Jenner in the bathroom, well, that is some scary stuff. Totally disqualifying to the bowtie-sporting political class. Some grizzled senior citizen goes under the knife, dons a dress, might use the wrong toilet on public property, and suddenly it's the end of the world.

That's really the most critical issue America's facing right now, is it?

But that wasn't the only thing the anti-Trump voices were lamenting, was it, my little children? The Rainbow Crowd had some colorful fever dreams of their own. They were seeing visions of government Jackboots kicking in their doors and reversing every cultural gain they had fought so hard for under the last President. And there was no possible way they would be giving back any of that ground. They somehow convinced themselves that mild-mannered Mike Pence was the bogeyman lurking under their beds at night. They imagined him waiting to hook them up to electroshock therapy ... for some insane reason.

Go ahead and ask them where they got the idea that Pence wanted to run a few hundred volts through the brains of anyone he catches wearing lavender in public. They can't answer. The whole idea is as bogus as a three-dollar bill.

That didn't stop activists from "protesting" his inauguration as Veep by throwing the world's most fabulously irritating dance party on his lawn to accomplish, well ... something. What that something was, who knows, I couldn't tell ya. I'll bet the neighbors were really impressed by all the glitter, noise and strangers on their street well past midnight. That's perfectly normal behavior for people supposedly scared to death of Pence, eh?

That fact that Pence and Trump are not some movie monsters coming to drink their blood doesn't stop people from freaking out. People like Ellen went way over the top and brought others with them. Here's Ellen DeGeneres using her name recognition to gin up some fear among her audience against the Trump/Pence White House:

> I just, you know, he is who he is and he has enough attention and he has his Twitter account and he has ways to get his message across. There's nothing that I am going to say to him that is going to change him and I don't want to give him a platform because it just validates him. And for me to have someone on the show, I really, I have to at least admire them in some way and I can't have someone who I feel is not only dangerous for the country and for me personally as a gay woman but to the world. He's dividing all of us and I think I don't want him on the show.[95]

Dangerous? Pence's integrity prevents him from even eating a meal alone with a woman other than his wife, and you're afraid he'll put you in danger? Puh-lease.

However aggressively inarticulate her word salad was, she's pretty clear about one thing. She imagines an army of civil servants will be throwing pink-haired lesbians off the top of every tall building in town. He's been in office two years now. There's got to be a long list LGBTQ refugees streaming out of America by now. What's that? They're coming to America and claiming asylum from South America? That can't be right, can it?

Dan Savage – Cry-bully, attack dog, and gay activist provocateur from Obama's administration – looked at the Pulse Shooting in Orlando and immediately piled on Trump, "He is the enemy of the LGBT community just as he is against the Muslim community."[96]

Trump is the "enemy" of the LGBT community, now? Oh? Are you so sure about that, Dan? Was it Donald J. Trump that waltzed through that nightclub, with a Sig Sauer and a Glock, punching holes in infidels at something like 1200 feet per second? Call me crazy, but if it had been Trump, I'm pretty sure he'd be in prison by now, not the White House.

Last we checked, that dance macabre was the personal handiwork of some worthless punk named Omar, who shouted something that rhymes with "Aloha snackbar," and whose dad made headlines when he showed up in the backdrop at a Floridian Hillary campaign. His dad? At a Hillary campaign stop? Well, isn't that special? Yes, little kiddies, Seddique Mateen was spotted in the crowd of Democrat plants behind Hillary on stage in Kissimmee, Florida in August 2016.

Why should the LGBT crowd have to worry about any threats from Trump? They're having enough trouble getting along with each other lately. Even among the "community" there is trouble in paradise. Flip open to the Daily Beast, and you'll read a 2016 study that bisexuals aren't fitting with the cool kids in the LGBT crowd. It's "biphobia."[97] If you think they're ostracized now, just wait until the rest of the LGBT crowd remembers that "bi" means "two." You're named after the idea of binary gender? Oh, heck no!

The rise of trans activists threw a stick in the spokes of an already uneasy alliance. Everything you thought you knew about men and women is now wrong. Like this gem that Teen Vogue is teaching the young'uns "If a woman has a penis, her penis is a biologically female penis."[98] You think I'm joking? Nah, even I'm not that funny.

It started with washrooms, a visit to Obama's White House, and the bizarro celebrity status of Bruce/Caitlyn Jenner. Then there were women chased out of changing rooms at the local fitness clubs because they didn't want to change with some hairy-back Mary leering at them.

Bradley Manning was convicted of espionage and sent to prison. He came out as "Chelsea" after Obama cut down his sentence so that he'd be free after Trump took office. When old Brucie got the 2018 Woman of the Year award, we should have known a storm was coming.

Cracks in the intersectional alliance were already forming, and the different factions were already starting to pull in different directions.

Remember when women's shelters were sacrosanct ground that no man was permitted to set foot on? Well, those are the old rules; transgenderism has changed everything.

In Toronto, one woman was traumatized and suffered from rape flashbacks when her new "roommate" was a dude with facial hair who identified as female and spoke about his former wife, his pregnant fiancée as well as other women he found "hot." Kristi Hanna was told she had to share a bedroom with someone who could stand up to pee. When she complained, Hanna was hit with a human rights complaint by the roommate with a johnson. The kicker? The Human Rights complaint was because Hanna dared to call the dude who still has his original wedding tackle a "man."[99]

Lawdy, folks. It's enough to make your head spin, and outsiders to the cause are expected to keep up? But that's just the beginning.

The crybullies set their sights on sports. Sporting their Adam's Apples, some dudes took the easy way to success. They threw on a skirt and fought against girls. Literally. Fallon Fox took on a female MMA fighter, Tamikka Brents. It was "just another fight" until Fox shattered her skull with his fists ... and kept swinging until the ref called the fight.[100]

In women's competition, record after record is falling to the upstart trans athletes. It's costing young women their shot at athletic scholarships.

One of the most famous tennis players of all time spoke up. Martina Navratilova is a legend. She's also seen as a hero and trailblazer among lesbian athletes. How do you think that went over? Do you think being an LGBT icon would make it safe for her to weigh in on the trans trends in sport? At one time, maybe it would have, but not anymore. Now, they've lost that lovin' feeling. It's not even close. The LGBT advocacy group "Athlete Ally" tossed her like leftover gas station sushi.

What was her grave sin? She said this:

> Letting men compete as women simply if they change their name and take hormones is unfair — no matter how those athletes may throw their weight around.[101]

And that's not even getting into the Log Cabin Republican crowd. They feel more persecuted among gays for being conservative than they do by conservatives for being gay. Their website has quite a list of reasons they prefer Republicans to Democrats. Here's just one:

> Senate Republicans flipped the script on gay rights Thursday by confirming Richard Grenell as U.S. ambassador to Germany after months of Democratic opposition and with virtually no support from liberal LGBT groups.

> The Senate voted 56-42 to confirm President Trump's nomination of Mr. Grenell, an openly gay conservative who headed the communications office for four ambassadors to the United Nations, including National Security Adviser John R. Bolton.

> A handful of Democrats joined all Senate Republicans in voting to confirm Mr. Grenell, whose confirmation was described as a gay rights milestone.[102]

Meanwhile, other gay conservatives also tell us that they take more heat from gays for being conservative than they do from conservatives for being gay. Go figure, it's the 'tolerant' liberals that are the one persecuting them because they're different.

As for Trump, on a personal level? Do you think he really cares who someone else hooks up with when he's not around? Probably not. His own life is busy enough that he doesn't need to micromanage everyone else.

I guess now that Trump's in power, San Francisco and New York's Lower East side must be ghost towns, eh? The Pride Parade packed their bags and ran for the border begging Trudeau to let them in?

What's that? It never happened?

Oh, that's right. The asylum cases we really heard about were the *chicas* and *hombres* in South American caravans trying to find safety here in America.

The Trump-is-a-homophobe crowd are truly grasping at straws. Now they're angry at that same gay ambassador to Germany Trump finally got to appoint. Why? Because he is trying to decriminalize homosexuality worldwide.

Here's the story: Grenell flew in activists from across Europe for a strategy dinner at the US Embassy to discuss how to change life for people in the 70 countries where gay sex can still get you thrown from a tall building or sent to jail.

If anyone else did this, they'd make him the Grand Marshall of San Francisco's Pride Parade and fête him with Rainbow-colored keys to the city. But we can't forget 'Orange Man bad.' Trump can't be trusted. It's somehow a sham. The so-called bumbling oaf they tell us can barely tie his own shoes is suddenly a Sinister Svengali who can trick a gay Ambassador to fake concern about the human rights of gays abroad.

Sorry, Dinky, you can't have it both ways.

Here's the Catch-22 every national politician faces now that this Pandora's Box has flipped its lid. It's tough to thread that needle in a world where one-time lesbian icons are no longer "woke" enough, and abused women in a shelter find themselves on the wrong side of a hate speech complaint.

The left's solution is simple pandering. Kiss the feet of whichever victim group is top dog and pray not to become an accidental heretic. (Spoiler Alert: in that system, everyone will eventually become an accidental heretic.) But that gives you a butt-kisser as a leader, and you're giving the country away to the whiniest and most petulant factions in society. It gives you the sort of folks who don't mind outsourcing their politics to Blackshirts in Antifa masks. That's a really great plan – If you want to see a society collapse into itself and sink into civil war.

What does a leader who isn't brain-dead do in a political minefield like this one?

Let's remember who's stacked up in this fight.

We've got religious people who want to be left alone by their government, or if they care, just want the government to stay out of the 'redefining marriage' and compelling language business.

On the side of Woke Activists, we've got women, gay men, lesbians, transsexuals, bisexuals, and whatever other groups we've not even named yet pushing for special rights, and sometimes even fighting among themselves.

What you really want is a leader who can cut the Gordian knot.

Well, guess what? Trump did exactly that.

How'd he do it? Did he consult with a focus group from the Gender Studies department at Berkeley? Did he ring up JoJo's psychic alliance? Crack open one of the books by Hillary's beloved mentor, Saul Alinsky? Nope. He fought their radicalism the old-fashioned way, by being ... American.

He answered their radicalism with a healthy dose of "Life, Liberty and the Pursuit of Happiness." He answered by not pandering to any of the interest groups. He answered by promoting ... the individual. He answered by getting the government to stop picking winners and losers. He focused, instead, on moving government in the direction of providing the maximum possible freedom he could offer everybody, precisely the opposite of micromanaging life in the Social Justice Warrior model.

Does Trump really look like a guy who cares who you want to bump uglies with?

If you think he does, I've got some bad news for you. In a country somewhere North of 300 million people, your sex life really isn't that important to anyone besides you. That's a soul-crushing truth, I know.

Deal with it.

But that's also the good news.

We. Don't. Care.

You aren't "oppressed." Knock yourself out. What you do in your personal life is between you and God. God will have something to say about it. Your Pastor should have something to say about it. Your loved ones might care.

But your Government doesn't care. Nor should it.

This takes us right back to those red-letter words of Jesus that we started with.

The President is nobody's final moral judge. Nor is your Senator, or Hollywood. That job is already taken.

Hollywood paints Christians as whiny hall monitors handing out citations.
That's not what Santo Paulo had to say about Christianity. We're a rag-tag mess of humanity from every background. He said this:

> Do you not know that the unrighteous will not inherit the kingdom of God? Do not be deceived. Neither fornicators, nor idolaters, nor adulterers, nor homosexuals, nor sodomites, nor thieves, nor covetous, nor drunkards, nor revilers, nor extortioners will inherit the kingdom of God. And such were some of you. But you were washed, but you were sanctified, but you were justified in the name of the Lord Jesus and by the Spirit of our God. (1Co. 6:9-11, NKJV)

It's one of those verses that the activists love to hate, but only because they stop too soon, they miss the point.

Some people will spend a long time rethinking their life choices in Dante's Easy-bake. Sorry, there's no getting around that, it's in The Book. But look a little more closely. It lists some of the sins that will haunt you. Nobody disagrees about extortionists or thieves, but when he brings up homosexuals and sodomites, that rattles some chains. But keep reading. This is not a "Go Directly To Hell, Do Not Pass Go" card. This is a message of hope.

"And such were some of you. But you were washed, but you were sanctified, but you were justified in the name of the Lord Jesus…"

Let me key in on an important point that often gets lost.

"Such were some of you…"

Whatever you think about Christians, the real deal isn't that much holier than thou Church Lady from SNL.

"Washed … Sanctified … Justified…"

Even if I was a thief? Yes.

Even if I was an extortionist? Yes.

Even if I was a – yes. Even that. That's the point.

A politician's job is clear. They need to run the country. Preachers tend to the souls of men and women.

It's not your President's job to get in the pulpit on a Sunday. He would suck at that job.

But drawing upon that Christian example of treating every man and woman, slave and free, Jew and Gentile as equally worthy of dignity, and letting it guide how you govern a nation, now that's something a President can do. Unless you're a Democrat. They have to pick winners and losers.

CHAPTER SIXTEEN

Yes, The Son Of David Still Supports Israel

Brandon Vallorani

O Jerusalem, Jerusalem, the city that kills the prophets and stones those sent to her! How often I wanted to gather your children together, just as a hen gathers her brood under her wings, and you would not have it!
Luke 13:34 NASB

J esus knew exactly the fate that awaited Him, and that many of His own people would not see Him for what He was. But that did nothing to diminish His great love for the people of His own nation, the nation with whom God made a special covenant. That great love was passed along to His disciples and apostles, even the one that was specifically sent to bring His Gospel to the Gentiles.

Romans chapter 9 opens with the following lines:

> *I am speaking the truth in Christ—I am not lying; my conscience bears me witness in the Holy Spirit— that I have great sorrow and unceasing anguish in my heart. For I could wish that I myself were accursed and cut off from Christ for the sake of my brothers, my kinsmen according to the flesh. They are Israelites, and to them belong the adoption, the glory, the covenants, the giving of the law, the worship, and the promises. To them belong the patriarchs, and from their race, according to the flesh, is the Christ, who is God over all, blessed forever. Amen.* (Ro. 9:1-5, ESV)

And then again in Romans 11, he gives a stern warning to the Gentile believers who he calls "wild branches" that Gentiles have no right to be arrogant because they are by nature outsiders brought in and that the Jewish people are those who are by nature part of the promise given Abraham. That's not the language of someone replacing Israel, as some might suggest, so much as people being added to it.

> *But if some of the branches were broken off, and you, although a wild olive shoot, were grafted in among the others and now share in the nourishing root of the olive tree, do not be arrogant toward the branches. If you are, remember it is not you who support the root, but the root that supports you. ... And even they, if they do not continue in their unbelief, will be grafted in, for God has the power to graft them in again. For if you were cut from what is by nature a wild olive tree, and grafted, contrary to nature, into a cultivated olive tree, how much more will these, the natural branches, be grafted back into their own olive tree.* (Ro. 11:17-18, 23-24, ESV)

Jesus has a particular love for the people of Israel, and what did the Triune God say about anyone who messes with Israel?

That same blessing that was given to the man Abraham in Genesis 12:3 is also the blessing extended to the entire nation in Numbers 24:9 during Balaam's prophesy:

> *He crouched, he lay down like a lion*
> *and like a lioness; who will rouse him up?*
> *Blessed are those who bless you,*
> *and cursed are those who curse you.*
> (Nu. 24:9, ESV)

There is a common thread from Moses ...

> *Then you shall say to Pharaoh, 'Thus says the Lord, Israel is my firstborn son, and I say to you, "Let my son go that he may serve me." If you refuse to let him go, behold, I will kill your firstborn son.* (Ex. 4:22-23, ESV)

To Jeremiah...

> *With weeping they shall come,*
> *and with pleas for mercy I will lead them back,*
> *I will make them walk by brooks of water,*
> *in a straight path in which they shall not stumble,*
> *for I am a father to Israel,*
> *and Ephraim is my firstborn.*
> *"Hear the word of the Lord, O nations,*
> *and declare it in the coastlands far away;*
> *say, 'He who scattered Israel will gather him,*
> *and will keep him as a shepherd keeps his flock.'*
> (Jr. 31:9-10, ESV)

231

Again and again, throughout scripture, the thrice-holy God makes it clear that if you mess with Israel, He takes it very personally. It becomes *His* score to settle. Even after He used the bloodied sword of foreign nations to judge Israel for her apostasy, He punished Edom for taking advantage of her in that time of weakness.

> *I have heard all the revilings that you uttered against the mountains of Israel, saying, 'They are laid desolate; they are given us to devour.' And you magnified yourselves against Me with your mouth, and multiplied your words against Me; I heard it. Thus says the Lord God: While the whole earth rejoices, I will make you desolate. As you rejoiced over the inheritance of the house of Israel, because it was desolate, so I will deal with you; you shall be desolate, Mount Seir, and all Edom, all of it. Then they will know that I am the Lord. (Ez. 35:12b -15, ESV)*

If there was any doubt as to how seriously we should take these admonitions, we know from history that Edom was scattered and entirely disappeared as a people in the 5th Century BC. This is as serious as a heart attack.

Turning our attention to the Twenty-First Century, what does America's recent relationship with Israel look like?

Since politics does not occur in a vacuum, let's take a step back. While the 2016 election was still in progress, what trends did we see developing with the prior administration in their dealings with Israel?

A guy by the name of Barack Obama was in charge. Remember him? He charted a rather different course in direction than our previous presidents had. Like most other things he did, Obama started with all the right and conventional platitudes, promising to move the American embassy to Jerusalem ... someday. As he got bolder, he dropped the pretenses. The further he got into his presidency, the more he polished the apple of Islamic Dictatorships. And by the end of his presidency, his behavior toward Israel was openly hostile.

Look at the Iran Deal he worked so hard on. Against all of Israel's objections, Obama put all his chips on the table trying to make the Iran deal work. It was only after the fact that we learned just how much Obama was willing to sacrifice to make this work.

Politico's Josh Meyer wrote a devastating piece about Project Cassandra entitled, *The Secret Backstory Of How Obama Let Hezbollah Off the Hook.*[103] As juicy as that title sounds, it doesn't even begin to tell the half of it.

As the DEA was monitoring the transformation of Hezbollah from regional political and military focussed terror network to an international crime syndicate, they followed the trafficking of cocaine into the US, and then cars into Africa while it blossomed into a billion-dollar-a-year criminal syndicate. US investigators had solid leads on who the big players were. They were poised to break it all up. Until the Obama administration pumped the brakes.

They had traced it all the way back to state sponsors in Iran. That was a problem for Obama's diplomatic objectives. When it came time to arrest, prosecute or place sanctions on key players, they got stonewalled, delayed or even stopped by the Justice Department and the Treasury Department. The State Department was no better; they refused to cooperate in luring targets to the U.S. where they could be charged.

Obama ran his first campaign on the claim that Bush's strong-arm approach toward Iran wasn't working, and that the solution required warming of relations. Obama's team were so hell bent on making that nuke deal with Iran work that they turned a blind eye to the growth of Hezbollah into a proper international crime syndicate ... and gave stand-down orders to projects already underway.

What kind of things do they deal in? Besides the drugs (multi-ton loads of cocaine), cars and money laundering I've already referenced ...

There was something else they were trafficking in: "the new and lethal IED known as the 'Explosively Formed Penetrator.' The armor-piercing charges were so powerful that they were ripping M1 Abrams tanks in half."[104] There's even a Russia connection. Putin-linked Hezbollah operative and arms dealer Ali Fayad was arrested in Prague in 2014 ... but Presidential pressure was not brought to bear to extradite him to America.

Not just Russia, either. Syria's Bashar Assad and Venezuela's Nicholas Maduro were also implicated, and we all know what wonderful people they have turned out to be.

Iran – which even liberal-friendly PBS acknowledged in 2017 as "still the world's leading State Sponsor of Terrorism"[105] – was of particular concern with Israel because of their obnoxious habit of funding proxy wars throughout the region. Their annual festival calling for "Death to Israel" and Death to America didn't help with their trust issues any.

While Obama's administration was bending over backward to keep Iran happy, what were they doing for the one free and Democratic state in the region, Israel? They were throwing every spoke in the wheel that they could. Obama showed himself overtly hostile to Israel's Prime Minister. *The Atlantic* reported that Obama "tried to force a rupture in the governing coalition" that would force them to broker a deal with the centrist Kadima Party.[106] That failed. A 2016 bipartisan Senate report found that $350K in taxpayer dollars were given to a group called "OneVoice Israel" that used said funds to "support a political campaign to defeat the incumbent Israeli government."[107] With friends like these, who needs an enemy?

But that wasn't all.

In the transitional period, while Trump was getting ready to assume leadership, Obama showed us all just how petulant he could be. Ignoring the usual "don't make any drastic policy changes" position during his final month in office he gave Israel the finger ...

In a December 2016 vote, USA abstained from UN Security Council Resolution 2334 demanding an immediate halt to all Israeli settlement construction in the West Bank and East Jerusalem. Because America voted "present" instead of invoking the veto, the measure passed 14-0. Perhaps more importantly, the wording in the resolution "to distinguish, in their relevant dealings, between the territory of the State of Israel and the territories occupied since 1967" could be used to justify and intensify the anti-Israel BDS movement.[108]

How did Israel feel about that decision? One minister after the vote lamented: America has, "abandoned Israel, its only ally in the Middle East" and said its behavior was "not that of a friend."

Obama's team had been working overtime for years to strike a deal with a hostile regime in a nation that literally has an annual festival calling for "Death to Israel" and "Death to America"; so Obama treating the only Democratic nation in the region with hostility shouldn't really have surprised anybody. Obama waited eight long years before pulling this rug out from under Israel and only did so once he had nothing left to lose.

Until Obama, American Presidents had quite a warm relationship with Israel – notwithstanding the unrivaled diplomatic stupidity of President Carter.

Did Obama's deal with the devil solve the Nuclear Iran problem? Not even close, as evidenced by the midnight raid by Mossad in which they broke into a warehouse and stole literally half a ton of Iran's Nuclear secrets out from under their nose: 50,000 pages and 163 compact discs containing files, videos and plans.

So here we were, in 2016 with two choices before us. We had Hillary Clinton – Obama's Former Secretary of State and a de-facto Third Term of Obama's presidency versus ... Donald J. Trump.

But would Trump do any better? After all, there's been a lot of chat about Trump being a RacistSexistHomophobe. Is that just the Drive-by media up to their usual tricks, or is there something of substance to those accusations of bigotry?

There are so many different ways to deflect or even wave this question away as unimportant. But since it's central to the attack on his character, and it's even been repeated in the foreign press, let's dig into the allegations a little and see what they're really made of ... they claim he is racist generally, and white supremacist, specifically.

Donald Trump – until the time he declared an interest in politics, or more specifically *Republican* politics – was generally liked and accepted by the political in-crowd. Whether they liked Trump or they liked his money, who can really tell, but try to think back: Before he came down that famous escalator, did anybody seriously accuse him of racism?

Before there was an (R) after his name, the Rap culture loved the man. He was the standard by which other would-be musical success stories would be measured. Any number of songs celebrated his wealth.

Before there was an (R) after his name, he received an Ellis Island award alongside Mohammed Ali and Rosa Parks.[109]

Before there was an (R) after his name, he "dispatched his plane to fly a sick Jewish boy for special care when he heard no airline would accommodate his medical equipment."[110] (It was 1988, and the boy was 3-year-old Andrew Ten.)

The keystone allegation in claims of Trump's racism is one "gotcha" quote after Charlottesville, which was both malicious and deceptively edited. The clash between one group protesting the removal of a statue of Robert E. Lee with protesters that wanted the statue removed occurred in Charlottesville on Saturday, August 12, 2017. The two groups both had some peaceful protesters, but they also had agitators that got pretty aggressive. The media had a field day blaming Trump. They ramped up into high gear when a white supremacist drove his car into a crowd killing pro-removal protester, Heather Heyer.

There were several separate times President Trump addressed the press in the days that followed. First was Saturday's statement, then a formal one on Monday, after he'd been briefed by officials. Then was the Tuesday press conference from which the "gotcha" quote is taken. On each of those days he made statements – hard to miss – where he *explicitly* denounces racial hatred. As one example among several:

> As I said on Saturday, we condemn in the strongest possible terms this egregious display of hatred, bigotry and violence. It has no place in America.
>
> And as I have said many times before: No matter the color of our skin, we all live under the same laws, we all salute the same great flag, and we are all made by the same almighty God. We must love each other, show affection for each other, and unite together in condemnation of hatred, bigotry and violence. We must rediscover the bonds of love and loyalty that bring us together as Americans.
>
> Racism is evil. And those who cause violence in its name are criminals and thugs, including the KKK, neo Nazis, white supremacists and other hate groups that are repugnant to everything we hold dear as Americans.
>
> We are a nation founded on the truth that all of us are created equal. We are equal in the eyes of our Creator. We are equal under the law. And we are equal under our Constitution. Those who spread violence in the name of bigotry strike at the very core of America.[111]

President Trump condemned the driver:

> I think the driver of the car is a disgrace to himself,
> his family and this country. You can call it terror-
> ism. You can call it murder. You can call it what-
> ever you want.[112]

He was asked leading questions to place all blame on one racist group, and despite making distinctions in who and what
he meant, those distinctions were deliberately twisted.

To summarize, the President recognized that apart from the
Neo-Nazis, who he explicitly denounced, some people present in Charlottesville were simply protesting the removal of a
statue and renaming of a landmark park with no racial component whatsoever.

Because of Richard Spencer's views, he drew a counter-pro-
test, including some black-clad Antifa agitators. Tensions
flared. Violence erupted. One racist rammed his car into a
crowd, killing someone, was charged and convicted for the
crime. But to say everyone was there to participate in violence
is obviously false.

His "very fine people" comment takes on a different tone in
its full context:

> I think there is blame object both on both sides.
> I have no doubt about it. You don't have doubt
> about it either. If you reported it accurately, you
> would say that the neo-Nazis started this thing.
> They showed up in Charlottesville. Excuse me.
> They didn't put themselves down as neo-Nazis.
> You had some very bad people in that group.

You had some very fine people on both sides. You had people in that group – excuse me, excuse me. I saw the same pictures as you did. You had people in that group that were there to protest the taking down, of to them, a very, very important statue and the renaming of a park from Robert E. Lee to another name.[113]

And still, staffers at CNN and MSNBC would have us all believe that Trump is a racist and friendly toward White Supremacists.

Give your head a shake, people. Step back and look at the big picture. Trump's daughter married a Jewish man – Jared Kushner – and she herself converted to Judaism. The President has Jewish grandkids. If he's a closet Klansman, that alone would be enough to get his membership revoked in a hurry. How much more so the fact that Kushner has become one of his more trusted advisors?

They say David Duke endorsed DJT. So what? Now he hates Trump and David Duke has moved on to supporting other people like Ilhan Omar, and Tulsi Gabbard, in the party that cannot quite bring itself to directly denounce anti-Semitism.

On the day he was elected, Benjamin Netanyahu called Trump a "true friend of Israel."[114] He concluded that after sitting down with Trump for 90 minutes in Trump Tower on a visit to the UN that September.

Has Trump's policy reflected his rhetoric? Said differently, has Trump put his money where his mouth is? Absolutely.

To name just a few key examples:

The Iran Deal is gone and heavy sanctions on the terror-ist-friendly regime are back.

Trump finally moved the US Embassy to Jerusalem – despite enormous objections from the "global community." Not only that, but he made the switch almost immediately.

And who can forget Nikki Haley, the firebrand nominated to the United Nations that absolutely torched the stuffed shirts over there for the endless hostility to exactly one nation: Isra-el, while ignoring the *real* problem nations around the world.

> Members of the Security Council have heard me say this many times. The problems of the Middle East are numerous, and yet we spend vastly disproportionate amount of time on just one of them. And the UN has shown itself to be hopeless-ly biased, as we witnessed again just two weeks ago when the General Assembly failed to con-demn Hamas's terrorist activity against Israel.

> Over the past two years, I have attempted to provide more value in this monthly meeting by using my time to speak about other pressing problems in the Middle East. I have spoken about Iran's illegal weapons transfers and destabilizing support for terrorism throughout the region. I have spoken about the barbarism of the Assad regime in Syria. I have spoken about Hamas's illegal and diabolical use of human shields. I have spoken about Hezbollah jeopardizing the safety of the Lebanese people and its violations of Israeli sov-

ereignty, which have come to light even more clearly in the last month. I have spoken about Iraq and Yemen, about refugees and humanitarian crises.[115]

She went on, and described the Trump administration's proposed peace deal, yes – peace deal:

It is time we faced a hard truth: both sides would benefit greatly from a peace agreement, but the Palestinians would benefit more, and the Israelis would risk more.

It is with this backdrop in mind that the Trump Administration has crafted its plan for peace between Israel and the Palestinians. I don't expect anyone to comment on a peace proposal they have not read. But I have read it. And I will share some thoughts on it now.

Unlike previous attempts at addressing this conflict, this plan is not just a few pages, containing unspecific and unimaginative guidelines. It is much longer. It contains much more thoughtful detail. It brings new elements to the discussion, taking advantage of the new world of technology that we live in. It recognizes the realities on the ground in the Middle East have changed – and changed in very powerful and important ways. It embraces the reality that things can be done today that were previously unthinkable. This plan will be different from all previous ones. The critical question is whether the response will be any different.

There are things in the plan that every party will like, and there are things in the plan that every party will not like. That is certainly true for the Israelis and the Palestinians, but it is also true for every country in the world that has taken an interest in this subject. Every country or party will therefore have an important choice to make. They can focus on the parts of the plan they dislike. For irresponsible parties, that would be the easiest thing to do. Just reject the plan because it does not satisfy all of your demands. Then we would return back to the failed status quo of the last 50 years with no prospects for change. Israel would continue to grow and prosper. The Palestinian people would continue to suffer. And innocent people on both sides would continue to be killed.

The other choice is to focus on the parts of the plan that you do like and encourage negotiations to move forward. And I assure you there is a lot for both sides to like.[116]

Israel has thanked President Trump for his support of Israel by naming the train station near the Western Wall after him. Prime Minister Benjamin Netanyahu went further still with his public statements, putting him in with some very elite company:

I want to tell you that the Jewish people have a long memory, so we remember the proclamation of the great king, Cyrus the Great, the Persian king 2,500 years ago. He proclaimed that the Jewish exiles in Babylon could come back and rebuild our Temple in Jerusalem. We remember a hundred years ago, Lord Balfour, who issued the Balfour Proclamation that recognized the rights of the Jewish people in our ancestral homeland. We remember 70 years ago, President Harry S. Truman was the first leader to recognize the Jewish state. And we remember how a few weeks ago, President Donald J. Trump recognized Jerusalem as Israel's capital. Mr. President, this will be remembered by our people through the ages.[117]

Bibi tweeted on March 21, 2019:

At a time when Iran seeks to use Syria as a platform to destroy Israel, President Trump boldly recognizes Israeli sovereignty over the Golan Heights. Thank you President Trump! @realDonaldTrump[118]

"Blessed are the Peacemakers," Jesus said. How much more so when that attempt at making peace touches the lives of the very people He first made that covenant with? People who have bomb shelters built in their homes to protect from rocket attacks. The Divine author reserves harsh language for those who despise and mistreat Israel. What about those who seek the well being of Israel? He promises to thoroughly bless them. So, let's recap:

Trump isn't racist. (Obviously)

He has affirmed Jerusalem as Israel's capital.

He is working towards a peace deal that will not sacrifice key interests in Jewish sovereignty.

He has slapped down Iran's regional ambitions.

Looking at the casual attitudes toward anti-Semitism in the Democrat ranks, and their eagerness to push the anti-Israel Boycott Divestment Sanctions (BDS) agenda, is there any politician on the Left whose positions on Israel Jesus would possibly support more than Trump's?

CHAPTER SEVENTEEN

Woman, Thou Art Loosed!

Doug Giles

*Then His mother and His brothers arrived, and standing
outside they sent word to Him and called Him. A crowd was
sitting around Him, and they said to Him, "Behold, Your mother and Your brothers are outside looking for You." Answering
them, He said, "Who are My mother and My brothers?"
Looking about at those who were sitting around Him, He said,
"Behold My mother and My brothers! For whoever does the
will of God, he is My brother and sister and mother."*
Mark 3: 31-35, ESV

D onald J. Trump certainly has quite the history with the
fairer sex. Can anyone seriously question whether or
not he loves women? After all, he's been married to
three of them, dating the next wife while still married to the
previous one. Trump has reveled in his Billionaire Playboy status, which has become a significant part of the mythos of The
Donald. Trump's penchant for beautiful women is just as well

known as his signature golden comb-over. Back in the pre-White House days, DJT was immortalized by rappers in song for his cash, bling, and seemingly tremendous success with bedding beauties.

Trump critics love to cite that he has appeared on the cover of Playboy and gone along with Howard Stern's shock jock shtick by rating women's bodies and discussing his sex life. Trump has boasted about his conquests and missed opportunities (he claims he could have been with Princess Di,) on his many appearances on Stern's show over the years. One of the more scandalous comments Trump made to Stern was that Ivanka is so beautiful, if she weren't his daughter, he'd date her. Now, for the anti-Trump peeps that can't seem to understand the world according to DJT this isn't to imply some sort of incestuous lusting on his part, but rather, as the pinnacle of achievement for a beautiful woman -- to become arm candy for The Donald.

Trump has also had multiple women come forward and accuse him of sexual assault, (which he denies,) and then there was that infamous Access Hollywood blather with Billy Bush, where, after admitting to making the moves on a married woman, he said, "when you're famous, they let you do anything. You can grab 'em by the p***y." Trump was pilloried for that little nugget. While being a gross statement, when you think about it for a minute, and don't ignore the *consensual* implication, it actually says less about The Donald than about the women he is surrounded by. There are a startling number of women looking for a Sugar Daddy, and Trump, with his abundant fame and fortune, would be the ultimate prize.

Let's face it; it's Trump's history with women that makes a whole lot of religious folk so queasy about him as a person that they can't seem to look past it. To the NeverTrumpkins, especially of the evangelical Christian variety, it is Trump's inability to keep his junk in his pants that makes all of his conservative policies on border security, abortion, taxes, Obamacare, and everything else completely irrelevant. *This* was the deal-breaker.

As Bible-believing Christians, however, we can see from Scripture that God has used men to accomplish His plans who have succumbed to far worse sin than what Trump has ever admitted to doing. (And, he's admitted to *quite* a bit.)

You want to talk about The Donald getting around? I raise you King Solomon with his 700 wives and 300 concubines. (1 Ki. 11:3) How that bro had any energy left to ensure the building of the Temple and enshrine his wisdom into Holy Writ is beyond me.

How about Samson? A cursory glance at Judges 14-16 reveals that Samson made some pretty *mondo* mistakes when it came to the ladies. First, he spied a Philistine woman and he demanded, Veruca Salt-like, that his parents get her for him to marry. Unfortunately, it didn't work out so well for Samson and his blushing bride. After she told her countrymen the answer to a riddle Samson had posed to them to win a bet, he walked out on her. That's some super-spiritual stuff from a God-appointed Judge of Israel, eh? When he eventually decided to come back to her, he found that his father-in-law had handed her over to Samson's best man. Yikes. Samson didn't take kindly to that, so he started some trouble with the Philistines by setting fields and vineyards ablaze via foxes. Yes, *foxes*. Look it up. Samson then had a Stormy Daniels interlude with a prostitute in Gaza. It was immediately after this that scripture tells us he fell in love with Delilah. We all know how *that* particular story ends — Samson was captured by the Philistines and had his eyes gouged out.

Samson really knew how to pick a woman. Both his wife and Delilah were feckless, nagging traitors who pestered him day after day and when he finally gave in and told them the truth, they quickly handed the newfound intel over to his enemies. Ironically, the woman that caused him the *least* amount of trouble was the whore. Being led by his crotch really bit him in the *tuchus*. And yet — God still used Samson to accomplish His purposes, later calling him "faithful" in Hebrews 11. As we covered in a previous chapter, God really does use the base things to confound the wise. (1 Co. 1:27)

But if we're going to look at a man whose lust for the ladies got him into deep doo-doo, we cannot find a better example than shepherd, Psalmist, and the "man after God's own heart" -- King David.

David, after he became King, sent his men off to war and stayed back where it was safe. He then saw the bodacious babe Bathsheba bathing on a rooftop and asked who she was. When he was told that she was married (by one of his mighty men, by the way) that made zero difference to him. King David used his kingly authority to have her brought to him so that they could get down'n'dirty. Frankly, having her husband away at war — where David should have been — made the adultery easier. Unfortunately for David, his sin couldn't be kept secret because Bathsheba found herself pregnant. Oops. In 2 Samuel 11, you can see how the story plays out; David brought back Uriah from the battle, but Uriah, being a faithful man, slept at the entrance of the king's house and not with his wife. David even tried to get Uriah drunk to go home to Bathsheba, but that didn't work, either. (2 Sa.11:13) So, David did the unthinkable — he had Uriah placed on the front line while the other warriors pulled back. King David, the "man after God's own heart," ordered the assassination of the husband of his lover using an opposing army, and it was all done to hide the paternity of Bathsheba's child. There's a pretty hefty example of "there is none righteous, no not one." (Ro. 3:23)

Would those same folks that say that Trump is unfit for office because of his philandering past have been "NeverDavids" back in 1000 BC? Maybe. And yet, God still used David, counted him as righteous, and Jesus is descended directly from his line.

Last time I checked, Trump hasn't *schtupped* a chick then had her husband knocked off to hide the fact that she was in-the-family-way with a mini-Trump.

I also read somewhere that we are to "judge not lest ye be judged" and "let he who is without sin cast the first stone" and I'm pretty sure it was written in red. It's quite rich that some of these NeverTrump peeps condemning The Donald for his womanizing would fold worse than their own cheap suits if a Victoria's Secret model flaunted her voluptuous ta-tas at his Crisco-sweating self.

As for the pearl-clutching Neo-Puritans on the Left who are suddenly offended by sex ... Donald Trump is a product of the morality of our age, which, last time I checked has shifted towards the libertinism that is promoted by their lot. It's the Left that pushed for free sex unshackled from monogamy, commitment, or even knowing first names. These are the same folks that made excuses for credibly accused rapist Bill Clinton, big-time Democrat donor and serial sexual abuser, Harvey Weinstein, and the "moral superiors" in Hollywood on

251

their 8th marriages. Heck, they were even buddy-buddy with The Donald back when he didn't have an "R" after his name. These same Leftists that were so outraged that Trump was allegedly unfaithful have nigh-unto sainted the porn star that broke the non-disclosure agreement and cashed-in with a tell-all book which includes her claim of a one night stand with the current President of the United States.

Besides, Trump seems to have mellowed out in the last few years. No one can know what is in a man's heart, (hence the whole "judge not" thing) and his repentance or lack there-of, to his own past deeds are between him and the God that made him. Whether you believe him or not, Trump has denied the claims of extra-curricular sexual exploits made by both Stormy Daniels and Karen McDougal.

At first glance, it seems like Donald J. Trump and Jesus are on completely different planets when it comes to women. But our premise here is whether or not Jesus would vote for Trump, so we've got to delve a little deeper into how Trump treats women *outside* the bedroom.

Trump isn't one of those fake feminists like the global Left's new hero, Prime Minister of Canada, Justin Trudeau, who made sure that fifty percent of his cabinet ministers were women simply because we're in the 21st century. By the way, speaking of Trudeau, it seems that he got a little "handsy" with a female reporter back before his political life, but the Canadian media largely ignored the story. Meanwhile, President Trump was pilloried in the press for his braggadocios claim that women allowed rich, famous men to grope them. (I guess the media hasn't heard of a Kardashian.) Despite his frequent appearances on Howard Stern, his multiple marriages, and the inspiration that he was to rap stars prior to becoming a Republican, President Trump has appointed people based on merit, and many of those worthy individuals happen to be of the female persuasion.

Despite his predilections, President Trump has actually been very good in his working relationships with women. He has appointed more women to senior positions within the government and the West Wing than any other president in history. An op-ed in The Hill boldly declared, *"Trump's First Year In Office Was The Year Of The Woman."*[119] Somehow CNN missed that memo.

We could write a whole other book on the worthy women that POTUS DJT has appointed, but let's just look at one high-profile example – Kellyanne Conway.

Kellyanne Conway's success is a result of her hard work, dedication, and a go-get'em attitude. This chick is an absolute badass. She was raised by a single mom in New Jersey and decided to make it in a male-dominated field — which she did. She's a mom with four young children, a husband that has open Twitter-feuds with her boss, the President, and she still keeps her cool. She also has the distinction to be the first female campaign manager to see her candidate become President.

Of course, because she was a Republican, this meant nothing to the Media(D) that normally shouts those kinds of accomplishments from the rooftops. Kellyanne was an incredible surrogate for Trump as he ran, continuing to get his message out, and not backing down when pushed by the vapid, anti-Trump Media(D). After bringing Donald J. Trump to the White House, Conway was given the position of Counselor to the President. If she had done nothing else, her on-camera verbal dropkick calling CNN's perpetual whiner and White House Correspondent, Jim Acosta, a "smartass" alone is worthy of a job in the West Wing.

President Trump has appointed many other talented women in major positions of leadership within his administration.

Here's a partial list for the pink, knit-hat-wearing "I'm With Her" crowd that absolutely insists that Donald J. Trump is anti-woman:

1. Sarah Huckabee Sanders — White House Press Secretary.
2. Nikki Haley — U.S. Ambassador to the United Nations. First Indian-American woman appointed to a presidential cabinet.
3. Gina Haspel — CIA Director. She is the first woman to lead the CIA.
4. Kirstjen Nielsen — Secretary of the Department of Homeland Security.
5. Elaine Chao — Secretary of Transportation. First Asian-American woman to serve in a presidential Cabinet.
6. Dr. Heather Wilson — Secretary of the Air Force.
7. Betsy DeVos — Secretary of Education.
8. Linda McMahon — Administrator of the U.S. Small Business Association.
9. Mercedes Schlapp — Senior Communications Advisor.
10. Hope Hicks — Communications Director.
11. Sema Verma — Administrator of the Centers for Medicare and Medicaid Services.
12. Jovita Carranza — U.S. Treasurer.
13. Jessica Ditto — Deputy Director of Communications.
14. Heather Brand — Associate Attorney General.
15. Dina Powell — Deputy National Security Advisor.
16. Neomi Rao — Regulation Tzar, Now appointed to the D.C.

District Court of Appeals to fill the seat left by Justice Kavanaugh's appointment to the Supreme Court.

17. Kelly Sadler — Director of Surrogate and Coalitions Outreach.

18. Ivanka Trump — Advisor to the President.

This list doesn't even count the numerous lower court appointments that have been women. Nearly a third (28%) of all of President Trump's judicial picks have been women.[120] This is far more than any other GOP President in history – even Michelle Obama's buddy, Dubya. We're still just two years into his term and a number of his court appointments have been stalled due to severe cases of Trump Derangement Syndrome in Congress. Oh, and that TDS is bipartisan. (Thanks for nothin', Jeff Flake.)

There is also the chance that Justice Ruth Bader Ginsburg may hang up her robes and give President Trump a third Supreme Court pick, who would likely be a woman. That would make the anti-Trump peeps shout louder than a troop of howler monkeys!

Trump treating women as equals isn't anything new. DJT has been honoring women's accomplishments even *before* he became POTUS.

Barbara Res was the Vice President of the Trump Organization and was the first woman to oversee the construction of a skyscraper. And what a skyscraper it was — *the* Trump Tower. In her new role as anti-Trump activist writer for HuffPo, she even accidentally admits that The Donald had surrounded himself with several strong women way back in the late 1970s and early 1980s, and her opposition to him is largely based on her own progressive political views. She even writes that in Trump's view, "men are better than women, but a good woman is worth ten good men"[121] which she uses to show his alleged misogyny. If he's so misogynistic, why would he say that in a work environment, one good woman is better than ten good men? Now, I just went to public school, but it sounds to me like The Donald respects strong, hard working women.

Under the Trump Administration's policies, women are winning. The unemployment rate for women is at record lows, women's wages have risen, and more women are opening up businesses. Trump has also dealt with one of the major hurdles that women face in going to work — childcare. The Trump tax bill included tax cuts to offset the cost of childcare. In Trump's America truly, "Woman, thou art loosed!" to go and do and be anything her heart desires.

So much for the dystopian "we're living in *The Handmaid's Tale!*" fever dream that the Left keeps pushing.

Trump and Jesus seem to be on the same page with their treatment of women as equal to men. In the first century, Our Lord went against the cultural norms and didn't treat women as the inferior of the sexes. Jesus swam against the flow and would oft engage in conversation with women in public, which was *verboten*.

When Jesus met the woman at the well, not only did He speak with her, He asked her to share some of her water, which would have meant sharing a cup with a Samaritan. This was seriously *not* kosher, in the colloquial sense, of course. Jesus then has an extended chat about theology, her relationship status, and within that convo, He revealed that He was the Messiah — to a woman. Not just a woman, but an outcast Gentile woman who had been married five times and was shacking up with yet another man. When Jesus' disciples come back, they're clearly uncomfortable, but don't question Him on the interaction. The Samaritan woman then left the water at the well and brought half her village to Jesus. Yes kiddies, she became an evangelist. (See John 4)

When Jesus healed a woman who had been crippled for 18 years on the Sabbath, He called her a "daughter of Abraham" (Lk. 13:16) making her equal with the male heirs of the Covenant known as the "sons of Abraham." He also called the woman with the issue of blood "daughter." This was a deliberate ditching of societal norms and a return to the way things were in the Old Testament, where women were included in the Covenant and active participants in worship.

In the first century, society had marginalized women almost exclusively to the home, even excluding them from public prayers. Although admitted to the Temple for worship, at the time, women were not permitted to read, let alone learn the scripture. When Jesus taught, He welcomed both men and women to sit at His feet and listen to Him.

Our Lord's interactions with women weren't exactly conventional at the time. When He went to the house of a Pharisee and a prostitute washed His feet with her tears, dried them with her hair, then anointed them with oil, Jesus didn't send her away or call her unclean. Instead, He chastised His host for *his* judgmental thinking. (Lk. 7:36-50)

Jesus also had several followers that were women that traveled with Him and the disciples. Luke names a few of them, Mary Magdalene, Joanna, Susanna, and says that there were "many others." (Lk. 8:1-3) Our Lord reiterates this idea when He is told that His mother and brothers are outside waiting for Him. He asks, "Who are my mother and my brothers?" Looking at those seated around Him, He said, "Here are My mother and brothers! Whoever does the will of God is My brother and sister and mother." (Mk. 3:31-35) Jesus includes the word "sister" as an indicator that there were some women in the group gathered listening to Him. Scripture speaks of the sisters of Lazarus, Mary and Martha, who Jesus would visit, and Mary would be sitting at His feet and listening to His teaching. (Lk. 10:38-42)

Women were with Jesus during His trial and crucifixion. (Jn. 19:25) After He had risen from the dead, the first people that Jesus appeared to were the women coming to the tomb to prepare His body for burial. It was those women who were the ones to bring the news of the Resurrection to the disciples.

It seems that DJT's treatment of women as equals and his rewarding those that have worked hard to achieve their success is indeed consistent with the way that Lord of All Creation treated women.

CHAPTER EIGHTEEN

Would Dulce Jesús Make
ISIS WAS-WAS?

Brandon Vallorani

*But bring here those enemies of mine, who did not want me to
reign over them, and slay them before me.*
Luke 19:27, NKJV

When we speak of Jesus, we normally speak of His love and His tenderness. Gentle Jesus, meek and mild. Truly, this is part of who He is. But that is not the entirety of who He is. One can have no greater friend and defender than God himself, but you can have no greater foe, either.

We are so accustomed to His kindness and compassion that when we read passages like the one above, they seem a little jarring to be coming from the mouth of our Lord. In fact, part of Him being both good and just is that He is a righteous judge, and a terror to the wicked. In His first coming, He came as a Lamb. But in His return, He will come in glory as a conquering king.

> *Now I saw heaven opened, and behold, a white horse. And He who sat on him was called Faithful and True, and in righteousness He judges and makes war. His eyes were like a flame of fire, and on His head were many crowns. He had a name written that no one knew except Himself. He was clothed with a robe dipped in blood, and His name is called The Word of God. And the armies in heaven, clothed in fine linen, white and clean, followed Him on white horses. Now out of His mouth goes a sharp sword, that with it He should strike the nations. And He Himself will rule them with a rod of iron. He Himself treads the winepress of the fierceness and wrath of Almighty God. And He has on His robe and on His thigh a name written: KING OF KINGS AND LORD OF LORDS.*
> (Rev. 19:11-16, NKJV)

His people have been explicitly taught to spread the gospel message peaceably ... but that job is different from the role of political leaders. Their role is that of governing and maintaining public peace. That is good news for law-abiding civilians and very bad news indeed to those who are not.

> *For rulers are not a terror to good works, but to evil. Do you want to be unafraid of the authority? Do what is good, and you will have praise from the same. For he is God's minister to you for good. But if you do evil, be afraid; for he does not bear the sword in vain; for he is God's minister, an avenger to execute wrath on him who practices evil. Therefore you must be subject, not only*

because of wrath but also for conscience' sake. For because of this you also pay taxes, for they are God's ministers attending continually to this very thing. Render therefore to all their due: taxes to whom taxes are due, customs to whom customs, fear to whom fear, honor to whom honor. (Ro. 13: 3-7, ESV)

Governmental leadership has a divinely appointed role in society. Not of pastoral leadership, but of bearing the sword of justice against those who practice evil.

Let's have a look at that role in our nation's recent history.

One otherwise ordinary Tuesday morning in September changed the course of U.S. history. It was the day – September 11, 2001 – when four hijacked passenger planes were turned into weapons of war by people who hate us. We all know what happened next: two planes struck the Twin Towers of the World Trade Center in NYC, raining death and destruction into the heart of New York, and bringing those towers, and some other nearby buildings crashing to the ground below. A third plane slammed into the Pentagon. And yet another was headed toward Washington D.C. when some defiant Americans, realizing their own lives were already forfeit, died as heroes preventing that plane from realizing its intended target.

Todd Beamer, trying to call home from Flight 97 before his last act of defiance, explained the situation to the airphone customer service representative who took his call. The pilots were dead, their throats were cut. Todd was going to "jump on the attackers" and fly the plane into the ground so that nobody else would die. Beamer recited the Lord's Prayer and the 23rd Psalm with airphone supervisor, Lisa Jefferson, prompting others to join in, asked that his family be told he loves them, and then Beamer's voice on the line for his final recorded words, "Are you ready? Okay. Let's roll."

"Let's Roll" encapsulated the resolve and defiance that characterized the attitude toward the terrorists who sought American blood throughout the period immediately after the attacks. Follow-up attacks like the "shoe bomber" were foiled. The 2002 Beltway Sniper attacks had an affinity for jihad mentioned in the trial, even though no official motive was given. A dirty bomb plot in Chicago was foiled. But not everyone shared that initial resolve, and it began to waver over time.

In the time afterward, Dubya was denounced by the press as a "war criminal" (a vicious charge that was conveniently forgotten when he and his family stood opposed to the election of one Donald Trump). Before long, a new word was introduced to the national conversation: Islamophobia.

Suddenly, even mentioning the "Religion of Peace" (as it had curiously come to be known) as a possible motivating influence by attackers -- suicidal or otherwise -- who had begun killing civilians in the name of religious devotion became politically incorrect ... even when there were such tell-tale signs as a cry of "Allahu Akbar" during the attack itself.

We began to see a clear change in how our media and political classes responded to such attacks.
They became very reluctant to assign the motive "terror" to any attacks ... unless of course, the attacker did not appear to be associated with an ethnic or religious minority.

In fact, the pendulum had swung so far under President Obama that he was often accused of being afraid to utter the phrase "Islamic Terrorist attack."

Such deliberate and willful blindness to a dangerously hostile ideology (dangerous, at least, in its radical form) would be like a 20th Century nonchalance toward Fascistic or Communist ideologies. In fact, history saw just such a complacency during the Cold War among a number of our academics, actors and journalists. (See: Hanoi Jane.) The more things change, the more they stay the same.

A prime example of this willful blindness is the 2009 attack in Fort Hood. It was at Fort Hood that Major Nidal Malik Hasan unleashed the worst mass murder we had ever seen at a U.S. military installation. Thirteen victims were shot dead, and another thirty were wounded. And the worst part of it was that this was preventable. There were warning signs.

The Pentagon and US Senate looked into the situation and concluded that, "Hasan's superiors had continued to promote him despite the fact that concerns had been raised over his behavior, which suggested he had become a radical and potentially violent Islamic extremist." Maybe his belief that America's war on terrorism was really a "war on Islam" should have been a tip-off. He shouted that infamous line "Allahu Akbar" during the attack, but how did President Obama respond to the incident? He and Eric Holder described it as "workplace violence."

The press even noticed a pattern forming in his reaction. The 2009 Christmas Day bomber was "an isolated extremist." The Benghazi attacks in Libya (that just "happened" to be on the anniversary of 9/11) were attributed to an Anti-Islamic video ... despite solid evidence to the contrary.

The shooting of a Kosher supermarket in Paris by Islamic radicals? That was a "random" shooting. Obama did acknowledge that the Boston Marathon Bombing was an act of terrorism, but – despite the literature linking the terrorists to Al-Qaeda – did not step out on a limb and specify it as "Islamic" terrorism.

As for San Bernardino, Obama said it was "possible" the shooting was terror related, but it was also possible it was workplace related.

Again, in Chattanooga, Mohammad Youssef Abdulazeez opened fire on a military recruiting center before moving on to and targeting a Navy Reserve center. Speaking from the Oval Office just hours after the attack, President Obama did not once use the word "terrorism."

U.S. Attorney Bill Killian, on the other hand, had no such difficulty. The situation "is being treated as a terrorism investigation," he said. "It is being led by the FBI's Joint Terrorism Task Force. And we will continue to investigate it as an act of terrorism until proof shows us otherwise."

Obama had a strange aversion to speaking plainly about this issue. This paired poorly with his tendency to over-correct to show the world how "tolerant" he really was.

The ridiculous tweet to Clock-boy comes to mind, "Cool clock, Ahmed. Want to bring it to the White House? We should inspire more kids like you to like science. It's what makes America great." That tweet didn't age well at all.

Instead of taking seriously the threat of an identified group of people (jihadis) who have both the intent and means to do us harm, Obama had a very different plan.

In an interview with Al Jazeera, Charles Bolden said:

> When I became the NASA administrator, he [Mr. Obama] charged me with three things. One, he wanted me to help reinspire children to want to get into science and math; he wanted me to expand our international relationships; and third, and perhaps foremost, he wanted me to find a way to reach out to the Muslim world and engage much more with dominantly Muslim nations to help them feel good about their historic contribution to science, math, and engineering.

He added, "It is a matter of trying to reach out and get the best of all worlds, if you will, and there is much to be gained by drawing in the contributions that are possible from the Muslim [nations]."

In the wake of Benghazi, Obama blamed the attacks that killed American Ambassador Stevens, Sean Smith, Tyrone S. Woods, and Glen Doherty on American provocation, when they knew for a fact that no American "provoked" this attack.

Obama stood in front of the United Nations and said, "The future must not belong to those who slander the prophet of Islam."

Not only did #44 not take real threats seriously, he could not properly distinguish between friend and foe. We've covered it elsewhere, but it bears repeating just how far Obama was willing to turn a blind eye to substantial threats in his pursuit of that desperately-longed-for treaty with Iran.

Politico broke a story about "Project Cassandra" where stand down orders were given to American crimefighting agencies who had been gathering information on Hezbollah bringing tons (plural) of cocaine into America, buying used cars to launder the money, shipping them to Africa, and using the funds to transform Hezbollah from a political organization to a full-blown criminal cartel with business dealings in the billions of dollars. They also had business connections with such charming leaders as Putin, Maduro, and Assad. Known associates were held in prison elsewhere and could have been extradited here to face US charges -- but weren't. This group was making advanced IEDs that could rip an M1 Abrams tank in half, and using them to arm groups aligned against Western interests.

But, as that Politico piece, *The Secret Backstory of How Obama Let Hezbollah Off the Hook*[122], explains, most of those leads went cold. The investigations were for naught. The bad guys got away, and the criminal cartels got stronger, wealthier, and even more dangerous.

In the end, Iran had become so emboldened by Obama's weakness that they even scored a serious PR win against "the Great Satan" when they captured and humiliated some American sailors in 2016 without ever facing real consequences for it.

We saw more of the same when we look at Obama's handling of Gitmo. A trade was arranged between Bergdahl, a deserter, for as many as five Taliban commanders, who are now all serving in leadership roles in a Taliban office in Qatar. Bergdahl, on the other hand, has since entered a guilty plea to charges of desertion and misbehavior before the enemy.

Obama's policies helped lead to the destabilization of an entire region. The same Obama who cheered and welcomed the "Arab Spring" that led to a Muslim Brotherhood leadership in Egypt, and governments overthrown in Yemen, North Africa and Syria. That, in turn, precipitated the Syrian refugee crisis in Europe and elsewhere.

Hillary chortled at her own "joke" when she said of Gaddafi, "We came. We saw. He died." Libya has since become a dangerous failed state. Only one year after Gaddafi died, the Libyan city of Benghazi made its way into the news.

Meanwhile, Obama's military decision to leave a power vacuum in Iraq led to that supposed "J.V. team" (ISIS) seizing a power base, amassing weapons, murdering, raping and selling locals into slavery, and becoming a dangerous political-criminal enterprise that served as a magnet for other would-be warriors for "the cause."

That "J.V. team" quickly metastasized into a real and serious threat. Obama didn't even rise to his own standards of right and wrong – for example, he said the use of chemical weapons would constitute a "red line" that would obligate him to act militarily. When that line was eventually crossed, he hemmed and hawed and did a whole lot of nothing. Leading from behind is about as close to a perfect opposite of Reagan's 'Peace Through Strength' policy as one could possibly get.

All of these things had a shared root cause – leadership that refused to acknowledge as serious an armed and motivated ideological threat – even when clues were right there before their very eyes. That the blindness was willful is entirely obvious in that leaked Podesta email after the jihadi attack in San Bernardino.

"Better if a guy named Sayeed Farouk [sic] was reporting that a guy named Christopher Hayes was the shooter," Podesta wrote in a Dec. 2, 2015 email to Karen Finney, a Clinton campaign spokeswoman. [123]

This is where Donald Trump entered the political scene. He was refreshing in the fact that his instinctive response to a criminal threat like ISIS or a jihadist was to crush it. These violent malcontents are an enemy to be opposed and destroyed, and their ideology should be discredited and held in near-universal contempt as Nazism was in its day.

Even Trump's use of "losers" to describe the jihadis was a strike right at the heart of an idea whose cultural currency is measured with words like "honor." In an ideology where dying for the cause is one of the selling points, making the idea itself contemptible is part of the process of both discrediting it and discouraging others to join the cause. That's only part of the equation. The other part is in hitting the threat head-on. There are a few different dimensions to this approach, and he addressed them all.

"When you look at Paris – you know the toughest gun laws in the world, Paris – nobody had guns but the bad guys. Nobody had guns. Nobody," Trump said at a rally here. "They were just shooting them one by one and then they (security forces) broke in and had a big shootout and ultimately killed the terrorists."

"You can say what you want, but if they had guns, if our people had guns, if they were allowed to carry –" Trump said, pausing as the crowd erupted into raucous applause, "– it would've been a much, much different situation."[124]

Trump echoed the Second Amendment argument that citizens should have both the right and the means to defend themselves if facing an attack like this one.

Trump made a very blunt statement about how he would handle ISIS. He would bomb the s**t out of them. Which is exactly what he did once he took office. According to *Task & Purpose* in September of 2017:

> The operational tempo of U.S.-led air campaigns has increased dramatically against terror groups across the region since Trump took office: So far this year, U.S. aircraft have deployed 2,487 munitions against enemy targets in Afghanistan, nearly double the number dropped during all of 2016, according to CENTCOM data.[125]

Similarly, aircraft in August dropped some 5,075 munitions on ISIS targets as part of Operation Inherent Resolve in Iraq and Syria, up from 3,439 in February and the most deployed in a single month since the beginning of Operation Inherent Resolve there in August 2014. Putting an Exclamation point on that policy would be his use of the MOAB.

At least 94 Islamic State fighters were killed when the US military dropped America's most powerful non-nuclear bomb on ISIS targets in Afghanistan, an Afghan official said Saturday.

> "The number of Daesh fighters killed in the US bomb in Achin district jumped to 94, including four commanders," Nangarhar provincial spokes-

man Attaullah Khogiani told CNN, using an alternative name for ISIS.[126]

And not a single civilian died in that blast.

When a "red line" issue came up for Trump, he did not hesitate. He hit back ... and hard. Even his critics on CNN admired his "presidential" response when Syria was hit with what was believed to be a Ricin attack.

Perhaps the most controversial of his policies on how to deal with credible threats has been his policy of "extreme vetting." It has been falsely characterized as a Muslim ban despite the fact that the nations mentioned happen to be from Obama's list of failed states, plus Venezuela, which has slid into chaos. It also has absolutely zero restrictions on a great many nations with either majority-Muslim status or a significant Muslim presence in the nation. The fact that a court upheld that so-called ban should be sufficient to disprove the claim that it's somehow motivated by bigotry.

Where Obama traded 5 high-value members of a foreign military force for one deserter or pallets of cash that were timed suspiciously close to the release of American hostages, Trump had a very different approach to the return of US hostages. As reported in the Daily Caller in May of 2018:

> Since President Donald Trump took office, his administration has secured the release of 17 prisoners foreign governments had detained.
>
> "We've had 17 released, and we're very proud of that record. Very proud. And we have others coming," Trump said Saturday evening as he wel-

comed home Joshua Holt, an American citizen who had been detained in Venezuela for two years without trial.

Unlike his predecessor, the president has managed to bring these prisoners home without freeing terrorists or paying millions of dollars in suspected ransom payments.[127]

This includes hostages returned from North Korea, besides which, he has paved the way for the repatriation of fallen US soldiers from the Korean War.

As willing as he is to use force when it is necessary, he would rather use pressure or persuasion to get results. Economic sanctions are a key tool in Trump's diplomatic toolkit, and he is putting them to good use in different places around the world.

That is how he has gotten North Korea to the negotiating table. While talks may be currently stalled, those economic pressures have not been reduced, and the American leverage point is still there if and when Kim comes back to the negotiating table.

And even the more conventional military rivals have reason to take notice. Trump is pressuring other member countries in the EU to step up and maintain funding levels. We are giving Ukraine lethal force with which to repel Russian advances on their territory.

Meanwhile, Trump is pouring money back into our military readiness and capacity in all aspects of military strength so that we could stand ready if one of our rivals should get any grandiose ambitions.

Trump prefers to crush wicked and violent individuals or regimes, to compel or persuade rivals that are open to reason, and to do everything possible in standing ready to oppose any threats that may arise against the safety of the people.

He is tough where he needs to be tough, fair where he can be, open to negotiations where they can be had, and always vigilant for the safety of those under his care.

The wicked are judged while the rest are protected. Is there anything in such a straightforward approach to leadership that stands contrary to the biblical picture of what is expected of political leadership?

Yeah, I didn't think so.

CHAPTER NINETEEN

What Do Melania's Accusers And The Pharisees Have In Common?

Doug Giles

*Now when the Pharisee who had invited Him saw this,
he said to himself, "If this man were a prophet, He would have
known who and what sort of woman this is who is touching
Him, for she is a sinner." And Jesus answering said to him,
"Simon, I have something to say to you."
And he answered, "Say it, Teacher."
"A certain moneylender had two debtors. One owed five hundred denarii, and the other fifty. When they could not pay,
he cancelled the debt of both. Now which of them will love
him more?" Simon answered, "The one, I suppose, for whom
he cancelled the larger debt." And He said to him, "You have
judged rightly." Then turning toward the woman He said to
Simon, "Do you see this woman? I entered your house; you
gave me no water for my feet, but she has wet my feet with her
tears and wiped them with her hair. You gave me no kiss, but*

from the time I came in she has not ceased to kiss my feet.
You did not anoint my head with oil, but she has anointed my
feet with ointment. Therefore I tell you, her sins,
which are many, are forgiven—for she loved much. But he
who is forgiven little, loves little." And He said to her,
"Your sins are forgiven." Then those who were at table with
Him began to say among themselves, "Who is this,
who even forgives sins?" And He said to the woman,
"Your faith has saved you; go in peace."
Luke 7:39-50, ESV

Jesus' parables were never *just* telling an informative story. He was making a surgical strike on someone's ideological strongholds. They were a sneak attack on ways of thinking His audience didn't just accept as correct, but would be deeply offended by anyone who said otherwise.

It's a way of sneaking past the defenses of a hostile audience not just hopelessly ignorant of any better way of thinking, but that would fight to their dying breath to defend that ignorance as incontrovertible truth.

Jesus, with His use of these parables, was in good company. David's prophet Nathan used the same tool to get King David's attention after the Bathsheba fiasco. David could have faced the fact that he had abused his authority and betrayed the trust of a loyal friend (one of his mighty men, Uriah), knocking up his wife while Uriah was off fighting Israel's enemies in the king's name. When he was busted, David had that honorable friend killed instead.

Do you really think Nathan would get away with blasting king David with full frontal assault, calling him an adulterer? Or is there a chance that David would have found a way to make Nathan disappear, too. He took an indirect approach.

In order to reveal God's moral outrage over David's sin, he told David a story about a rich man with many flocks and a poor man with a single lamb. When a traveler came by, the rich guy didn't want to slaughter one of his own flock to feed the visitor, so he took the poor guy's lamb, instead. David was outraged and pronounced fierce judgment against the rich man. Only then, after David had accepted the premise of guilt needing punishment, did Nathan hit him with the truth – "you are that man." (2 Sa. 7) That anger led him to first a realization of the seriousness of his sin and then, more importantly, a desperately needed change of heart.

This is the point where we ask – hold up, what does King David have to do with Jesus talking to a Pharisee? That's a great question. Let's break it down.

Jesus *could* have sat Simon down and told him a direct lesson about everyone being guilty of sin and needing forgiveness. He could have gone into a speech about judging people. But He used a story about two people, who were *both* debtors, who were *both* forgiven debts. Initially, Simon sees the story at a safe distance. That was exactly the point. Since he doesn't yet see himself in it, he is able to hear the lesson without pushing back against it until Jesus hits him with the "you are that man" moment.

Jesus pointed to ways in which this "sinful woman" had expressed moral excellence – in the short time of that meeting at Simon's house – to which even "righteous" Simon could scarcely hold a candle. That was hardly a problem unique to biblical times. Since people haven't really changed much, it continues today. And there are few places where these sorts of failings are more obvious or public than in our political interactions.

Before and after Trump's election, Melania has a complex role in how she's portrayed by the media. The goalposts keep shifting depending on whether they are trying to make her look complicit or make her look like Trump's "victim."

In today's telling of the story, the role of the Pharisees gets played by more than one character. The political Left is the easy and obvious one since they find fault with everything Republicans do anyway – why should they just call our ideas wrong when they can denounce us all as "evil" instead?

But there are many others competing for that same role. We see it with the Media(D) and their #PartisanPress. We see it with the pure-as-the-driven-snow NeverTrumpkins who think Melania has a sketchy past that forever disqualifies her as beneath them. We see it in the Feminists who think a stay-at-home mom just isn't woman enough by their measurement. We even see it among the Elite of the elite – the "pretty people," A-listers, celebrities, and even fashion designers who were tripping over themselves to be seen with her until that day her husband came down the escalator with the Scarlet Letter beside his name – (R).

The same celebrities who fawned over Hillary and Michelle for their leadership and style, splashing them over every conceivable magazine cover have stiff-armed Melania, and have tried to down-play her sense of style. It wouldn't be sour grapes, would it? After so many years of propping up aggressively unlikable feminists like Hillary and Michelle as "fashion-forward'" thought leaders, Melania made them all look like chumps by showing up on Inauguration Day with a level of feminine elegance and class that immediately invoked whispered references to – can it be? – the Queen of Camelot herself, Jackie Kennedy!

How. Dare. They.

Fashion designers scrambled to prove how "woke" they were by announcing their disdain for our new FLOTUS before anyone bothered to ask their opinion. Despite being a former model, high fashion designers have shunned her. Tom Ford, Marc Jacobs, Christian Siriano, and Michelle's former designer, Sophie Theallet, have all refused to dress the First Lady. Ralph Lauren, who made the now-famous powder-blue Inaugural day dress and jacket for Melania, was laughing all the way to the bank when sales rose after her outfit wowed the world. Yet again, it was a lesson in get woke, go broke. Well done Ralph Lauren!

Not long afterward, women in high positions around the world – including Europe's royals – morphed from frumpy to fab when they began to emulate her clean, elegant style preferences. But that still didn't land her on the cover of magazines. The only time they would do that was if there was some kind of negative message attached, preferably one they could use to hurt Trump.

Magazine cover space was to be reserved for other things, like Russian Collusion or the old head of Planned Parenthood, Cecile Richards. Now that the Democrats have a toehold on political power again, they're putting political gaffe-factories like Alexandria Occasional-Cortex, Ilhan Omar, and Rashida Tlaib on the covers of magazines like *Time* or *Rolling Stone*.

When they did tell stories about Melania, the press didn't even care if it was true or fair, so long as it could be politically damaging to Trump.

One perfect example of this is a scandalous story the *Telegraph* wrote about Melania. They ran a hit piece against her so egregious that someone squeezed an article of apology and retraction ... as well as a settlement for damages. We covered it in our January 2019 ClashDaily.com piece titled, *Defamation: 'News' Org Writes Apology To Melania, Pays Damages For Hit Piece.*

> Following last Saturday's (Jan 19) Telegraph magazine cover story *"The mystery of Melania"*, we have been asked to make clear that the article contained a number of false statements which we accept should not have been published. Mrs. Trump's father was not a fearsome presence and did not control the family. Mrs. Trump did not leave her Design and Architecture course at University relating to the completion of an exam, as alleged in the article, but rather because she wanted to pursue a successful career as a professional model. Mrs. Trump was not struggling in her modelling career before she met Mr. Trump, and she did not advance in her career due to the assistance of Mr. Trump.
>
> We accept that Mrs. Trump was a successful professional model in her own right before she met her husband and obtained her own modelling work without his assistance. Mrs. Trump met Mr. Trump in 1998, not in 1996 as stated in the article. The article also wrongly claimed that Mrs. Trump's

mother, father and sister relocated to New York in 2005 to live in buildings owned by Mr. Trump. They did not. The claim that Mrs. Trump cried on election night is also false.

We apologise unreservedly to The First Lady and her family for any embarrassment caused by our publication of these allegations. As a mark of our regret we have agreed to pay Mrs. Trump substantial damages as well as her legal costs.[128]

"As a mark of our regret ..." Riiiight. You're genuinely contrite now, holding yourselves to new ethical standards. Let's run it through the weasel-speak-to-English dictionary. Roughly speaking, that statement translates to, "our lawyers tell us that if this case goes to court, Melania will take us to the cleaners, and we could never afford the kind of settlement a judge might hand down."

Let's look at some other examples of how the Media have been reporting about Melania. Do you remember her health scare? She needed kidney surgery in May of 2018. Not surprisingly, she took some down time to recover after going under the knife. Did the media step back and give her time to recover? Or did they use her absence as an opportunity to crank up the rumor mill? The answer is obvious, isn't it?

I gave the bogus Melania narratives a good hammering on ClashDaily.com, but in case you missed the article, *Fake News: Here's All The Bogus 'Missing Melania' Stories Spawned By 'The Media(D)'*[129], here are some of the key takeaways.

CNN's Brian Stelter – nicknamed "Helter Stelter" by the Associate Editors on ClashDaily.com for how disconnected he is from reality – tried to mock Trump's tweets about media rumor-mongering by passing off the conspiracies as just the work of Twitter trolls. This guy is supposed to be a "Chief Media Correspondent"? Here's how boy wonder got it so very, very wrong.

NYT published a story breathlessly wondering why FLOTUS hadn't been seen in three weeks.[130]

The Root suspected she had a "body double."[131]

A writer at *Rolling Stone* hinted that she was a victim of domestic abuse. (With zero evidence.)[132]

Politico ran a laundry-list of theories that included cooperating with Mueller, leaving Trump for NY, hanging out with the Obamas and drafting a tell-all against The Donald, and plastic surgery ... but it's the White House that was responsible for stoking conspiracy theories.[133]

HuffPo suggested a "breakdown," "plastic surgery" and "a scam."[134]

NeverTrumpkin David Frum tweeted a macabre scenario where Donald Trump punched Melania in the face, had the Secret Service conceal it, and – under Seculow/Dowd – it would not be obstruction of justice.[135]

And on Stelter's own dishonestly-named show *Reliable Sources*, David Zurawik of *The Baltimore Sun* completed the set by suggesting she didn't have control of her own Twitter account.[136]

This is the same Brian Stelter who – on June 3, 2018 – Tweeted a "last seen May 10" graphic and a link to a CNN discussion, "if any First Lady disappeared, you'd want to know where she is."

Jerry Dunleavy, a reporter for *The Washington Examiner* set him straight on Twitter that same day:

> Hey @BrianStelter — @CNBC's Washington correspondent @EamonJavers — who I would call a Reliable Source — says he saw @FLOTUS in the West Wing on May 29th, yet the graphic you shared claims that she was last seen on May 10th. You are sharing Fake News right now. Delete your Tweet.[137]

Did Stelter delete or retract it? Of course not. As of this writing, it's still there. CNN is the most *busted* name in news for a reason.

Days later, our First Lady was back on her feet and as dazzling as ever ... driving the Left clean crazy.

One thing that really tweaks the Left is how clearly happy she is to be a devoted wife and mom. She even – are you sitting down for this? – seems to enjoy motherhood! She didn't rush off to Washington after Inauguration Day – she let her son finish out the school year. Naturally, the Left found reasons to be outraged. If Michelle Obama had done the same thing, they'd be calling her Mom of the Year.

What else did they go after her for? High heels. Yes, kiddies, they lost their minds over her ... stiletto heels. When they went to visit after Hurricane Harvey our FLOTUS got onto Air Force One wearing high heels – to go to a flood zone! What a horrible, stupid mistake she had made! (Because who could possibly imagine the possibility of a grown woman changing shoes on Air Force One?)

They didn't like one jacket she wore, either. Most folks on the Right took it as her quiet way of flipping a middle finger at a hostile press without getting down in the muck with them. But the #PartisanPress saw it as catnip – and openly speculated about secret coded messages like they were hosting some overnight talk radio show. She wore an off-the-rack jacket while boarding Air Force One that said, "I really don't care, do u?" Just like that, all Hell broke loose.

The Amazing Kreskins in the press consulted their psychics – or whatever they do to read minds – and announced that Melania was sending a message about the "kids in cages" border narrative.

Sure, she was, Spanky.

They'd have us believe that the same woman whose face lights up when she's surrounded by children at schools and hospitals has a heart of stone when it comes to kids too young to have any say about whether they should be carried across an international border.

What, haven't you heard about her social work? Of course not. That wouldn't help them demonize anybody, would it? No, for them, #BeBest is a punch line to mock people with, not a goal to aspire to.

In fact, in the past two years, Mrs. Trump has visited several hospitals, both at home and abroad, and visited with children in immigration facilities in Texas and Arizona. In the wake of the hurricanes that devastated Texas, Florida, Louisiana and

Puerto Rico, she traveled to the affected areas to support re-
covery efforts – and she partnered with the Federal Emergency
Management Agency to issue a public service announcement.
Mrs. Trump comforted shooting victims in Las Vegas, Park-
land and Pittsburgh, and thanked law enforcement personnel
and first responders for their heroic efforts during times of
national tragedy. She has carried her "Be Best" message – a
message of hope and empowerment – to children in the United States and around the world. She has emphasized the ur-
gency and severity of our nation's opioid crisis with visits to
Lily's Place in West Virginia and multiple newborn intensive
care units, where she conducted listening sessions before the
cameras to shine a light on successful Neonatal Abstinence
Syndrome programs across the country. As part of the broader effort to reduce addiction, she has spoken to thousands of
young people about the dangers of drug abuse. She has met
with major technology companies to understand the challenges that each faces in the effort to address unsafe or irresponsible behavior online, and has encouraged children to
practice digital civility. Each event in her comprehensive "Be
Best" initiative is focused on helping children with the many
issues they face today. Yet, somehow, she is still characterized as a "reluctant" first lady, *Melania Trump's spokeswoman
speaks out.*[138]

And what is her "Be Best" movement about, anyway?

It's about well-being. (That's where the children's charities
she loves to visit come into play ... she brought gifts of supplies to schools and orphanages. That was the trip where she
went through Africa and paid a visit to Ghana's "Door of No
Return"– a sad testament to the history of slavery, but the
press, naturally, was more interested in faking outrage over
her clothes.)

It's about Social Media and how to use it for positive change.

It's about opioid abuse, and the impact this crisis has had on families and kids.

But why would her political enemies want to talk about any of that when they could exaggerate her "sordid" past (she was a model, with some fully nude photos of the artistic rather than the scintillating variety), ignore her business successes completely, skip over the fact that she speaks six languages, and falsely assert that she once worked as an "escort." The *Daily Mail* was ordered to pay damages for that last allegation. They won't be making that mistake again.

The *Morning Joe* duo has been especially ruthless with their open speculation about the state of both the marriage and mental health of the President and First Lady – as though that were any of their business to spitball about in the first place.

Mika Brzezinski said in an interview, "Melania's got the worst job in the country and I don't think she wants to do it a lot longer. I think she will do it for as long as she has to for her son, and that's it."[139] Melania answered with more grace and class than Mika Brzezinski deserved, "It is sad when people try to further their own agenda by commenting on me and my family, especially when they don't know me."

But doesn't that precisely sum up what we admire – and so many others despise – about her. We finally have someone with the grace and class expected of the (informal) office she holds – she has a heartfelt warmth toward the nation that put her there, and she doesn't feel obligated to diminish herself by coming down to the same level as her critics.

Disgruntled Hollywood talent mock her for speaking "with an accent" in one of the *six languages* she speaks – without finding a single thing they can praise about her.

We're talking about the same people that couldn't help but hold up her Christmas decorating to open contempt and ridicule. Even that, she handled with warmth and grace. "We are in the 21st century and everybody has a different taste,"[140] Melania said, "I think they look fantastic." Melania then invited the large student audience to visit the White House. "I hope you will all come over to visit. In real life they look even more beautiful. You are all welcome to visit the White House, the people's house,"[141] the first lady said to cheers. *The Peoples' House.* Exactly. Her position has not blinded her to the institutions she and her husband represent ... or more specifically ... *who* they were sent there to represent.

Can you even imagine Michelle Obama – who was noted for saying she wakes up "every morning in a house built by slaves"[142] – ever calling it "the People's House"?

The pharisaical Resistance movement sees Melania as an odious wretch, like so much mud to be scraped from the sole of their shoes. The sneer they make at Melania is a lot like the one Simon the Pharisee would have given the woman we began this chapter with. To them, Melania is tainted by Trump, her modeling photos make her morality suspect, and she's simply beneath all contempt.

That doesn't mean everyone has their knives out for a piece of Melania. Some visitors took Melania up on that invitation; their reaction was entirely different than the angry and bitter ones we've looked at here.

"Are you the first lady?!" a boy asked as he embraced Melania Trump during a White House Christmas event. "She seriously looks like an angel," another child said.[143]

Isn't it funny how even Jesus noticed that sometimes children can see truth that the grownups can't? (Lk. 10:21)

CHAPTER TWENTY

How Trump Defends Justice With "Filthy Lucre"

Brandon Vallorani

And so it was that when he returned, having received the kingdom, he then commanded these servants, to whom he had given the money, to be called to him, that he might know how much every man had gained by trading. Then came the first, saying, "Master, your mina has earned ten minas.' And he said to him, 'Well done, good servant; because you were faithful in a very little, have authority over ten cities."
Luke 19:15-17, NKJV

Jesus could have used any parable He wanted to explain what faithfulness was expected of believers waiting for the Second Coming. He chose *this* one. Why?

He chose an example of servants who had been entrusted with wealth and the master measured the faithfulness of his servants in how they made good use of it. How did the master reward those who had been found faithful with the master's money? They continue as servants, only with increased responsibility and authority. He doubles down on that image with the harsh words given to the unfaithful servant.

> *Then another came, saying, "Master, here is your mina, which I have kept put away in a handkerchief. For I feared you, because you are an austere man. You collect what you did not deposit, and reap what you did not sow." And he said to him, "Out of your own mouth I will judge you, you wicked servant. You knew that I was an austere man, collecting what I did not deposit and reaping what I did not sow. Why then did you not put my money in the bank, that at my coming I might have collected it with interest?" And he said to those who stood by, "Take the mina from him, and give it to him who has ten minas." (But they said to him, "Master, he has ten minas.") For I say to you, that to everyone who has will be given; and from him who does not have, even what he has will be taken away from him. (Lk. 19:20-26, NKJV)*

"Why did you not put my money in the bank?" he asks.

That's a strange question for a sermon, isn't it? We can wax philosophical and describe exactly what spiritual principle Jesus was trying to teach people about, but it's easy to forget that He was talking to real people. If He wasn't talking about real-world things His original audience could understand, the lesson would have fallen flat.

It is a good thing to turn a small amount of wealth into a larger one. Jesus, in His parable, was not only praising the results themselves but the willingness to take results-oriented risks to *achieve* those results.

Nobody in the parable lost money. But if they had, who do you think he would have been more upset with? The guy who swung for the fences but failed – or the one who took no risks at all?

Ok, but what's this got to do with politics?

That same system of risk and reward is one of the big reasons that America is uniquely positioned in the world. Risk and reward is the heartbeat of trade and the engine of the American Dream. Where the Left sees evil and exploitation, the rest of us see a free and fair system. It's free and fair precisely because it is a purely voluntary system where one succeeds only by doing things that make someone else's life better in some way. For example, by giving them a product they want at a price they are willing to pay. If businesses failed to do that, if they were unresponsive to the needs of their customers, someone else would meet that need and their doors would close before very long.

This isn't a question of one guy hoarding all the wealth so much as new wealth being created as new products are invented. If you doubt that, just look at the enormous overall value of tech stocks, most of which didn't even exist before 1990.

The one thing the socialists *almost* get right is that the playing field isn't always a fair one. How can the economic playing field be unfair? Simple. Just ask the question: is everyone playing by the same rules? Domestically, this can happen a few different ways, for example – Corporatism. Over-regulation. Monopoly. Predatory practices. Business collusion.

We see one all-too-common example: one major player using their wealth or connections to lobby politicians to make laws that advantage one company over its competitors. Those politicians later find themselves – or their friends and relations – elevated to advisory roles in a board of directors or some other plum position. This is not free enterprise, this is corporatism or "crony capitalism" – which is not capitalism at all.

We see it internationally, too. Governments want – or need – a strong economy to fund their political aims. When it comes to international trade, governments have some tools in their tool belts to manipulate the markets to favor their own nation's companies. This can take all kinds of different forms. It might be punitive taxes on foreign goods, or other penalties right up to closing access to their markets completely. It might be strict ownership rules for national companies.

It might be other protectionist laws giving domestic companies unequal access to a domestic market. We might see things like currency manipulation – which would make input costs for manufacturing less expensive in one part of the world than another. Some tricks might be more subtle – favorable (or less burdensome) laws regulating a company's obligations toward worker safety, wages, or various kinds of environmental and regulatory compliance.

Some countries might have rampant corruption where authority figures need to be bribed periodically for anything to get done. A less obvious, but potentially devastating, inequality is corporate espionage and outright theft of intellectual property. (Think: China.) If a Western Country pays millions in Research and Development to create the next-generation widget – what happens to competition if a Pacific Rim company can reverse-engineer that widget and have knock-offs flooding the market just a few weeks later?

What happens in countries where swiping intellectual property isn't just ignored, but is acceptable business practice and is not punished by law?

This is where "fairness" really comes into play at an international scale.

There is another dimension where thumbs can be used to tip the scales: badly negotiated trade deals. And if anyone should know a thing or two about negotiating deals without getting taken to the cleaners, it would be someone who made his fortune doing exactly that.

It just so happens that bad economic deals were of particular interest to Trump, and have been for a very, *very* long time. In the 80s he took out an ad criticizing U.S. foreign policy of defending countries that can afford to defend themselves.

Ok, fine. But does God really care all that much about business practices? Isn't that a purely secular part of life?

Oh, He cares. It's a question of justice, after all. There are a few examples in the book of Proverbs that spell this out plainly. Here's just one example. "A false balance is an abomination to the LORD, but a just weight is His delight." (Pr. 11:1)

Trump has used trade in a way different from any other President before him. CNN called Trump's trade promises "impossibly ambitious" in June of 2017.

> "Probably one of the major reasons I'm here today – trade," he said two months after taking office. But nearly six months into his presidency – even as Trump's administration speeds into new

> talks with Canada, Mexico, China, South Korea, the United Kingdom and other countries – Trump is laying out a timeline that veteran trade negotiators say is impossibly ambitious.[144]

The question isn't so much "are they ambitious," we would expect nothing less of a risk-taking high-stakes Manhattan deal-making President. The key question is, can he make good on these promises?

He clearly identified Trade as a method to regulate and improve the health of the American working class, which he's done a fine job of so far, thank you very much. More than that, he obviously sees our trade position with other nations – whether ramping it up, or shutting it down – as a powerful alternative to direct military confrontation with other powers.

Our Trade policy is just as important in Trump's projection of national power and influence as a powerful military presence. Sometimes our trade policy is the carrot, and sometimes it is a very big and scary stick. The carrot is a pledge of new and more open trade (or reduced sanctions) for governments that play nice with us. The stick is exactly the opposite, closure of trade options, larger tariffs, or (in some instances) even targeted negative sanctions.

It's pretty remarkable what a change in US trade posture can do to a nation's currency. (Just ask Iran what happened to their economy when Trump pulled the plug on that deal.) When it came to Trade, Trump's very first priority was to identify deals he thought were not in the best interests of the country and either scrap them entirely or enter into negotiations. If you're paying attention, that's the same reason he was in favor of Britain's Brexit vote ... countries should be free to act in their own best interests. This approach to trade took us in unexpected directions that ruffled feathers.

Obviously, he had specifically named certain treaties – like the TPP and NAFTA – that were of particular interest to him. But there were other examples, too, where he saw America getting the short end of the stick. NATO, for instance.

What's NATO got to do with trade? That depends on how you look at the question. It's a mutual defense pact, right? American leaders have been complaining for years that certain European nations who have plenty of wealth have not been shouldering their share of the financial responsibility.

Should America really be more committed to the defense of Europe than the Europeans themselves are? Trump didn't think that was right – and said so. Trump held some feet to the fire, and has gotten something that American leaders have wanted for years. European countries are stepping up to carry their share of the load. Each NATO nation is supposed to spend 2% of their GDP on defense. But most countries have fallen far short of that number.

> Stoltenberg's comments come as U.S. Defense Secretary Jim Mattis is expected to pressure U.S. allies in Europe to increase military spending to levels targeted by NATO, fulfilling a key commitment sought by U.S. President Donald Trump.[145]

Gen. Mattis was rattling some chains.

> Stoltenberg said that in 2014, only three allies met the goal, but the number has increased to eight this year. The increase in the last four years has

added $19 billion to spending on weapons and equipment for the alliance, he said. An additional seven NATO members have laid out plans to meet the goal by 2024, he said.[146]

He also put some political pressure on Germany for their plans to build a natural gas pipeline to Russia -- the very nation they were looking to be defended from. It is, after all, bad strategy to make yourself economically dependent on the very people you are seeking protection from ... worse still if you're filling their war chest with revenue.

The Paris Accord was something Trump saw as harmful to US economic interests, among other reasons, so he announced we're withdrawing from there, too.

The TPP was another deal he blew off as bad for America. Part of the rationale for that one was because it was multi-lateral, you couldn't easily make deals that were in your own country's best economic interests in the same way you could in a bilateral trade agreement where you could just renegotiate or even end the agreement in the case of a serious dispute. True to his word, Trump pulled out of the TPP. In its place, he started negotiating direct deals with South Korea and China. Those negotiations had some very specific goals in mind. China has certain unfair practices that needed to be addressed, including theft of intellectual property and a lack of reciprocal access to markets.

Like most realists, he wasn't upset at the other party for exploiting our poor negotiating position so much as our side for having done such a pathetic job of representing our nation's interests in the first place.

Another way in which Trump was unlike previous leaders was his understanding of the power dynamics in negotiations. Politicians – cautious by nature – were afraid of making a misstep that would make them look bad at home. They were unwilling to walk away from the negotiating table without "results" and so negotiated from a position of weakness.

America, in Trump's view, is not in a position of weakness, and so should not have to come cap-in-hand to any other country. If they want access to our markets, they will play by our rules and agree to our terms. Period.

That view guided negotiations with NAFTA and his administration's approach to negotiations with China. He wasn't afraid to implement heavy tariffs on key industries like aluminum and steel – much to the shock and horror of free trade absolutists in his own party. Whatever the downside of those tariffs may turn out to be, they helped kickstart key industries in America again. IndustryWeek, in a June 2018 edition, announced a manufacturing "building boom" that included: a Mazda/Toyota auto plant in Alabama, an aluminum rolling mill in Kentucky ($1.3Billion), Volvo in SC, Nocor Corp making rebar, and "scores of other new plants that are underway, recently opened or freshly proposed."[147]

Whether his approach is considered orthodox or not, it has certainly been getting results.

It has also been getting the attention of China. They have hit us back with reciprocal tariffs, true enough, but their economy is more fragile than they are willing to admit, and U.S. trade is an enormous part of their business model. They have come to the negotiating table with us.

Even as this chapter goes to press, Chinese and American negotiators say they (think) they are moving toward a potential trade deal.

With NAFTA, Justin Trudeau's team wasn't playing ball. They were focused more on pushing social justice issues than actual trade, so Trump's team told Canada to pound sand while the USA and Mexico sat down like adults to discuss serious trade terms. Which they did. Canada, after being shut out of the conversation for a while, came back to the table, but they did so in a position that even Canadians criticized as a position of weakness.

In the end, the three countries came to terms in principle, and the agreement of those leaders now awaits ratification. But whether it gets ratified by the Pelosi's Democrat #Resistance or not, Trump has put himself in a win-win situation. He has no reason to be afraid of walking away from this deal. If it gets ratified, it's a good deal; if it does *not* get ratified, we revert to the deal we had before NAFTA.

How can that be a good thing? Simple. So far as Trump is concerned, NAFTA is the worst of the three trade deals. He would like to get the USMCA passed, that's the deal he most wants to see happen. But if not, hey, that's a win too. He'd much rather see us revert back to what we had before than work under NAFTA.

With USMCA we see Trump's trade philosophy in action. His goal was to get as level (or better still, advantageous) a playing field as possible for workers and businesses in America. The obstacles for that goal included, among other things, wages that substantially undercut American wages. What did Trump do? He negotiated for (and got) Mexico to set a minimum wage of $16 an hour for the auto sector. Suddenly the incentive to move Auto plants to Mexico for cheaper labor is no longer as strong, and reasons to keep the plant in America become more compelling.

Canada, for its part, had a protectionist policy of supply management in their dairy system. This is something Trudeau had insisted was not going to change under USMCA. Then they negotiated. And it changed. Trudeau sent lightweight negotiators, to do business with America, and when all the dust had settled, the USMCA provides that the Canadian market be opened to U.S. dairy markets in a way that it had never been before. That's how negotiating for your nation's best interests is supposed to work – "America First," one might even say.

He's also inked a deal with South Korea, is in talks with Europe, and has already made overtures to the U.K. if they ever finally figure out what to do about Brexit.

Good examples of the "stick" approach to economic diplomacy include tearing up the Iran Deal and dropping sanctions on Russia.

With Russia sending troops to back up Venezuela's despot Maduro, another round of sanctions against key Russian officials or companies is likely to follow. With so much of Putin's power directly connected to the wealth and influence of the corrupt oligarchs he surrounds himself with, hitting their wealth and ability to travel internationally matters. Likewise, the Treasury has slapped a series of sanctions against Venezuelan companies and industries that would be propping up Maduro's regime, and a Russian-backed bank which was "attempting to circumvent U.S. sanctions on Venezuela."[148]

But the most interesting application of his economic approach to negotiation as diplomacy would be with his approach to North Korea.

When Trump first took office, North Korea was known as the "Hermit Kingdom." It had been in an unresolved war since the unofficial conclusion of the Korean War in 1953. During previous administrations, North Korea managed to become a nuclear power. More recently, it was making very public tests of a delivery system. It was doing so while making some pretty aggressive threats to its neighbors, and America in particular. Trump (infamously) reminded Kim that POTUS also had a "button" on his desk ... a button that was a lot more effective and reliable than anything Kim had access to.

But Trump didn't just hammer him with threats, he used a sophisticated coordination of crushing global sanctions together with what can only be described as a sales pitch of what life could look like for his country if Kim took steps toward normalized international relations. There was even a very Trump-y promotional video of North Korea catching up to South Korea in terms of tech and lifestyle.

It's too early yet to see where these one-on-one talks and negotiations will lead – *The Art of the Deal* famously requires that you always be willing to walk away – which Trump showed himself willing to do at their meeting in Vietnam.

But some early positive signs are there – a cessation of missile testing, for one. That famous handshake between leaders of North and South Korea is another. And Trump has already gained some real benefits – namely the return of U.S. citizens, together with the mortal remains of U.S. veterans of the Korean War. The heavy sanctions against North Korea are still in place, so Trump is in no rush to sign the first offer that comes his way. He'd rather wait, and do this right.

Potentially ending the longest unresolved war on the planet is worth taking the time to do it right, wouldn't you say?

One prior President famously said, "speak softly, but carry a big stick." Trump has proven that while the military is certainly one such big stick (just ask ISIS), economic policy can be powerful in different ways.

Trump is rolling those high-stakes dice to see if the tools he's honed in a lifetime of financial negotiations could succeed in cracking the tough nut of the Hermit Kingdom where everything else has failed.

And didn't another Famous Person once say, "Blessed be the Peacemakers?"

CHAPTER TWENTY-ONE

The Fear Of The Lord Is The Beginning Of Wisdom

Doug Giles

And Jesus came and said to them, "All authority in heaven and on earth has been given to Me. Go therefore and make disciples of all nations, baptizing them in the name of the Father and of the Son and of the Holy Spirit, teaching them to observe all that I have commanded you. And behold, I am with you always, to the end of the age."
Matthew 28:18-20, ESV

F amous last words. There's a reason people call them that. If you're rocking up to take your final bow, that's the time to say the things that really need saying.

What you say in that moment will be how you are remembered. Jesus was no different. This was His chance to drive home the key takeaway. He gave us "The Great Commission."

Go. Make disciples. Teach.

You've gotta be pretty thick to miss the point when He makes it so clear. Fortunately for *El Diablo*, humanity specializes in being "pretty thick."

The Christian life, says Jesus, will be very much built on key ideas. They are the foundation for everything else. *San Pablo* drove the same point home in 2 Timothy 2:22. "And the things which you have heard from me in the presence of many witnesses, these entrust to faithful men, who will be able to teach others also." If that chain gets broken, everything else goes off the rails.

Why else do you think the apostles spent so much time and effort kicking false teachers to the curb?

It's right there in black and white (or red, when Jesus was talking): Peter, Paul, John, Jude, and even Jesus Himself – again and again we heard warnings about false teachers who would lead us astray.

Yep, Jesus actually cares about what we fill that tub of mush between our ears with. ("and with all your minds..." Mk. 12:30)

It matters. Why? The ideas in our heads define us. The cerebral sanctification of Romans 12:2 is central to scaring Satan stiff with Christian courage, confidence and yes, even cheerfulness.

Remember when the Apostle Paul was still little ol' Saul, and "breathing threats and murder" against Christians? He figured he was even doing God a favor, scoring some extra credit for his zeal.

Then one day, God flipped His script. How did God get the attention of a zealot like Saul of Tarsus? Oh, it didn't take much. Saul got knocked off his horse, blinded for three days, and was told by the same Jesus whose name he was trying to wipe from history that he's been called to proclaim the same message he'd been trying to suppress. Oh, and he's got a new name, too.

This new idea eventually took his head from his shoulders courtesy of a Roman soldier. He truly *lived* his life for the cause until that final day. Floggings, prison sentences and shipwrecks he had the scars to prove. For what? Once he believed – really believed -- that Jesus was the promised Messiah – *everything* else in his life changed.

Ideas matter. And what you do with them matters, too. What's a "Christian" approach to ideas? The Good Shepherd didn't keep us guessing. He said:

> *"Whoever receives one such child in My name receives Me, but whoever causes one of these little ones who believe in Me to sin, it would be better for him to have a great millstone fastened around his neck and to be drowned in the depth of the sea. Woe to the world for temptations to sin! For it is necessary that temptations come, but woe to the one by whom the temptation comes!"* (Mt. 18:5-7, NKJV)

Need another hint? How about what the Lord said right after the verse Jesus called "The First And Great Commandment":

> *Hear, O Israel: The Lord our God, the Lord is one. You shall love the Lord your God with all your heart and with all your soul and with all your might. And these words*

303

that I command you today shall be on your heart. You shall teach them diligently to your children, and shall talk of them when you sit in your house, and when you walk by the way, and when you lie down, and when you rise. You shall bind them as a sign on your hand, and they shall be as frontlets between your eyes. You shall write them on the doorposts of your house and on your gates. (Dt. 6:4-9, NKJV)

Teach your kids about God.

And for those of us who went to public school, and take just a little longer to pick up what YHWH is putting down, Proverbs 22:6 gives us the final piece of the puzzle: "Train up a child in the way he should go; even when he is old he will not depart from it."

Yes, my little children, education is a big deal to the Lord of Life. Those folks who stepped off the Mayflower thought so, too. They could tell you exactly why the literacy and learning were a top priority.

Back then, school wasn't a boring business building better cubicle drones. It churned out citizens with a sharp mind and a keen sense of justice. The earliest American law providing for Education in 1642 (look up "Old Deluder Satan Act"[149]) provided for a literate public to achieve two goals – an informed laity who could read Holy Scripture for themselves and sniff out any clod selling spiritual snake oil, and also so that they could be an informed citizenry who would understand and obey the law and sniff out any clod selling tyranny.

Serious education served the public good. It was crafted with purpose: informed citizens and stable traditions. How well is education serving that purpose today?

Do we ever stop and wonder what we have an education system for, anyway? Is it just job skills training? Or is it aiming higher? Education used to help children seek the three virtues most highly praised in antiquity: Truth, Beauty, and Goodness. How many of use even knew those were once the goals of education? Or that kids used to finish their education with a better grasp on wisdom and goodness than they began with in the folly of their childhood?

There was a time when that was exactly what the school system was set up to do, and in some Classical Schools – it still is.

One of the big differences between the old way of teaching and the kind pushed since the 20th Century is how ideas are introduced.

Revisionist historians will tell you that buckle-shoes Puritans are so narrow-minded they could look through a keyhole with both eyes. That they are allergic to ideas and are natural book-burners. Internet Atheists, ignorant of history, enjoy taunting Christians with memes about how Christians like one book, but atheists like many.

Cool story bro, except that it's a lie. If you know anything about these early Americans, you also know that they could switch freely between English, Latin, and Greek. They could cite the works of Cicero, Plato, or Homer as easily as Augustine of Hippo or St. Thomas.

If you look at the old Masters, their art is filled with examples from grand stories of antiquity that we'd be hard-pressed to even recognize today. We might still know what a narcissist is, but how many still remember Narcissus? We might still know a story about a wooden horse, but how many know why Paris and Agamemnon were fighting ... or even who they were? Who would still know the difference between Thucydides and Telemachus? Or between Aeneid and Aeschylus? Our "backward" forefathers did.

If you were wondering why their rhetorical style dwarfs our own, there's your reason. They were exposed to some of history's greatest minds through the greatest literature of past centuries. They sat at the feet of the masters and learned to copy their style. Until the method of teaching that produced the soaring rhetoric of Churchill was kicked aside for something new.

Remember that the next time some slug sells you the line that newer is always better. "Innovations" are *not* always advancements. Plutarch's expression: "The mind is not a vessel to be filled, but a fire to be kindled," nails the difference between the old way and the new one.

If you ask people today why kids go to school, the answer will almost always have something to do with "career path" ... and that sets up the modern changes to our education.

The good guys weren't the only ones who understood the importance of training children. Vladimir Lenin had a saying of his own, "Give me four years to teach the children and the seed I have sown will never be uprooted."

Yes, Dinky, education really *does* matter.

We *had* a solid school system, until a Progressive wizard came along and decided to "make it better." He's not the Dewey Decimal system guy, by the way, that was Melvil Dewey. But John Dewey did reorganize the education system. He was a

Progressive in the early 20th Century. He toured Soviet Russia between the world wars, and he liked what he saw there. He came back and helped to lead 'reforms' in the American education system.

Worth noting is the fact that this influential man responsible for the redesigning of education slapped his name on an important historical document of the era, *The Humanist Manifesto*.

Here are a few of the original *Manifesto*'s fifteen affirmations:

> FIRST: Religious humanists regard the universe as self-existing and not created.
> FIFTH: Humanism asserts that the nature of the universe depicted by modern science makes unacceptable any supernatural or cosmic guarantees of human values ... Religion must formulate its hopes and plans in the light of the scientific spirit and method.
> SIXTH: We are convinced that the time has passed for theism, deism, modernism, and the several varieties of "new thought."

Yada, yada, yada ... You get the idea. Here's another juicy nugget:

> FOURTEENTH: The humanists are firmly convinced that existing acquisitive and profit-motivated society has shown itself to be inadequate and that a radical change in methods, controls, and motives must be instituted. A socialized and cooperative economic order must be established to the end that the equitable distribution of the

means of life be possible. The goal of humanism is a free and universal society in which people voluntarily and intelligently cooperate for the common good. Humanists demand a shared life in a shared world.[150]

So basically, the explicit goals of this guy who helped redesign the education system are to: dethrone God, neuter religious belief, and push Marxism. Does any of that sound familiar? Stalin would be so proud. Taking a look at the state of public education today, how would you say his vision is taking shape so far?

Since the *Humanist Manifesto* was signed in 1933, what changes have we seen to the school system? Suddenly, the educational system that was explicitly launched so that a literate population could read the Bible for themselves no longer has room for books that conflict with their secular way of thinking.

For these cats, it's not enough that the school day no longer begins with the Lord's Prayer; the Bible should no longer be taught at all. Not as a source of learning and wisdom in its own right, and not even as a necessary historical backdrop to comprehend much of our own culture. How will we understand what those "dead white guys" thought about the world we live in if we can't even grasp the allusions and concepts that form the raw material upon which later thinkers, writers and artists have built? Who cares? They don't want us to know any of that "old" learning anyway.

In the name of "tolerance" the Bible and Christian belief have been crowded out of the curriculum. But that's not all. In the name of secular "fairness," it is being exiled from the schools entirely.

One example of this in practice is the case of Ohio teacher John Freshwater. He had his personal Bible on his desk in the 8th Grade Class he taught. He had been teaching for 24 years, and his own students credited him as a fair and even-handed teacher, even on topics like evolution where he allowed the class discussions to explore not just the state-sanctioned official view of evolution, but also some of the commonly-held beliefs that are – in one way or another – skeptical of the official explanation.

John Freshwater committed the grave sin of having his personal Bible on his desk at school, and he was fired for it. In 2013, a 4-3 decision at the Ohio Supreme Court upheld his firing for his "refusal to eliminate religious symbols in the classroom."

This was no isolated incident. A Washington State assistant HS football coach would kneel after games – he did not expect anyone to join him – and was fired for it. SCOTUS recently refused to hear his appeal.

Remember those *Humanist Manifesto* points? This is sounding familiar, eh?

Students and parents are no freer than their teachers. Just ask Donna Busch, mother of then-kindergarten student, Wesley. His teacher had invited Mrs. Busch because Wesley was that week's featured student of "All About Me." It highlights a different student each week to emphasize that student's personal characteristics, preferences and personality in classroom activities. Other students discussed Christmas and Passover, during their turn she was not permitted to read the selected passage from Psalm 118. The Third District upheld that decision 2-1.

A Florida Teacher even told a 12-year old he couldn't read his Bible during the free reading time during the school day. The Supreme Court has since slapped that stupidity down. How sad is it that it took a Supreme Court ruling?

Now that we think about it, it isn't the religious people that are most inclined to book burnings and censorship after all, is it? Historical Christianity loved the great works of Homer and the ancient Greek playwrights, despite their pagan roots. Today's secularists have no such tolerance for the heresy of believing in traditional Christianity. But the secular snarl doesn't rage against *all* religions equally, does it? Somehow, special accommodations are given to *special* religions like Islam in the name of "tolerance."

Universities – many built by Christians – now wage war against both conservative and Christian values. Unsuspecting students, unprepared for the assault on their values, find themselves questioning or even abandoning the sincerely-held traditional beliefs they began with within their first year of college.

Not only is our education system actively undermining the reason it was first established, but it is failing to give the most basic kinds of education to many of its students. For example, the Baltimore Sun reported that only 13% of fourth and eighth grade students are proficient in reading. Math is even worse: 14% proficient in fourth grade, 11% in eighth grade.

Should this really surprise us? The system seems more intent on protecting the interests of unionized teachers than the students they are supposed to be teaching. How many more stories of teachers (male and female) seducing their public school students will we have to see before the wizards we keep electing get a clue and can finally admit we've got a problem?

Then we hear stories about unions pressuring school administrations who ought to fire teachers that have shown themselves incompetent or otherwise worthless. The case of Albert C. Virachismith in Seattle is one example. The teacher reportedly had a past history of showing up smelling of alcohol – if he showed up at all – and putting a special needs kid in a headlock. But he kept his job. Now he's been fired and charged with the rape of a 9-year-old boy.

With the curriculum in the service of an agenda, and unions in service of teacher's interests – who is looking out for the kids?

Trump and the policies on the right rock up to the rescue.

Trump has already pushed back, with policy and his Trumpian personality. Indirectly he has brought anti-Christian and anti-conservative biases to the attention of the public. Campuses, after having shown themselves no friend to the free speech of dissenting (i.e. conservative) opinions have a decision to make. They have been told by Trump that a commitment to free speech of students on campus would be a consideration for the awarding of (literally) billions of dollars some of these same schools are requesting in Federal Grants.

Trump's administration has also stood up for the due process rights of students who have been accused of sexual assault on campus. Changes to Title IX have even been hailed by Bloomberg's Ramesh Ponnuruso as a "victory for due process."[151]

Conservatives likey freedom. We have been pushing forever to give students the right to vote with their feet. Set them free to abandon craptastic schools through a voucher system that follows the student.

Unions and administrators can argue all they want about their big plans for the schools. But when you put purchasing power in the hands of the students, money talks and BS walks.

Schools that don't care about the quality of children's education and protect the jobs of teachers that suck can argue about their priorities in an empty building. Are student needs and failures in education more complicated than just a bad school or a bad teacher? Sure. But it never hurts to put power in the hand of the *customer*.

For all the times Democrats blather about representing "grassroots" and the "rights" of little people, it would sure be nice of them to start here. Few things would empower those "little people" on an issue that hits as close to home as this one.

Trump did another thing that caught heat from both parties. Six states announced their intention of introducing electives in school which teach the Bible in terms of historical context – that is, give a broad understanding of the Bible as an influential book in history, literature, and the forming of modern culture. Predictably, the "civil rights" agitators that have, for decades, carried water for Dewey's totalitarian secular humanist vision were positively outraged.

Trump didn't care. He brought the idea into the national conversation by endorsing it on Twitter:

"Numerous states introducing Bible Literacy classes, giving students the option of studying the Bible. Starting to make a turn back? Great!"[152]

Two ideas of what to fill our kids' heads with are duking it out.
Should we teach our kids what to think, or how to think?

Team indoctrination offers a regulated curriculum of acceptable politically-correct ideas and thought. When their fun-
house ride finally rolls to a stop on graduation day, the entire
student body steps off with a politically uniform grid of social
and cultural beliefs that just *happens* to match the goals and
interests of a single political party.

Team Freedom teaches students *how* to think. It emphasizes
exposure to a wide range of ideas, to develop a skill set of
comparing and evaluating one in light of another, and deciding which idea is of greater worth and benefit. This is 'riskier'
than indoctrination because it allows the student to have a
mind of his own. He might even draw different conclusions
than his teacher.

But that's ok. If that student can think straight, those differences are exactly what will push society forward to new advances in anything ranging from philosophy and ethics at the
more abstract, to building the proverbial "better mousetrap."

That system turns out the kind of minds that might see Democrats and Republicans wrangling over energy and ecology,
and ask a question like, "what about 'trash-to-energy' or nuclear fusion as a solution?"

It's the kind of mind that dreams up desalination plants to solve
global water supply problems. Or invents ride-sharing apps and

lets homeowners rent out their basement apartment on Airbnb. They dream up university-level lectures streamed freely to the public. Or kids' games that can teach basic coding skills.

It's the kind of mind a nation of innovation like America was built on in the first place.

Most importantly, it is a kind of mind that has *not* been squeezed into the amoral mold of a secular state – accepting all the current "conventional wisdom" as Absolute Truth, morally speaking.

If Jesus stood among us, bodily, would He toast the current state of our education system? Or would He denounce it in the harshest possible terms? What of the changes that Trump and the Republicans have proposed – they aren't magic bullets, obviously. But would the Divine Word call them corrective steps in the right direction?

The Old Testament's report card for when one of Israel's kings were good or wicked, graded the sort of incremental change they made in their culture. Look at how kings like Asa, Azariah, Hezekiah, and others had their virtue as leaders measured mostly by where their hearts were toward God, and which direction the pendulum swung while they held office.

Who would Jesus give His holy fist bump to? Officials suppressing and undermining the Christian faith children receive at their parent's knees, to have it replaced with the supposedly neutral "religious humanism" embraced by men like Dewey? Or Trump and others calling for wider freedom of belief and diversity of opinion in our education system? Which approach best squares with the good news being freely proclaimed to a world so desperately aching for the peace that it offers?

CHAPTER TWENTY-TWO

Trump's Appealing And The Left Is Appalling

Brandon Vallorani

After this He went out and saw a tax collector named Levi, sitting at the tax booth. And He said to him, "Follow Me." And leaving everything, he rose and followed Him. And Levi made Him a great feast in his house, and there was a large company of tax collectors and others reclining at table with them. And the Pharisees and their scribes grumbled at His disciples, saying, "Why do you eat and drink with tax collectors and sinners?" And Jesus answered them, "Those who are well have no need of a physician, but those who are sick. I have not come to call the righteous but sinners to repentance."
Luke 5:27-32, ESV

They say everyone is able to brighten a room. Some do it by entering, others – by leaving. There was a certain "something" about Jesus that left no room for neutrality. People either loved Him or loathed Him. Powerful insiders and defenders of the status quo, threatened by His popularity, didn't like Him at all. That eventually led to His betrayal and crucifixion. But it doesn't tell the whole story.

As we know, Jesus was given a King's welcome in Jerusalem on Palm Sunday. Even on ordinary days, everyone else – the ordinary man, the outsider, men and women with a sketchy past – all flocked to Him. The crowds following Jesus got to be so enormous that it created logistical problems for people who wanted Him to heal their sick friends and relations – logistical problems that found their way into the text of scripture itself.

> *And many were gathered together, so that there was no more room, not even at the door. And He was preaching the word to them. And they came, bringing to Him a paralytic carried by four men. And when they could not get near Him because of the crowd, they removed the roof above Him, and when they had made an opening, they let down the bed on which the paralytic lay.* (Mk. 2:2-4, ESV)

It wasn't just Jesus, either. Jesus proved to the crowds how some people would always find a way to be the Debbie Downer, always find some reason to complain and find fault. He used their hostile reactions to both Himself and John the Baptist – who were so very different in their life and example – to make His point.

> *When John's messengers had gone, Jesus began to speak to the crowds concerning John: "What did you go out into the wilderness to see? A reed shaken by the wind? What then did you go out to see? A man dressed in soft clothing? Behold, those who are dressed in splendid clothing*

and live in luxury are in kings' courts. What then did you go out to see? A prophet? Yes, I tell you, and more than a prophet. This is he of whom it is written, 'Behold, I send my messenger before your face, who will prepare your way before you.' I tell you, among those born of women none is greater than John. Yet the one who is least in the kingdom of God is greater than he." (When all the people heard this, and the tax collectors too, they declared God just, having been baptized with the baptism of John, but the Pharisees and the lawyers rejected the purpose of God for themselves, not having been baptized by him.) "To what then shall I compare the people of this generation, and what are they like? They are like children sitting in the marketplace and calling to one another, 'We played the flute for you, and you did not dance; we sang a dirge, and you did not weep.' For John the Baptist has come eating no bread and drinking no wine, and you say, 'He has a demon.' The Son of Man has come eating and drinking, and you say, 'Look at him! A glutton and a drunkard, a friend of tax collectors and sinners!' Yet wisdom is justified by all her children." (Lk. 7:24-35, ESV)

The pompous windbags could find fault with everyone but themselves. John the Baptist was too austere. Jesus was too jovial and friendly ... even with "those" people. Neither Jesus nor John fit into their neat little grid, so they found reasons to reject both men.

Does that sound familiar? Could the same thing be happening with today's media and even the NeverTrumpers? Of course, it could. You remember how they came up with all kinds of crazy reasons why Bush, McCain, and Romney were the embodiment of evil – until they were no longer standing between their team and the levers of political power. But now that Trump is in office, and each has stood opposed to him, all is forgiven?

Could the moral high ground they pretend to stand on be more than a little bit suspect?

What "champion" did the left send us in answer to Dubya, Romney, and McCain? They gave us Obama. If you believed the Press, you'd almost think he was the Second Coming. Even he seemed to think so. Remember when he knocked off Hillary as DNC nominee? He told us, "... this was the moment when the rise of the oceans began to slow and our planet began to heal ..."

How nice. Good to see he has no God complex there.

When he landed in D.C. what kind of a person was he? The "cool kids" in the Beltway and Hollywood all loved him – no surprise there. But what about everyone else?

What was Obama's attitude to the non-elites? Who really captured his attention? Who did he make time for? How did he speak of the ordinary person? When it suited him, Barack had all the right words and declared to the world just how much he cared about – whichever issue he was supposed to be caring about on a given day. He was a great friend to the poor and the oppressed – in principle. Just don't look too carefully at his policies, or who he spent his time with.

He loved America – or at least his idea of what it should become once it was "fundamentally transformed" into something worthy of his love. He loved America so much that he immediately took what his critics began to call a "Blame America" tour.

He loved the "ordinary folks" – except when he disparaged them as bigots, "It's not surprising, then, they get bitter, they cling to guns or religion or antipathy to people who aren't like them or anti-immigrant sentiment or anti-trade sentiment as a way to explain their frustrations." Yeah, that line went over really well, didn't it?

He cherished the faith of the ordinary person – except for the fact that he had a nasty habit of pitting one religion against another. He didn't hesitate at all to scold Christians for "getting on a high horse" and invoking the Crusades. (Even though the Muslim conquest of Spain and North Africa predated the Crusades by nearly five centuries.) He scolded Christian belief in the context of the Prayer Breakfast.

This is the same Barack Obama who couldn't bring himself to utter the words "Islamic Terrorism" (radical or otherwise), dismissed Ft. Hood as "workplace violence" and stood in front of the UN – knowing full well that Benghazi had nothing to do with a sad little YouTube video – and declared that, "the future must not belong to those who slander the prophet of Islam."

What about those who have served to protect the nation, at home and abroad? We saw how ongoing deployment coupled with spending cuts gutted military readiness. When Clinton or Dubya would address the U.S. Military, the troops seemed happy to see them. By contrast, if you can get past the Google safeguards protecting Obama from any wide shot of his final address to the troops, (try a different search engine) it is telling just how few people actually showed up for his event.

The same disconnect carries through to law enforcement. At the Beer Summit – he assumed the cop "acted stupidly" without knowing a single fact about the case. He jaundiced an open criminal case saying, "If I had a son he would look like Trayvon." He sided against honest police officers who responded to a bomb hoax in a school by inviting Clock-boy to the White House with his "Cool clock, Ahmed" tweet. Only later did we learn just what an upstanding and patriotic family Clock-boy really came from.

But the real kicker was after the shootings in Dallas, when police officers stood by to protect marchers in a BLM rally – a movement that was often so very critical of police that other protests had called for violence against law enforcement. At the conclusion of that march, police officers were shot dead one by one. They were murdered by a man with a rifle and a burning hatred. One witness to the tragedy, Shetamia Taylor, said that "several" of the murdered cops died shielding her and her kids from the assassin.

What did Obama do? In a speech where he admitted the killer was motivated by racial hatred, he took time to point fingers at the racism of cops who had literally just laid down their lives to save people of a different cultural background than their own.

Who did Obama really love to spend his time with? He liked to host A-list celebrities from film or music. In fact, *Vanity Fair's* Hilary Weaver wrote a story about it in the last days of his presidency: "The Obamas Have Outdone Themselves with Star-Studded Parties." The article went on to describe how it "follows years of star-packed soirées." The list was a long one.

He surrounded himself with wealthy stars and political activists like Al Sharpton, who had something like 80 visits to the White House, and Robert Creamer (342 visits, including 47 with Obama) who is best remembered from the undercover *Project Veritas* videos as the bridge between the Clinton Campaign (which he was part of) and Scott Foval – who successfully provoked violence at Trump rallies.

The "Community Organizer In Chief" pretended to be a great supporter of grassroots movements, but he weaponized the IRS against Patriot and Tea Party Groups (which he mockingly mispronounced to describe a specific homosexual act). He ran the DNC into the ground and left it near bankruptcy.

What sort of picture is coming together here? Obama was an opportunist that mostly surrounded himself with people that could benefit his ego or his ambitions. But the Media stood guard over him – like the Praetorian Guard once did over Caesar – to guard his image and legacy at all costs.

Hillary, as we all saw, picked up where Obama left off. Routinely accusing Trump, and Republicans generally of being racist, sexist bigots – a "basket of deplorables" – she once scolded the public for not lining up in support of Her Highness. In a scene that was only missing flying monkeys or a bubbling cauldron, she croaked her lament into the camera "why aren't I fifty points ahead right now you may ask." You just answered your own question, Hillary. That's a hard pass, thanks.

As hard as they worked trying to sell Hillary as a palatable candidate, they just couldn't get past the complete disconnect she had with most of America. Spending more time with donors than with voters didn't help any. (By the way, has she found Wisconsin yet?)

In case there was still any doubt, Bill and Hillary went on a stadium tour through North America to pitch her *What Happened* book, and try to get her political mojo back. Humiliated by the lack of interest – tickets dropped to six dollars apiece in Toronto. And that's in the colorful Canadian funny money that's worth about ¾ of the Greenback. Good luck even watching a movie matinee for that price in Toronto! From the vaunted heights of running almost unopposed for President in 2016, to drawing sparse crowds that could scarcely fill a photo booth, Hillary has crashed and burned in a spectacular way.

The people had spoken.

But while Hillary struggled to imagine why she couldn't shame and abuse the public into supporting her campaign, another candidate took the field. You might expect someone of his background, a jet-setting billionaire with his own star on the Walk of Fame, to be stuck up and unapproachable. But somehow, he isn't. He has a rare showman's talent for connecting to a crowd on a personal level. Maybe you remember the throngs of people that were lined up to see Trump speak in his 2016 rallies – and long after.

Maybe it was because he took action in the Louisiana flooding, filling an 18-wheeler with supplies and helping unload it to the people. Maybe it was because he went into neighborhoods in Michigan where he didn't stand a chance, and he asked them point-blank "what do you have to lose?" Maybe it had something to do with an interest in the suffering of "flyover country," lost industries, drug addiction issues, dangerous neighborhoods, and failing schools with the intent of not just "organizing" them behind a political movement, but actually making their lives better.

Candace Owens and Kanye made a lot of waves when they told America that black voters are free to vote for whoever they want – they have no moral obligation to stand behind Democrats if the Democrats are not actually serving their interests. Between that – and the fact that Trump's policies were starting to catch the attention of those "safe" Democrat voters, the polls have started shifting in the President's favor.

Trump even listened to the issues that ordinary Americans brought to him. Trump didn't run on a platform of prison reform, but after sitting down with some community leaders, he let them make the case for what changes needed to be made. Not only has he delivered on the *First Step Act* – which showcased some amazing success stories of people who had clearly turned their lives around, and deserved a shot at returning to society, he has followed it up with a *Second Step Act* – which aims to match those who have paid their debt to society with gainful employment. "A job," as Reagan used to say, "is the best social program."

As you might expect, Trump has a specific goal: he is aiming for single-digit unemployment for those with criminal records within five years. Ambitious? Yes. And it's also compassionate. Helping these people get matched up with honest work could go a long way to breaking some of the negative cycles these people have found themselves trapped in.

The same trend we saw with the "Blexit" movement – they adapted the "Brexit" name for black activists turning their back on the Democrat party – is not the only sign of Democrat Defections. There is also a "Jexodus" (Jewish Exodus) movement by people who have noticed that elected Democrats are increasingly indifferent to anti-Semitism in their midst. Another movement, called "Walk Away," was intended for long-time liberals who no longer recognize the party they were once part of ... with the party taking an aggressive tilt to the Left, we might expect more like it.

Another of Trump's signature issues is border security. As a President, is there anything more fundamental to his role than keeping America safe? He identified two threats. One, which was peaking during the 2015 Refugee crisis, was the mass migration of people with unknown motives and backgrounds from one place to another. The other was our southern border.

After eight years of being run by a party that dismissed Jihadi attacks as "workplace violence," the potential impact of unrestricted mass migration was a real concern to him. Especially when we saw a spike of ISIS-inspired attacks like the bloodbath in Paris.

Meanwhile, Hillary's campaign manager, Podesta, got busted in a leaked email complaining about the San Bernardino attack, "Better if a guy named Sayeed Farouk was reporting that a guy named Christopher Hayes was the shooter."[153]

Sadly, the Democrats cared more about leveraging racial politics than they did about identifying and neutralizing threats. When Democrats fought to defend chain migration and maintaining *de facto* open borders with Mexico, Trump had a different priority. Just like you don't treat a houseguest who comes in through the front door and a burglar who breaks in through the window as moral equals, Trump has a high opinion of legal immigration – through ports of entry – while being absolutely opposed to border-jumpers who want to break our laws and game our system. Democrats prioritized illegal border-crossers while Trump prioritized American citizens.

The rule of law. A strong border. He acknowledged a suffering group that everyone had previously ignored – the "Angel moms."

Trump drew attention to the somber fact that there are real victims to this lawless policy. People who had no right to be in America have cut short the lives of honest citizens. Perhaps no story so powerfully illustrated the very real and important distinction between legal and illegal immigration than the 2018 Christmas killing of Ronil Singh. Ronil, a young police officer who left behind a wife and newborn son, at the hand of a Mexican national who was unlawfully in the country. Ronil Singh was not born here either. But he came here the right way – legally. He immigrated to America from Fiji and set out to be an officer of the law.

These are the sorts of the issues that energize Trump – individual stories of heroism or hardship. His first State of the Union speech led Americans to cheer the North Korean national who fled to freedom on his crutches and ache with the grief of the parents whose teenage daughter was cut down with machetes by MS-13 gang members.

Trump saw the viral video of Hayden Williams getting sucker punched on the campus of the home of the "free speech" movement -- Berkeley, and invited him to CPAC, saying, "He took a hard punch in the face for all of us."

For all the effort the media is taking to demonize Trump, his fans and his policies, they're missing the big picture.

Democrats have staked their claim in a divide-and-conquer approach to politics: splitting us into rival factions and collecting as many pieces as they can as "voting blocks." The

Democrats need us divided into factions: us-and-them, race-baiting, Occupy Wall-Street types with a manifest hatred of successful business owners.

But Trump strikes a chord with ordinary Americans because, on a fundamental level, he shares our values. He loves America, its people, and its institutions. He elevates us all by drawing on what really unifies us -- an America whose contributions to the world have been both remarkable and undeniable.

This wouldn't be the first time in history that powerful elites reject someone the crowds intuitively embraced. When they got tired of being kicked around and taken for granted, they reached out for someone who would truly represent them the way they deserve to be represented.

In Trump – they have found just such a man.

CHAPTER TWENTY-THREE

A Bad Tree Doesn't Produce Good Fruit

Doug Giles

But let your "Yes" be "Yes," and your "No," "No."
Matthew 5:37, NKJV

When you say you are going to do something, do you deliver on that promise ... or not? In our ordinary relationships, that question can make or break a friendship. But when a politician flips on us and works against the very promises he ran on, we aren't the least bit surprised. We've grown accustomed to having politicians lie to us.

Once he showed up at 1600, we kept hearing the joke about Trump being a different kind of politician. *Usually* politicians are hated for the promises they break, but DJT kicked a hornets' nest with the promises he kept.

His critics got him totally wrong. They had him pegged, or so they thought. By the time they realized they'd been played, the genie was already out of the bottle.

They looked him up and down, sized him up as a misbehaving Billionaire Playboy who liked pretty women and expensive toys – and they wrote him off. That was a mistake, and it's one we've seen in the Good Book.

> *The Pharisee, standing by himself, prayed thus: "God, I thank you that I am not like other men, extortioners, unjust, adulterers, or even like this tax collector." (Lk. 18:11, NKJV)*

The stick God uses to measure our actions isn't the one we use when figuring out how we measure up against other people. Maybe that's why we're told not to be like the Pharisee in his public prayer, eh? Sure, the Pharisee may have been the hero in the story he told himself, but to the Lord, he was the villain -- that's serving up a double-helping of humility for the rest of us.

When the Lord has strong words – and, eventually, punishments– for those in authority, He doesn't waste time messing around with petty moral failings and peccadilloes. He goes straight for the big game: the leaders' abuse of his God-given authority.

> *Her priests have done violence to my law and have profaned my holy things. They have made no distinction between the holy and the common, neither have they taught the difference between the unclean and the clean, and they have disregarded my Sabbaths, so that I am profaned among them. Her princes in her midst are like*

wolves tearing the prey, shedding blood, destroying lives to get dishonest gain. And her prophets have smeared whitewash for them, seeing false visions and divining lies for them, saying, "Thus says the Lord God," when the Lord has not spoken. (Ez. 22:26-28, NKJV)

The Lord didn't leave a lot of grey area in the right and wrong use of political power. Don't fleece the public or pad your own wallet. Don't enable corruption or deny justice to the ordinary citizen. Politicians are supposed to faithfully serve the interests of the nation they govern. Basically, don't do Deep State stuff.

Ok, then, let's look at what Trump has done with his time in office so far. How does he score on that scale? This isn't about his braggadocio bluster or truculent tweets, just what he has accomplished during these initial two years of his time in office.

To set this up, properly, let's measure what he *has* done in light of what went before, what he said he was setting out to do, and what his critics said about his bold claims and predictions.

Some leaders blunder their way through their time in office. They make vague, optimistic promises (think: "Hope and Change"), which is handy later, because if nobody knows what you've promised, nobody can complain when you fail to deliver. It also helps by making it easy to move the goalposts, taking credit or casting blame when the political winds shift.

Not Trump. He has made his key issues and objectives clear, specific, and measurable. More than that, he has predicted the specific impact of the policies he has promised to make.

Like Babe Ruth did on that famous World Series home run, Trump pointed to the bleachers *before* he took his swing. He told us just what was going to happen to the American economy when he took office. He told us a *lot* of things that would happen in America once he took office.

Compare this epic rant to the hopey-changey nonsense:

> We're going to win. We're going to win so much. We're going to win at trade, we're going to win at the border. We're going to win so much, you're going to be so sick and tired of winning, you're going to come to me and go 'Please, please, we can't win anymore.' You've heard this one. You'll say 'Please, Mr. President, we beg you sir, we don't want to win anymore. It's too much. It's not fair to everybody else.'" Trump said. "And I'm going to say 'I'm sorry, but we're going to keep winning, winning, winning, We're going to make America great again."[154]

That paints a pretty clear picture of what he wants to see happen in America. He wants a roaring economy, plenty of jobs, safe streets. He wants Americans from coast to coast to grab life with both hands and squeeze. To see everyone (who dares to) live out the promise of the American Dream.

His key promises were real things that you could measure. Things like border security, Obamacare repeal, faithful judges, and the unleashing of America's economic engine – namely jobs.

Even before the election, dire predictions were being made about just how "devastating" a Trump economy would be, not just for America, but for the entire world. Experts predicted doom and gloom on an enormous scale. Calling Trump the "mother of all adverse effects," the Nobel Prize-winning economist, Paul Krugman, predicted that the GOP nominee's administration could quickly undo the progress that the markets around the world have made in the eight years since the financial crisis.

"Under any circumstances, putting an irresponsible, ignorant man who takes his advice from all the wrong people in charge of the nation with the world's most important economy would be very bad news," he wrote. "What makes it especially bad right now, however, is the fundamentally fragile state much of the world is still in." [155]

Krugman wasn't the only dope betting against Trump's economic optimism. WaPo predicted that a President Trump could "Destroy the World Economy." [156] Obama's chief Economist predicted doom. (Remember ... Obama later claimed credit for the Trump economy – which is exactly what we meant about moving the goalposts.) "Under Trump, I would expect a protracted recession to begin within 18 months. The damage would be felt far beyond the United States," said former Clinton and Obama chief economist Larry Summers. [157]

Destroy the World Economy? Thanks for that prediction, Nostradamus. Take a seat. We won't be needing any more of your "advice."

It wasn't just the political left saying so, either. How about this gem? "Trump's domestic policies would lead to recession." That quote came from no less a luminary than Mitt Romney.

Let's see how someone who really "puts his money where his mouth is" reacted to the Trump election. Warren Buffett added to his stock portfolio at Berkshire Hathaway Inc. in a big way after Nov. 8.

> "We've, net, bought US$12 billion of common stocks since the election," he said in an interview with Charlie Rose that aired on Friday. Buffett didn't identify the securities that he picked. Purchases of that magnitude represent a major pickup in activity for Omaha, Nebraska-based Berkshire. During the first nine months of last year, the company bought US$5.2 billion and sold or redeemed roughly US$20 billion worth of stocks, according to a regulatory filing.[158]

Well, well, well. That's quite a turnaround from what his investments looked like under Obama, isn't it?

The sort of gloom-and-doom predictions concerning Trump's economic policies were also said about his political platform more broadly. It was a rehash of the favorite retread criticisms of Dubya, only bigger. The way they contradicted each other would be comical if it weren't so serious.

They claimed at various times that:
Trump's an ignorant oaf.
He's the puppet of [insert name].
He's a dangerous cowboy who won't listen to reason.
He's a Machiavellian Svengali
He's a Pied Piper with dangerous sway over the MAGA hat-wearing public.
He's going to get us all killed.
He can't be trusted with the nuclear football.

On and on it went.

It wasn't long before the "Literally Hitler" quotes came out. His election was even compared to Pearl Harbor by the ever-so-impartial Partisan Press.

But let's move on and measure the man by his deeds, shall we? He made promises – did he do his part to keep them?

Iran
The President openly despised the Iran deal, he said it was bad for America.

Amid protests and pressure from other nations who did not approve – and with John Kerry secretly meeting with Iranian leaders to oppose him – President Trump tore it up, and slapped heavy sanctions back onto the World Leader In State Sanctioned Terrorism.

Paris Accord
Trump was also opposed to the Paris Deal that Obama had committed the American people to; he said it unfairly penalized American interests and companies, while asking very little from the major polluters like India and China.

We were told the Paris Accord was "nonbinding." Of course we were told that. They would have to tell us that. Otherwise, Obama – the self-described Constitutional Law Professor – would have somehow managed to commit America to participate in a binding treaty without the approval of two-thirds of the Senate. But if it was so very "non-binding" why did the Left squeal like a stuck pig when Trump said no mas to the plan? Could it be that the penalties lurking in there, unequally targeting America really were intended to be binding?

Now that we've pulled out, is the sky falling like we were told it would? Not so much – here's a headline from Gizmodo's climate change section, *U.S. on Track to Meet Obama's Climate Targets Despite Trump Killing Them.*[159] That almost sounds like American businesses did not need some foreign-made Sword of Damocles hanging over our heads to force us into compliance. In fact, without any threat of punishment, private businesses and state governments are responding to public demands for greater energy efficiency. The dirty little secret is that – even without being in the Paris Accord – America is doing more to curb emissions than anybody else, bar none.

> Although the U.S. reduction seems low percentage-wise, it translates to a total annual reduction of about 760 million metric tons since 2005, almost as much as the reduction in the European Union as a whole (770 million metric tons).[160]

Trade
Speaking of "Bad Deals," he has been renegotiating trade deals around the world. He pulled out of the TPP, as promised. He went back to the drawing board over NAFTA, hammering out a new deal, the USMCA, that has been agreed to in principle and awaits ratification as I write this. He has been in talks with China to hash out our differences – with special attention being given to their abuses of intellectual property.

That Clinton campaign line from the '90s, "It's the economy, stupid!" sure came back to haunt Hillary.

Employment numbers – Abracadabra!
Trump promised that jobs would be making a comeback. Obama scoffed at that, asking "what kind of a magic wand [Trump had]" that could accomplish that. Obama told us, you may re-

member, that such jobs were not coming back and that the meager growth numbers we saw under his administration were "the new normal." [Spoiler alert: he was wrong]

Obama's economic advisor Larry Summers wrote in 2017, "Apparently, the budget forecasts that U.S. economic growth will rise to 3.0 percent because of the administration's policies — largely its tax cuts and perhaps also its regulatory policies. Fair enough if you believe in tooth fairies and ludicrous supply-side economics."[161]

But Trump stepped up to that plate, pointed to the bleachers – and unleashed the powerhouse of the American economy. He cut back red tape – massively. Then he pushed for massive tax relief.

Hey Barack – "Abracadabra!"

Check this press release out, *Economic Growth Has Reached 3 Percent for the First Time in More than a Decade Thanks to President Donald J. Trump's Policies,*[162] White House

This marked the fastest fourth quarter to fourth quarter growth since 2005. 2018 was the second year in a row that the economy exceeded market expectations.

Second year in a row, you say? And Trump would like to see that number go even higher.

Trump Promised Jobs
The job numbers don't lie. We are now seeing employment numbers that (almost) nobody would have thought possible. So far, we've seen 5.3 Million jobs created since Trump took office, we've seen eleven straight months of unemployment

at or below 4%. And those jobs are going to the people who needed them most.

In particular, Black, Latino, female, and even disabled workers are seeing employment numbers that are at or near all-time highs. Demand is even opening up new opportunities for those who were once marginally employed or employable. As a result, the most dramatic wage growth is being seen at the lowest income levels.

And what about Manufacturing?
2018 was the best year for manufacturing job growth in the U.S. since 1997. Factories added 264,000 workers in 2018, up from 176,000 workers in 2017. [163]

Abracadabra ... again!

Repeal And Replace Obamacare
Trump saw that Obamacare not only failed to deliver on its promises, but it created more problems that it solved – especially with that Obamacare Mandate.

He made the repeal of Obamacare an early focus of his Presidency and took several runs at getting it repealed. He had a majority in both houses in Congress, but he didn't have enough for that magic "60 votes" in Senate to push legislation through unopposed. There were a couple of failed attempts to get rid of Obamacare, the most (in)famous of them was that eleventh-hour last act of defiance by McCain ... "thumbs down."

But he kept at it, and eventually Trump got the last laugh even without McCain's help. He killed the worst part of the "Affordable Care Act" by removing the enforcement mandate.

That had two benefits. The first benefit was that American citizens were no longer being bullied by their government to buy a product against their will. The second benefit was less obvious but had a far greater potential effect. By killing the mandate (which was written into the legislation as "inseverable" from the ACA) the rather dubious legal gymnastics arguing for why it was constitutional in the first place are no longer relevant or valid.

Now Trump's DOJ is agreeing with a recent Texas lawsuit about the "inseverability" of that mandate making Obamacare null and void without it. This battle is a long way from over, and the makeup of the courts has changed since Trump came to town.

Judges
He has nominated a boatload of judges and has leaned heavily on the list of candidates nominated by solid conservative and Originalist groups. The stand he took in defence of Judge Kavanaugh when they dragged his good name through the mud speaks for itself. And if it hadn't been Trump picking judges, it would have been Hillary.

ISIS
Trump minced no words on his intention to bomb them back to the stone age, strip them of the legitimacy of their "Caliphate" by stripping them of their territorial holdings, and help to publicly discredit them as a group – which includes holding them up to public ridicule as "losers."

Pro-Life
Trump has led the most aggressively Pro-life administration since Roe v. Wade – bar none. Refer to his 2019 SOTU speech as well as the closing of loopholes in the Mexico City policy.

The Big, Beautiful Wall

Border Security and especially the Wall has been a central promise of his from the get-go. Which would explain the support he got from the 5,000 member "National Immigration and Customs Enforcement Council." But he has faced enormous opposition to that plan from both sides of the political aisle. The Left no longer opposes illegal immigration – they embrace and encourage it, supporting so-called Sanctuary cities and opposing ICE at every turn.

The GOP has been pretty useless. Until Trump insisted this issue was worth risking a Government Shutdown over, there was no political will to use the mandate and majority the American voter had handed them to extend the wall or to solve the underlying amnesty/family separation/catch-and-release issue that is driving a new kind of illegal immigration that endangers children and enriches the cartels controlling the Mexican side of the border.

The Democrat Congress flatly refused to give funding for the wall, but had no problem giving ten billion (twice what Trump had asked for Wall funding) in aid to Mexico and Central America.

Trump found areas where he had authority to assign funding toward building the wall. He used laws on the books – including Emergency spending – and some of the Pentagon budget (which has since been approved) toward cutting off some of the known smuggling corridors. The only veto Trump has yet used in his presidency has been on legislation that would have blocked border wall spending.

'Bad Hombres', indeed ...

As for the claim Americans face no real threat coming across our Southern Border, perhaps they might want to explain why Brian Mudd was able to cite a new study by Citizens' Council for Public Security and Criminal Justice identifying the six most dangerous cities by homicides per capita. Number three was Caracas. The other five were in Mexico.

Why That "Extreme Vetting" Policy Matters

If people come to our country, we have a right to know whether they are honest citizens looking to live the dream, or if they are known criminals fleeing justice from their own land – or worse, people with known connections to criminal or even terrorist organizations. We're happy to welcome one group in our midst, but we have the responsibility to keep the other group out. We have too many "Angel families" whose loved ones have been murdered by foreigners here illegally to not take this issue seriously.

The tragic murder of Ronil Singh stands as a perfect example of the difference between immigration done the right way and the wrong way and why we need to keep *bad hombres* out.

But Isn't It A "Muslim Ban"?

Donald Trump was exercising his very clearly defined Article II powers in making determinations about who can and cannot enter the country. Critics called it a "Muslim Ban" because it is politically expedient to paint Trump as a racist to hurt him politically and to discredit his policy. But what did his so-called "Muslim Ban" call for?

The US Supreme Court has upheld a ban by President Donald Trump on travel to the US from seven countries: North Korea, Syria, Iran, Yemen, Libya, Somalia, and Venezuela. Depending on the country, it either suspends entry as immigrants and non-immigrants – Syria, Iran, North Korea; as immigrants and non-immigrants on tourist or business visas – Libya, Yemen; suspends entry as immigrants – Somalia; or restricts entry to specific government officials.

Venezuela and North Korea are not even close to being Muslim-majority countries, and each of the five remaining countries were already on a list of seven countries (which included Iraq and Sudan) that had been identified as "Countries of Concern" under Obama.

Disproving the "Muslim Ban" claim is as straightforward as looking up the largest Muslim populations in the world and seeing how many of those countries do not make this list.

We've got a President who has spent his time in office – when he wasn't being badgered over unfounded allegations of "Russian Collusion" – doing some very specific things.

Trump has been Reinvesting in the Military readiness to protect his citizens from any future conflict – which includes modernizing and recognizing the vulnerability of satellites and cybertechnology – while using a balance of diplomacy and force to protect our national interests worldwide.

The physical territory of ISIS has been smashed, North Korea has returned hostages and has moved toward possible reconciliation with South Korea and the U.S. He has led the free world in supporting the Venezuelan rejection of their despot Maduro, and sanctions, rather than military strikes, have been the preferred method of bringing hostile nations to heel.

He has not only promised to breathe life into the American economy ... but has backed it up with sound policy that got us there, both in cutting red tape and slashing taxes. And with a rising interest in unvarnished socialism on the Left, he's taken direct aim at it -- "We will never be a socialist country."

DJT has been upholding the rule of law, while being receptive to solutions in reforming the justice system, and has himself worked within the scope of Article II powers and existing legislation.

Religious freedoms have been upheld and expanded.

Life in the womb has been defended with such tools as he has at his disposal.

Judges committed to the Constitution – not judicial activism – are being appointed.

Whatever you may think of his personality and bluster, his checkered past and his regularly scheduled beat-downs of self-aggrandizing blowhards on CNN, take a good long look at that list.

If someone *not* named "Trump" had a track record like that, wouldn't you consider him the best President in a generation? Perhaps even among our true leadership greats? If so, why should his name being Trump make any difference?

He already pointed to those bleachers and told us what kind of a president he was going to be. Then he got to work and started executing that plan. No wonder his 2020 run has been considering "Promises Kept" as the slogan.

In our crazy upside-down world of politics today, any politician who delivers on his promises is a rare find indeed.

You can judge him by the words of his critics – who openly hate him – or you can judge him by his accomplishments.

Or, if you prefer to use biblical language, "judge him by his fruit."

CHAPTER TWENTY-FOUR

The Christian Roots Of This Grand Experiment In Self-Governance

Brandon Vallorani

*Do not think that I have come to abolish the Law or the Proph-
ets; I have not come to abolish them but to fulfill them. For
truly, I say to you, until heaven and earth pass away,
not an iota, not a dot, will pass from the Law until all is accomplished. Therefore whoever relaxes one of the least of these
commandments and teaches others to do the same will be
called least in the kingdom of heaven, but whoever
does them and teaches them will be called great in the
kingdom of heaven.*
Matthew 5:17-19, NASB

I n one sense, there's a sort of parallel between the American
Experiment and Christ's first incarnation. Both were the beginning of something new, but neither was a rejection of the
faith that went before.

When He announced, "I have not come to abolish the law but fulfill it," Jesus was describing the kind of change that was coming, something new that was not a complete break from what came before.

America is a little like that. We wanted our independence -- we'd had enough with being British subjects. But we brought a lot of good things with us. British Common Law, for example, was the foundation for what came later. But a lot has changed since 1776. Many of us have forgotten what it means to be American. Are we a nation of laws rooted in Christian faith, or was Christianity just an artifact of what some dead white guys believed a long time ago, something of no real relevance in the 21st century?

That question is a key distinction between how the Democrats and Republicans see America. Even among Republicans, some have been so careful to avoid kicking the hornets' nest of the press that they mention our Christian heritage only if they really have to, and as far as policy goes, it rarely shows up except in the context of big-government catchphrases.

What set Trump's promises apart from most other politicians? He came with a different promise. He wants to bring the best parts of America's Yesterday forward into Today. His rivals, on the other hand, are more interested in erasing that history altogether.

Every election we hear that tired old Standard Political Promise of, "I will bring change." Obama's version, "Hope and Change" epitomized that attitude. But what does it really mean? In some sense, it is a rejection of everything that came before you. It is a call to revolution. It is the promise of someone who wants to "fundamentally transform" a system.

If you're calling to fundamentally transform something, what is your opinion, really, of its actual, current value? Probably not much.

What is your opinion of the distilled collective wisdom handed down through generations over hundreds of years of learning from societal success and failure? What kind of person tells himself, "I'm smarter than everyone that came before me -- let's throw it all out and start over." It's the same kind of person who would later brag about being able to bypass Constitutional limitations by using his "pen and his phone."

They haven't even been honest about the changes they want to cram down our throats "for our own good." Hidden agendas and complicit media have swept certain unpleasant realities – and the red flags that came with them – under the rug.

Obama's born-alive voting while a Senator.

Obama's affiliation with Jeremiah Wright's race-baiting church.

Obama (and other Democrats') "evolving" positions on marriage. Positions that conveniently evolved sometime between when they ran for office, and when they found themselves in positions of influence.

Every one of the changes they push on us takes us further away from all that was once called traditional.

Until recently, politicians still had to play the game and downplay their secularist tendencies in front of a religious electorate. Despite a natural hostility to Christianity, which they are quick to criticize, it has been necessary, until now, to give lip service to having some kind of Christian religious affiliation. This is so relevant that even in 2016, Hillary's leaked emails showed that her team had even looked at drawing attention to Bernie Sanders' atheism as a potential weakness to exploit.

Their real contempt for Christianity comes across when blocking Christian candidates, attacking Catholic teens from Covington, Kentucky, suing the Sisters of Mercy, and using the AG's resources in attempting to strip court-awarded asylum that had been granted to the Romeikes – a Christian family fleeing Germany over documented religious persecution at the hand of a secular state.

When these people actually darken the door of a Church, what do they do when they get there? Maxine Waters, for one, took over a sermon, telling congregants that God sent her to stop President Trump. (Why not go all-in and tell them she was Napoleon while she was at it?) Even that paled against the time she hijacked a eulogy at Dick Gregory's funeral to proclaim her hatred of, and opposition to, a duly elected President.

How can anyone forget their 2012 DNC convention? It takes a certain *chutzpah* to boo Yahweh while voting on the party platform at your national convention.

But it hasn't always been this way. Nor does it need to be the "new normal."

Trump has been pushing back since he arrived on the scene. He has signalled it's "safe" to say Merry Christmas again. He's been re-establishing a consciousness of our Religious Freedoms. He has led by example so that it is once again as socially acceptable to wish someone a Merry Christmas as it is to wish them a "Happy Hanukkah." He is actively advocating the protection of religious freedoms. For example, the *Presidential Executive Order Promoting Free Speech and Religious Liberty*[164], which other Presidents before him could have put forward, but did not.

Is a billionaire Playboy an unlikely hero for religious freedom? Sure. But, it's beyond question that, while he'd never claim to be a *moral* exemplar, he does understand that freedom generally – and religious freedom particularly – is absolutely critical to the American DNA. Unlike the spineless grifters populating Congress, he's willing to defend that DNA. As such, he has been stalwart in the defense of many Christian ideals, including some that his more traditionally "Christian" Presidential predecessors did not defend nearly as well as ... this unlikely hero.

The Masterpiece Cakeshop owner had his case heard – And won! – in the Supreme Court. Do you suspect that a Hillary appointee would have even voted in support of giving it a hearing?

Historical revisionists claim Islam is very much a part of America's history, offering seminars like, *Muslims in America: Denaturalizing Christian-centered Narratives of American History16* Meanwhile, some of these same scholars think they're doing us a favor by eroding all references to the very obvious Christian DNA in America's identity.

So, who has it right? The secularists who think Christian faith wasn't a big part of what it meant to be an American, or the people like Trump who want to take us back to a time where Christian belief is once again at least respected, even celebrated.

It wasn't so long ago that the secular crowd was yelling at the believers not to "cram our religion down their throat." Just a few short years later, with the political power dynamics flipped in their favor, they've lost any pretenses of being pro-freedom. They're calling the shots – or so they think – and they will destroy anyone and anything that stands in their way. They even had the CEO of Mozilla Firefox canned over a donation he made to a political campaign. What was that unforgivable exercise of his civil liberties? He supported the traditional definition of marriage.

That's today's fight in a nutshell.

Trump's MAGA vision borrows from someone before him. Someone who saw America, not as a nation that owes the world an unending string of apologies, someone who famously referred to America as a city on a hill: "I've spoken of the Shining City all my political life ... That's how I saw it, and see it still," said Ronald Reagan in his Farewell Address. Reagan was quoting from the Sermon on the Mount.

> *You are the light of the world. A city that is set on a hill cannot be hidden. Nor do they light a lamp and put it under a basket, but on a lampstand, and it gives light to all who are in the house. Let your light so shine before men, that they may see your good works and glorify your Father in heaven.* (Mt. 5:14-16, NKJV)

The whole Point of that passage was to be unashamedly Christian in front of a world that isn't, to live in such a way that would make others want that thing that makes you different. That same imagery was used before, speaking of what would later become America, by John Winthrop. In his 1630 AD sermon, *A model of Christian Charity*, he said, "We shall be as a city upon a hill, the eyes of all people are upon us."[166]

Christian tradition in America goes back much further than secularists might think. And more importantly, it goes much deeper. It isn't just our traditions -- our institutions and our system themselves were anchored in faith.

Secularists have a "progressive" belief that humanity is "basically good," and needs only the right education and opportunities to be the best versions of themselves. Put the right system in place, they argue, and society will be utopian.

The Framers, being Christian, had a much more pragmatic view of human nature. We're deeply flawed, each driven by our own unspoken motives. Humanity, as a species, is basically unchanged over the thousands of years of written history we can look back upon. We are habitually drawn to falling into the same sins. So, rather than chase a ridiculous dream of making men better, they flipped the script and made men work at cross-purposes from each other. One man's pride and ambition would work against another man's. Each would seek to oppose the other from getting what he should not get.

The checks and balances took the selfish inclinations of bad people and put them to profitable use. It doesn't take a Nostradamus or even a diligent student of history to know which view was the more realistic depiction of American politicians. We're not saying they solved every problem, but at least they weren't lying to themselves about the sort of people we'd be sending to Washington.

How what about the "separation of church and state"? This comes up every time we talk about religion and politics, right? Did you know that Jefferson's letter wasn't even looked at before the Everson case in 1947? And if it was such a great solution, should it have made the "religious test" less clear?

Even now, while SCOTUS tries to figure out what to do with a cross monument not far from Arlington, SCOTUS recognizes that the current formulas for testing religious laws are not only broken, but they aren't even applied to all cases.

What did they used to do? Before that, the courts held two ideas in tension. The Establishment clause "Congress shall make no law respecting an establishment of religion or prohibiting the free exercise thereof" in the First Amendment, and Article VI Section 3. "No religious test shall ever be required as a qualification to any office or public trust under the United States." Whatever the Left might tell you, the establishment clause was not an exercise in declaring the American Government "religiously neutral." On the contrary, the Framers were saying that one Christian denomination could not be elevated to the exclusion of all others. David Barton makes the case pretty clearly in *Original Intent*, but we can hit on a just a few points here. Like the one where he listed some of the alternate wordings proposed for the First Amendment.

George Mason: "[A]ll men have an equal, natural and unalienable right to the free exercise of religion, according to the dictates of conscience; and that no particular sect or society of Christians ought to be favored or established by law in preference to others."[167] He was a Signer and is referred to as "The Father of the Bill of Rights," but what would *he* know about the Constitution?

James Madison's was slightly different, "The Civil rights of none shall be abridged on account of religious belief or worship, nor shall any national religion be established."[168] Oh, yes, you can see that really staunch commitment to secularism, there, can't you?

The First Amendment was written to put limits on the federal government's powers, and the *federal* government only.

What about Education? Surely Americans have always agreed that schoolchildren should be given a secular education? How else could they carry on the way they do today?

Did you know the name of one of America's earliest laws concerning education was the "Old Deluder Satan" law? The rationale it gave for an educated public was that every citizen would know to read the Bible and the laws for themselves, as a counterweight for abuses of either. Opening clauses were, "It being one chief project of that old deluder, Satan, to keep men from the knowledge of the Scriptures, as in former time…"

It wasn't just the younger grades that celebrated the Christian faith. Even Harvard set Christian faith as the cornerstone of their teaching. Yale was similarly founded by ten ministers of the gospel in 1699, with the intent "To plant, and under the Divine Blessing, to propagate in this wilderness the blessed reformed Protestant religion."

But the actual governing of America, wasn't that at least always kept arm's length from religious practice? After reading this far, you don't still really think so, do you? But you'd like some proof. That's fair.

Continuing to borrow citations from the heavily-footnoted *Original Intent*, let's keep going. One of the problems our leaders had to solve was a shortage of Bibles. In 1781, Congress stepped in and provided a direct solution. A resolution was passed to print rather than import them. Congress approved and appointed a Committee to oversee the project.

That wasn't the first time a national shortage of Bibles was of concern to them. On Sept 11, 1777, Congress agreed to order the Committee of Commerce to import 20,000 Bibles from Holland, Scotland, or elsewhere into the different ports of the states of the Union. Can you even imagine Congress importing Bibles for distribution today?

Sir Richard Sutton addressed British Parliament, reading a letter from a Crown-appointed Governor in America. "If you ask an American 'Who is his master?' He will tell you he has none, nor any governor but Jesus Christ."[169]

The rationale [America's earliest law concerning education] gave for an educated public was that every citizen would know to read the Bible and the laws for themselves, as a counterweight for abuses of either.

During the Revolutionary War, the British called our clergy "The Black Regiment." Why? Because of so many stories like the formation of the Eighth Virginia Regiment, which was formed at the close of a sermon that consisted of a call to arms. The preacher removed his clerical robes, revealing a military uniform, and proceeded to call for recruits at the back door of the Church. How many men answered that call to arms? Three hundred Christian patriots.

Christianity is hardly a clever new innovation that Evangelicals have come up with. It's part of America. You can trace it straight back through the earliest original documents. For example, of the 200 words in the text of the Mayflower Compact, God was referenced no fewer than four times, five if you count the date. When we finalized our Treaty with Britain after the

Revolutionary War, that treaty began with the words, "In the name of the most Holy and Undivided Trinity."

Our politicians love to stand in public when they have lofty ideas about how we need to change to match their vision, where they throw around phrases like "this is not who we are" and "America is better than this." But an honest look at our history shows their new and improved ideas have nothing to do with who we have been as a nation historically. What's more, nobody has asked us if we actually want the kind of change they try to force down *our* throats.

But who are we, really ... today? Are we, as a nation, the new secular creature the Left wants to champion? Or are our roots pulsing with something that cannot be severed from the Christian faith without losing some sense of ourselves in the transformation?

John Adams had a clear opinion on whether our society could get far without the body politic being, in some sense, Christian. He said,

> We have no government armed with power capable of contending with human passions unbridled by morality and religion. Avarice, ambition, revenge or gallantry would break the strongest cords of our Constitution as a whale goes through a net. Our Constitution is designed only for a moral and religious people. It is wholly inadequate for any other.[170]

He wasn't the only one to make that observation. The prospect of liberty hinges on a free people who don't need a government constantly hounding them to act in a moral way one to another – that's a job for the preachers to work out. Government need not busy itself in micromanaging the people.

Of course, if the people aren't being steered into treating one another – or the rule of law itself – honorably, the whole system breaks down, as we see in that "like a whale through a net" quote.

Our system of freedom requires a people committed to using that freedom in very specific, morally just ways. When society breaks down into an exercise of every man for himself, it crumbles under its own weight. "Men, in a word, must necessarily be controlled, either by a power within them, or by a power without them; either by the word of God, or by the strong arm of man; either by the Bible, or by the bayonet," are the words of Robert Charles Winthrop.[171]

If we, as a nation, truly want to embrace the birthright of our freedom set out for us by the Framers, there is no surer way than for America to embrace the faith that led them to discover that freedom. From where would we seek the freedom of "life liberty and the pursuit of happiness" if those "cords of our Constitution" are no longer sufficient to direct the hearts of Americans, and our vices burst through them, as predicted?

Of all the Americans to weigh in on this topic, our first President was especially well-positioned to do so. Not only did he desire to become free, fight to become free, but he took part in the Constitutional Convention so that we could remain that way, and retired rather than accept a longer term in office, to lead by example. What did *he* have to say about Christian faith's role in America? At the conclusion of his public life, in his Farewell Address he said the following:

Of all the dispositions and habits which lead to political prosperity, religion and morality are indispensable supports. In vain would that man claim the tribute of patriotism, who should labor to subvert these great pillars of human happiness, these firmest props of the duties of men and citizens. The mere politician, equally with the pious man, ought to respect and to cherish them. A volume could not trace all their connections with private and public felicity. Let it simply be asked: Where is the security for property, for reputation, for life, if the sense of religious obligation desert the oaths which are the instruments of investigation in courts of justice? And let us with caution indulge the supposition that morality can be maintained without religion. Whatever may be conceded to the influence of refined education on minds of peculiar structure, reason and experience both forbid us to expect that national morality can prevail in exclusion of religious principle.[172]

If the question we are asking is "would Jesus have voted for Trump," we need to consider what kind of leader he became. He valued America's history of Christian faith, and welcomed it. He secured Christian freedoms including speech and worship. He pressed ahead with pro-life issues.

Whatever fingers someone may point at his private religious life – and Romans 14:4 cautions us all about playing that game – as a President, he has been very good for Christianity.

What did scripture say about praying for our leaders? Was it that they become perfectly orthodox, checking off all the right Christian boxes? Or was that bar set just a little lower?

I urge, then, first of all, that petitions, prayers, intercession and thanksgiving be made for all people— for kings and all those in authority, that we may live peaceful and quiet lives in all godliness and holiness. This is good, and pleases God our Savior. (1 Ti. 2:1-3, NIV)

If that's what the apostle Paul hoped a national leader would be for the Church ... well Trump has passed that test with flying colors. The Christian church only asks to be left alone, free to live as God calls us to live.

After that last guy took the *Little Sisters Of The Poor* to court, the distinctions between the parties could not be any more clear. Even among Republicans, Trump has been far more bold about these issues than other elected Republicans.

You didn't really believe God was a big fan of big, bloated government, did you? Have you forgotten that it was the Thrice-holy God Himself that gave that warning in 1 Samuel 8?

But the thing displeased Samuel, when they said, Give us a king to judge us. And Samuel prayed unto the Lord.

"And the Lord said unto Samuel, Hearken unto the voice of the people in all that they say unto thee: for they have not rejected thee, but they have rejected Me, that I should not reign over them." (1 Sa. 8:7, ESV)

The prophet Samuel then warned Israel what a king (i.e. big government) would do. He will take ... he will take ... he will take ... Six times he warned them about all the different sorts of things a bloated government would devour for its own use. Looking at just these issues among so many others we might mention, of the two parties on the ballot – was there ever any contest? He'd vote for the one that left Christians free to be, well, Christians. In light of all this, the better question is why *wouldn't* He pull the lever for Trump?

CHAPTER TWENTY-FIVE

A Special Word For Christians "Too Spiritual" To Vote

Doug Giles

Since the moment Trump came down that Golden Escalator, I've been McLovin' it. This isn't my first rodeo. I've been to enough "Christian" and "Conservative" shindigs to know just how deceiving looks can really be.

Anyone can say they're on the side of angels. But getting up close and seeing what some of the fools we've pushed onto pedestals really are is enough to cure you of hero worship forever. You never know which "hero" might be throwing up in the punch bowl, off in the back, doing blow off the stomach of a hooker, or doing Lord alone knows what else.

Face it, the swamp is real and it is soul-sucking. It sucks in critters from every walk of life, *especially* the ones who think they're too pure of heart to succumb to the sucking.

There's a long list of wanna-be white knights sent to DC promising to clean up this town, only to have been shipwrecked by promises the swamp can offer of power, wealth, prestige, pleasure or ... you name it.

Jesus took dead aim at this kind of people-pleasing when He compared how the crowds reacted to Himself vs. Juan el Bautista.

> *They are like children sitting in the marketplace and calling out to each other: "We played the pipe for you, and you did not dance; we sang a dirge, and you did not cry." (Lk. 7:32, ESV)*

Not Trump. He is a different sort of cat. The very thing people use as a criticism against him is his best protection against that siren song. He has never once pretended to have that "unassailable purity of heart." He even jokes about tee-totaling being one of his 'only good traits'.

Trump's resistance to the swamp doesn't come from a heart as pure as the driven snow. Not at all. He's got a different kind of defense against it. It isn't even all that complicated. The swamp can't offer him anything he doesn't already have. The promises the swamp uses to corrupt good men are things that Trump already has. He is not a bought man. Supposing the saying was true that "every man has a price," his snappy answer would be that nobody in Washington could afford his rates.

We've sent plenty of "good" men to Washington. How did that work out? Again and again they fell short. Sometimes, spectacularly.

Sure, Dubya was a genial guy who tried to work across party lines. McCain was a war hero. Romney was a boy scout. But all that and a couple of bucks will get you a cup of java at Dunkin' Donuts.

Ted Cruz, indisputably, is a "good man" by the common standard. He's a man of integrity. A man of faith. A man of conviction. But is being a "good man" enough in picking ourselves a representative to send into the dirty street fight we're seeing in DC?

Is that, alone, enough when the media will suck you into their mosh pit grinding you down as a "racist" or a "war criminal" day after day, probing for that weak point in your armor to destroy you? Did being a "decent man" help Dubya? Or was that, too, exploited by his enemies? Did being a war hero and a "moderate" help McCain? Or did they walk all over him? Romney was a perfect gentleman with moderate policies on health care. He even took the high road in his debates with Obama. Did Barack return the favor? Or did he jump him in the alley while the so-called moderator curb-stomped him into the dirt? Then the media got their turn, hammering him for the "sin" of having a collection of successful women's resumes at his disposal. "Binders full of women" became a proof positive that he was sexist.

The same feminist journos who beat the stuffing out of Sarah Palin, running her pregnant daughter through the media meat grinder and pointing their gnarled fingers at Palin when a schizophrenic shot Gabby Giffords, suddenly got the vapours over Romney's "outrageous treatment" of dear, sweet, helpless women. And what were these supposedly "good men" really like when their shot had passed them by?

Dubya? McCain? Romney? Washington ate them alive. Not a single one of them had the guts to back the GOP candidate in the 2016 election. There's gratitude for you. Thanks for nothing.

Dubya was ritually curb-stomped by the media as a "War Criminal" and "literally Hitler." Was it Stockholm Syndrome that had his family supporting either Hillary Clinton or nobody at all? Bush somehow found it in himself to forgive the Obamas for blaming him for every mistake Obama ever made. He stood in stoic silence through it all. Dubya forgave them for those slights and is BFF and "partner in crime" with Michelle Obama. Everything with Obama was water under the bridge, but suddenly the Presidential tradition of shutting up and letting the new President run the country without interference is forgotten once Trump blew into town. Again, thanks for nothing Dubya. If you couldn't speak up when #44 was setting fire to the Constitution, you've got nothing worth hearing now.

McCain was a Vietnam Vet. A war hero. He was a freaking POW at the Hanoi Hilton. That makes him a hero, right? Yes, it does. And ... No, it doesn't. It means he was a hero in the Vietnam Era. Nobody can take that away from him. But what was he like here at home, in peacetime, once elected?

Do we remember Benedict Arnold for his heroic leadership at Saratoga, or for selling us out to the British? Are there any grand monuments built to "Hero Benny?" Eh, probably not.

Should we remember McCain for what he endured in the Hanoi Hilton while somehow forgetting what he did as a Senator?

I remember – don't you? – that it was McCain's own staff that came up with the idea to weaponize the IRS against Tea Party and Patriot groups.[173]

I remember – don't you? – that it was McCain, who had explicitly campaigned on a promise of scrapping Obamacare, and then became an instant hero to the Left when he single-handedly salvaged it with his infamous thumbs-down.[174]

I remember – don't you? – that McCain's office was a key link in the chain that put the Clintonian "Dirty Dossier" into the hands of Buzzfeed, and if that weren't enough, he was the gleeful patsy who "leaked" to James Comey, serving in the role of "useful idiot" for those who wanted the credibility of a senior Republican bringing the Steele Dossier forward.[175]

What about Romney, the boy scout? He turned out to be among the bitterest of our "bitter" clingers. He actively opposed Trump during 2016. Then he came to DC, cap in hand hoping for a Presidential Appointment to Secretary of State. He didn't get it.

But Trump held out an olive branch when Romney ran for Senate. How did Romney thank him? By writing a scathing screed in the Washington Post the day after he took office.[176] All sweetness and light, that guy is. But that's not all. He was also one of the twelve Senators who voted in opposition to the lawful use of legislation already on the books granting Presidential authority to use Emergency powers for stemming illegal immigration.

Trump wasn't just a Trump Card -- he was truly a *Wildcard*. That scares people. It scares the ones whose knees we want to see shaking.

That wildcard, and the shakeup he promised to bring with him, is exactly what the doctor ordered for Washington's case of swamp fever. But not everybody likes a shakeup. Especially the old boys' clubs with their cozy relationships and their *quid pro quos.*

Democrats were getting nervous. And so were the RINOs. What did all the support for the upstart new guy mean for the established order? Trump was literally *promising* to smash their delicate system.

That is exactly the kind of cat I wanted to throw among the pigeons in DC. But it wasn't just me, was it? It was me, and some 63 Million of my closest friends.

Sure, Trump isn't the "safe" choice. But what good have those safe choices done for us lately?

The moderates we kept sending to DC fold like a dollar-store lawn chair under Michael Moore's blubbery backside. Time had come for a new plan. We want a fighter. Someone who won't yield to pressure. Who owes nothing to anybody. Who will fight back ... and *win.*

Trump's got spirit and fight a-plenty. But can this John-ny-come-lately carry the conservative banner? Even some of the writers in my rowdy mosh pit of a political website, ClashDaily.com, had their doubts. Cruz? His political dues are paid up and he has taken his lumps as a proven conservative, but Trump ...? The jury was still out. It took a little while, but they came to see that he meant what he said. He earned their respect. The more they saw of his campaign, the better they liked him.

Other "conservative" writers were having none of it. They began, and remained, solidly NeverTrumpkins. Nothing and nobody would change their mind. They would sooner vote Hillary to preserve the "ideological purity" of the conservative movement. Purity? Have these clowns looked up and down the bench of RINOs on our team? You're seriously siding with Jeff Flake in the name of "purity"?

Trump, to them, is the ultimate bad boy. These "spotless souls" in the Beltway can't be seen endorsing a billionaire Playboy with a penchant for pretty girls. That's inexcusable. Far better for these pure ones to vote for the party that gaslights conservatives with accusations of homophobe, misogynist and racist all day long.

Far better to put the wife of the guy credibly accused of rape back in office – electing the woman who managed the "bimbo eruptions" and intimidated Bill's female accusers into silence, than it is to vote for some guy who brags about his sexual conquests, and just how "forward" a pretty stranger will let him be with her -- just because he's rich and famous.

It's way more spiritual to look down your nose at your own party's elected nominee and back the party who will gladly shred our Constitutional rights. Way more spiritual to support the Lardy Hagfish and her Rainbow Revolution with their jackboot enforcement of who makes what cake for whom.

Look at Bill Kristol. There's a fine example of that Never-Trumpkin moral authority. It's the same moral authority that drove *The Weekly Standard* into insolvency, where Kristol popped up again, whack-a-mole style with some new fellow travelers on *The Bulwark*. *The Bulwark*'s funding comes from a group created by Left-leaning Ebay creator Pierre Omidyar. A real shocker, eh? And what important article did they run, right out of the gate, little kiddies? Why, it was a story about Miss Occasional-Cortex "owning" the conservatives, of course.

Whoa Nelly! Now there is a man of principal, showing his commitment to those conservative *bona fides*.

Conservative *bona fides*? Let's have a little fact-check on that, shall we?

His Conservative principles are such powerful motivators for him that he donated to an oh-so credible Democrat candidate who would stand by Kristol's convictions much better than anybody on the Right possibly could.

Maybe you heard of him: Governor Northam in Virginia.

Name not ringing a bell? He was that neurosurgeon who had a Blackface / KKK yearbook photo. He did the Moonwalk dressed as Michael Jackson with "a bit of shoe polish" on his cheeks. He talked about Infanticide like deciding whether a newborn should have its life saved or not is the most natural thing in the world.

Let's all hear more about your "principled support of infanticide," Bill.

Sean Davis, co-founder of *The Federalist*, fish slapped Kristol on Twitter with this line:

> Nothing conserves conservatism like @BillKristol donating money to blackfaced pro-infanticide Democrat Ralph Northam, taking cash from a left-

wing foundation that's given millions to Planned Parenthood, and then sending a nutjob abortion activist to mock pro-lifers at @CPAC.[177]

Jonah Goldberg was – and is – devoutly anti-Trump. He's not won over by any of the policies or appointments of the Trump administration. He and Steve Hays just launched a new Trump-skeptical media company. Bold move there, Captain Courage.

Would now be a bad time to bring up that, two years into his Presidency, the Heritage Foundation counted a 64% completion of the 334 "unique policy recommendations" on the Heritage Foundation's wish list to Trump? *Ronaldus Magnus* at the same point in his presidency managed only 49%, even though The Great Communicator presented their 'Mandate for Leadership' document to his cabinet.

Still too "controversial" for you is he, Jonah? Could it be the problem isn't ideology or policy? Maybe he's just not *good enough* to hang with you at your DC soirees? Or are you afraid that supporting him might mean that you might get disinvited yourself? A Democrat with integrity, Alan Dershowitz was willing to pay that price to support Trump where he was right.

But somehow NeverTrumpkins – not so much.

The tut-tutting NeverTrumpkins might as well be saying, "If only the ignorant rubes really knew what kind of a man they were dealing with, they'd never vote Trump again."

Why does that attitude sound so familiar? Oh, that's right. That's exactly how the Pharisees were talking to the Lamb of God when a "dirty whore" was worshipping Him. How dare she.

She kissed His feet, washed them with her tears, and dried them with her hair. The Pharisee thought the woman was too "unclean" to be seen with him, but the Pharisee didn't think to ask whether he – personally – was also too "unclean" for Jesus to hang out with. Funny how Jesus saw things through a different lens than the "experts" of His day.

Twenty centuries later, society still has their self-appointed hall monitors. Maybe nobody asked your permission, Jonah.

How about Yahweh? What's the Good Lord's pick of the pack going to look like if He were voting? Remember, the choices He makes aren't always the obvious ones.

Would an unschooled fisherman be your pick for preaching the Good News to the Jewish center of learning? What about Paul? He was an expert in the Jewish Law right? What a waste of learning that would be, shipping him off to the Gentile pagans.

Plot Twist! The Lord of Glory chose the base to shame the wise. He picked the Super-Jewish rulekeeper to teach grace to the pagans, and the dirt-under-his-fingernails fisherman to teach the legal scholars that faith is about more than just the book-learning and rituals.

Wouldn't it be just like Him to play the same kind of switcheroo with Trump? The Donald is not exactly the guy you'd expect to be a man of the hour to carry the conservative banner. That's for sure. He's got himself a sketchy past, and he's only recently joined anything resembling a conservative cause. Cue the Church Lady whispers: *gasp* "did you know Donald Trump is ... divorced? And he's an adulterer, dontcha know?"

Then again, who could have predicted a divorced and remarried B-list Actor would one day find himself listed among the greatest Presidents ever to take the Oath of Office? His generation of Church Ladies probably didn't like Ronald Reagan either.

All the experts and insiders warned us about how bad Trump would be. They staked their professional reputations on it. So, how bad *was* he? How much harm did he do to the Conservative brand during his first two years in office?

He has been easily the most pro-life administration since Roe v. Wade.

He has been appointing Constitutionalist judges by the boatload.

He has picked a fight on the issue of border security, spending a lot of his political capital defending this issue, with precious little help from any RINOs in Congress.

Jerusalem – he didn't just promise to move the embassy to their national capital like all the Presidents since Clinton ... he delivered. And, savvy realtor that he is, he delivered a creative solution that got the job done in a hurry and didn't break the bank.

He entrenched religious freedoms. He didn't just bring back the freedom to wish someone a Merry Christmas, he is actively pushing to protect religious freedoms. For example, the *Presidential Executive Order Promoting Free Speech and Religious Liberty*.[178]

The rejection of Socialism: At the very moment when the political left is excitedly embracing their inner Stalin, running

Bernie Sanders, and glomming onto a Green New Deal that abolishes air travel and cow farts, Trump has unleashed his inner Reagan and gone on the offensive against the scourge of socialism.

In a speech addressing the troubles in Venezuela, he made the following bold statement, "The twilight hour of socialism has arrived," Trump said, adding that the 50 nations that have recognized Guaidó as the legitimate leader of Venezuela have a "shared interest" in preventing the spread of socialism. "To those who would impose socialism on the U.S.," he said, "we again deliver a very simple message: America will never be a socialist country."[179]

He made ISIS into WAS-WAS and the caliphate is no more. He promised the destruction of the territorial stronghold ISIS held in the Middle East, which had spread like cancer during Obama's administration. He made good on that promise. There are only a few localized holdouts remaining, and they are being systematically taken apart.

Obama had hampered military investment and maintenance both by endless missions and by use of his sequestration to curb desperately-needed military spending. He also made the military lose face by declaring red lines without actually following through on them. Trump, on the other hand, follows through on any threat he makes. He looks for opportunities to disengage when a war footing no longer serves a national interest, and he motivates other allied nations to step up and pull their weight when it comes to mutual defense arrangements like NATO.

He pulls out of treaties that are harmful to our international standing or that have not been honored by our counterparts.

He is pouring money into expanding and improving our military readiness, to avoid unnecessary accidents and fatalities associated with funding related deficiencies in staffing and training. He has been establishing a presence in space – where our rivals have already made themselves active.

What else has Trump done?

Oh, nothing much, he's just:

Put a stake in the heart of climate cultism when he set fire to the Paris Accord.

He gave us the first comprehensive tax cut package since the freaking Cold War.

He took a buzzsaw through government red tape by instituting a 2:1 removal policy. (EO 13771, look it up![180]) Two bad government laws come out for every new one written. According to The Office of Information and Regulatory Affairs data, that works out to a savings of $33 billion in net regulatory savings as of the 2018 midterms.

He axed the Iran Deal.

He canceled some of Obama's Executive Orders.

Unlike the last couple of wizards in office before him, Trump has read Article II and is restraining his own actions as President to this little thing called "stuff a President is allowed to do."

He's championing Trade reform.

He's using sanctions and diplomacy more than bombs and missiles in his foreign policy and has seen some tentative steps back from the brink of a potential shooting war in North Korea.

The Spotless Lamb no likey some of Trump's peccadilloes, sure. But what was it He said to the last group who dragged a guilty party to Him, confident that His religiosity would drive Him to stone the sinner?

Now, I may have only gone to public school, but I'm pretty sure He said something along the lines of "let him who is without sin throw the first stone," didn't He?

I've seen enough holier-than-thou types on pedestals scorn all those hapless sinners, only to find themselves in an embarrassing headline involving drugs, a hooker, or someone else's money that I'm gonna take some of the Lord's advice on this one.

You might think I mean the one about the plank and the eye. That's good advice too. But I'm thinking about the tree and its fruit.

He gave it as a test for Prophets, but it works for Politicians, too. Let's measure a politician by what he does, not just by what he says.

And by that standard, Trump's doing better than just "alright."

APPENDIX

TRUMP ART
&
ABOUT THE AUTHORS

Doug Giles earned his Bachelor of Fine Arts degree from Texas Tech University. His preferred mediums are oil paint and charcoal. His online gallery is DougGiles.Art.

Enjoy the following political pieces he's cobbled together regarding President Trump, Beto and Ocasio-Cortez.

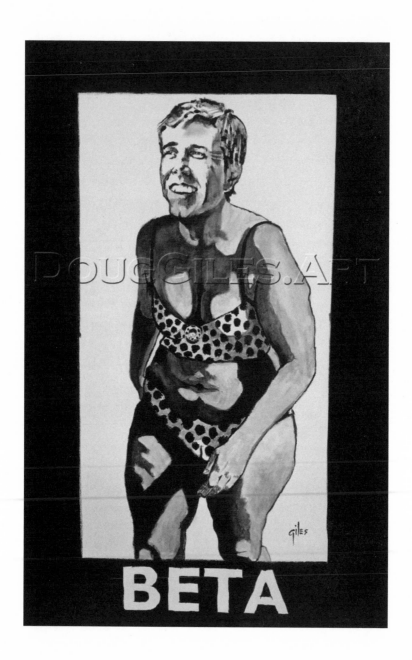

BETA

Doug Giles

Doug Giles is the co-founder and co-host of the Warriors & Wildmen podcast and the man behind ClashDaily.com. In addition to driving ClashDaily.com (250M+ page views), Giles is the author of the best-selling book, *PUSSIFICATION: The Effeminization Of The American Male.*

Doug's also an artist and his online gallery can be seen here at DougGiles.Art.

Doug earned his Bachelor of Fine Arts degree from Texas Tech University and his certificates in both Theological and Biblical Studies from Knox Theological Seminary.

Doug's articles have also appeared on several other print and online news sources, including Townhall.com, The Washington Times, The Daily Caller, Fox Nation, USA Today, The Wall Street Journal, The Washington Examiner, American Hunter Magazine and ABC News.

Giles and his wife Margaret have two daughters, Hannah and Regis. Hannah devastated ACORN with her 2009 nation-shaking undercover videos and she currently stars in the explosive, 2018 Tribeca Documentary, Acorn and The Firestorm. Regis has been featured in Elle, American Hunter, and Variety magazines. Regis is also the author of a powerful new book titled, *How Not To Be A #Me-Too Victim, But A #WarriorChick* (White Feather Press-March 2018). Regis and Hannah are both black belts in Gracie/Valente Jiu Jitsu.

DG's interests include guns, big game hunting, big game fishing, fine art, cigars, helping wounded warriors, and being a big pain in the butt to people who dislike God and the USA.

Accolades for Giles and ClashDaily.com include:

– Giles was recognized as one of "The 50 Best Conservative Columnists Of 2015"

– Giles was recognized as one of "The 50 Best Conservative Columnists Of 2014"

– Giles was recognized as one of "The 50 Best Conservative Columnists Of 2013"

– ClashDaily.com was recognized as one of "The 100 Most Popular Conservative Websites For 2013"

– Doug was noted as "Hot Conservative New Media Superman" By Politichicks

Speaking Engagements.

Doug Giles speaks to college, business, community, church, advocacy and men's groups throughout the United States and internationally. His expertise includes issues of Christianity and culture, masculinity vs. metrosexuality, big game hunting and fishing, raising righteous kids in a rank culture, the Second Amendment, personal empowerment, politics, and social change. Giles charges $5,000 per speaking engagement, plus food, hotel and travel expenses. For availability, please contact us at Clash@ClashDaily.com. Use 'SPEAKING ENGAGEMENT' for subject line.

Props.

"Doug Giles is a good man, and his bambinas are fearless. His girls Hannah and Regis Giles are indefatigable. I admire the Giles clan from afar." – Dennis Miller

"Doug Giles must be some kind of a great guy if CNN wants to impugn him." – Rush Limbaugh

"Doug Giles is a substantive and funny force for traditional values." – Ann Coulter, best-selling author

"Doug Giles speaks the truth ... he's a societal watchdog ... a funny bastard." – Ted Nugent, rock icon

OTHER BOOKS BY DOUG GILES

The Political Wisdom of Ocasio-Cortez (*Coming Spring 2019!*)

Pussification: The Effeminization of the American Male

Rise, Kill and Eat: A Theology of Hunting from Genesis to Revelation

Rules for Radical Christians: 10 Biblical Disciplines for Influential Believers

Raising Righteous and Rowdy Girls

Raising Boys Feminists Will Hate

My Grandpa is a Patriotic Badass

If You're Going Through Hell, Keep Going!

A Coloring Book for College Cry Babies

The Bulldog Attitude

Sandy Hook Massacre: When Seconds Count - Police Are Minutes Away

A Time to Clash

10 Habits of Decidedly Defective People: The Successful Loser's Guide to Life

Political Twerps, Cultural Jerks, Church Quirks

Brandon Vallorani

Brandon Vallorani is a practiced entrepreneur and accomplished CEO, recognized by peers and media outlets as a visionary leader and powerhouse executive who "knows a thing or two about marketing."

Brandon's background in graphic design, marketing, and executive management have resulted in continually increasing success. Colleagues have commended Brandon for creating an environment that not only allows but encourages people to succeed both professionally and personally. Brandon is an achiever and a positive thinker who is happiest when creating a new world to conquer.

Author of *The Wolves and the Mandolin: Celebrating Life's Privileges In A Harsh World (ForbesBooks; 2017)*, Brandon begins with the Vallorani family's modest beginnings in Italy, regales readers with legend-worthy stories of great-grandfather Luigi's first years in America, and culminates with his journey into entrepreneurship.

After graduating from West Virginia University with a Bachelor's Degree of Fine Arts in Graphic Design, Vallorani began his career in the non-profit sector in 1998. Within a window of 6 years, Brandon developed and led a number of strategic plans, improving online traffic by 151%, expanding radio network reach by 100%, and boosting annual company revenue by 700%.

Quickly rising through the ranks to Executive Vice President, he simultaneously earned his Master of Business Administration from Thomas More University in 2004.

He went on to another non-profit, boosting annual revenues from a few hundred thousand dollars to several million in a period of a mere three years, while co-founding Tolle Lege Press with his father, Ray.

As their first project, TLP raised over $100,000 for the reproduction of a historic masterpiece: The 1599 Geneva Bible, which bears much historical significance to the Reformation period, and came to America with the Mayflower. All but lost in obscurity and available only without modern spelling and punctuation, until the first updated reproduction was published and made available to the public in 2006 by Tolle Lege Press.

Brandon utilized his expertise in marketing to advertise this historic treasure in both traditional and modern media avenues, and since its publication, TLP has distributed over 140,000 copies in 13 different formats. Along with this stunning project, TLP published over 20 additional titles.

In 2007, Brandon branched out into yet another entrepreneurial endeavor, with the founding of a webstore that would eventually increase to a group of news commentary sites and explode into a network of websites and webstores known as Liberty Alliance.

Recognized on the Inc. 5000 list of America's fastest growing privately held companies for five consecutive years (2012-2016), Vallorani sold to Liftable Media in 2017, and shifted his focus to consulting through Romulus Marketing, LLC, specifically helping those in the conservative and religious markets build their empires.

Through a variety of sites and stores, Vallorani and team provide the American patriot with conservative-themed resources including Keep & Bear.com, RepublicanLegion.com, ThrasherCoffee.com, and content site FlagandCross.com, among others.

Brandon Vallorani is a legendary figure in the entrepreneurial world and an astute businessman who proves the American dream can be achieved with hard work and vision. A Forbes.com contributor, he has been interviewed by numerous podcasts, magazines, and online sites.

Vallorani resides in Metro-Atlanta, GA, with his wife with whom he shares seven children, a son-in-law, and two grandchildren. In his free time, he enjoys traveling, his dogs, and learning Italian.

NOTES

[1] Jack Shepherd, "Donald Trump wins: Video of MSNBC host Rachel Maddow reminding viewers 'you're not dead' resurfaces." *The Independent.* November 9, 2016.
https://www.independent.co.uk/arts-entertainment/tv/news/donald-trump-wins-msnbc-rachel-maddow-youre-not-dead-dreaming-a7406906.html.

[2] "Still The Best Election Night Compilation Video Of All Time." *YouTube video.* November 9, 2017.
https://www.youtube.com/watch?v=Lrpkxl4DXtk.

[3] "In 1997, Trump discussed Alicia Machado's weight." *YouTube video.* September 27, 2016.
https://www.youtube.com/watch?v=PpXsAoXZIMg.

[4] "Even Hillary wonders why she isn't '50 points ahead'." *YouTube.* September 22, 2016.
https://www.youtube.com/watch?v=tVCHU4wCBQg.

[5] "German home-school family will not be deported from US." *BBC News.* March 5, 2014.
https://www.bbc.com/news/world-us-canada-26454988.

[6] "Clinton Speaks Out Against Ban On Gay Marriage – 2004." *C-Span.* July 13, 2004.
https://www.c-span.org/video/?c4627199/senator-hillary-clinton-speaks-ban-gay-marriage-2004.

[7] "Remarks at the Annual Convention of Kiwanis International." *The Ronald Reagan Presidential Foundation & Institute.* July 6,1987.
https://www.reaganfoundation.org/ronald-reagan/reagan-quotes-speeches/remarks-at-the-annual-convention-of-kiwanis-international/.

[8] "CNN Late Edition With Wolf Blitzer: Interview With Ashraf Qazi; Interview with Donald Trump." *CNN Transcripts*. March 21, 2004. http://www.cnn.com/TRANSCRIPTS/0403/21/le.00.html.

[9] "Obama's NASA Chief: Muslim Outreach Is My Foremost Mission." *The Rush Limbaugh Show*. July 6, 2010. https://www.rushlimbaugh.com/daily/2010/07/06/obama_s_nasa_chief_muslim_outreach_is_my_foremost_mission/

[10] Ann Coulter, "Democracy Is Destiny." *Ann Coulter*. November 14, 2012. http://www.anncoulter.com/columns/2012-11-14.html

[11] "Witches cast 'mass spell' against Donald Trump." *BBC News*. February 25, 2017. https://www.bbc.com/news/world-us-canada-39090334.

[12] Rich Lowry, "Obama the abortion extremist." *Politico*. August 23, 2012. https://www.politico.com/story/2012/08/the-abortion-extremist-080013.

[13] Pema Levy, "Late-Term Abortion Debate Reveals A Rift Between Clinton and Sanders." *Mother Jones*. March 11, 2016. https://www.motherjones.com/politics/2016/03/hillary-clinton-late-term-abortions/.

[14] "Kathy Tran Presents Virginia Third Trimester Abortion Bill In Committee." *YouTube video*. January 29, 2019. https://www.youtube.com/watch?time_continue=5&v=OMFzZ5I30dg.

[15] Devan Cole, "Virginia Governor faces backlash over comments supporting late-term abortion bill." *CNN*. January 31, 2019. https://www.cnn.com/2019/01/31/politics/ralph-northam-third-trimester-abortion/index.html.

[16] Betsy McCaughey, "These abortion laws aren't what 'pro-choice' is supposed to mean." *New York Post*. February 13, 2019. https://nypost.com/2019/02/13/these-abortion-laws-arent-what-pro-choice-is-supposed-to-mean/.

[17] Jason L. Riley, "Let's Talk About the Black Abortion Rate." *Wall Street Journal*. July 10, 2018.

https://www.wsj.com/articles/lets-talk-about-the-black-abortion-rate-1531263697.

[18] Margaret Sanger, "The Eugenic Value of Birth Control Propaganda (Oct 1921)." *New York University, Margaret Sanger Project.* Copyright 2003. Margaret Sanger Project. https://www.nyu.edu/projects/sanger/webedition/app/documents/show. php?sangerDoc=238946.xml.

[19] Margaret Sanger, "My Way To Peace (Jan. 17, 1932)." *New York University, Margaret Sanger Project.* Copyright 2003. Margaret Sanger Project. https://www.nyu.edu/projects/sanger/webedition/app/documents/ show.php?sangerDoc=129037.xml.

[20] Anna Grossu, "Margaret Sanger, racist, eugenicist extraordinaire." *The Washington Times.* May 5, 2014. https://www.washingtontimes.com/news/2014/may/5/grossu-margaret-sanger-eugenicist/.

[21] Linda Long, "Abortion in Canada." *The Canadian Encyclopedia.* Last modified by Richard Foot, October 24, 2016. https://www.thecanadianencyclopedia.ca/en/article/abortion.

[22] Brandon Showalter, "The West Is Colonizing Africa With Abortion and Population Control, Obianuju Ekeocha Says." *The Christian Post.* July 14, 2018. https://www.christianpost.com/news/the-west-is-colonizing-africa-abortion-population-control-obianuju-ekeocha-says.html.

[23] Donald J. Trump, "Remarks by President Trump in State of the Union Address." *WhiteHouse.gov.* February 6, 2019. https://www.whitehouse.gov/briefings-statements/remarks-president-trump-state-union-address-2/.

[24] Adrian Norman, "2019 is the New 1984." *The Epoch Times.* Last modified March 10, 2019. https://www.theepochtimes.com/2019-is-the-new-1984_2827109.html.

[25] William Cummings, "'I am a nationalist': Trump's embrace of controversial label sparks uproar." *USA Today.* Last modified November 12, 2018. https://www.usatoday.com/story/news/politics/2018/10/24/trump-says-hes-nationalist-what-means-why-its-controversial/1748521002/.

26 Ronald Reagan, "Election Eve Address A Vision for America." *Ronald Reagan Presidential Library & Museum.* November 3, 1980. https://www.reaganlibrary.gov/11-3-80.

27 Ronald Reagan, "Farewell Address to the Nation." *Ronald Reagan Presidential Library & Museum.* January 11, 1989 .https://www.reaganlibrary.gov/011189i.

28 "Facts and Case Summary – Engel v. Vitale." *United States Courts.* https://www.uscourts.gov/educational-resources/educational-activities/facts-and-case-summary-engel-v-vitale.

29 "A History of Key Abortion Rulings of the U.S. Supreme Court." *Pew Research Center.* January 16, 2013. https://www.pewforum.org/2013/01/16/a-history-of-key-abortion-rulings-of-the-us-supreme-court/#regulations.

30 "Obergefell v. Hodges." *SCOTUSblog.* https://www.scotusblog.com/case-files/cases/obergefell-v-hodges/.

31 "Masterpiece Cakeshop, Ltd. V. Colorado Civil Rights Commission." *SCOTUSblog.* https://www.scotusblog.com/case-files/cases/masterpiece-cakeshop-ltd-v-colorado-civil-rights-commn/.

32 "Colorado baker back in court over second LGBTQ bias allegation." *NBC News.* December 19, 2018. https://www.nbcnews.com/feature/nbc-out/colorado-baker-back-court-over-second-lgbtq-bias-allegation-n949836.

33 "National Federation of Independent Business v. Sebelius." *SCOTUSblog.* https://www.scotusblog.com/case-files/cases/national-federation-of-independent-business-v-sebelius/.

34 Jonathan Turley, "Yes, Trump has authority to declare national emergency for border wall." *The Hill.* January 8, 2019. https://thehill.com/opinion/judiciary/424314-yes-trump-has-authority-to-declare-national-emergency-for-border-wall.

35 Adam Cohen, "The Supreme Court Ruling That Led To 70,000 Forced Sterilizations." *NPR.* March 7, 2016.

https://www.npr.org/sections/health-shots/2016/03/07/469478098/the-supreme-court-ruling-that-led-to-70-000-forced-sterilizations.

[36] "Facts and Case Summary, Korematsu v. U.S." *United States Courts.* https://www.uscourts.gov/educational-resources/educational-activities/facts-and-case-summary-korematsu-v-us.

[37] "Plessy v. Ferguson (1896)." *C-SPAN: Landmark Cases.* http://landmarkcases.c-span.org/Case/19/Plessy-v-Ferguson.

[38] "Dred Scott v. Stanford (1857)." *Cornell Law School.* https://www.law.cornell.edu/wex/dred_scott_v_sandford_%281857%29.

[39] "District of Columbia v. Heller." *SCOTUSblog.* https://www.scotusblog.com/case-files/cases/dc-v-heller/.

[40] Matt Vespa, "CNN And The Curious Case Of The 'Full Semi-Automatic' Rifle." *Townhall.* February 27, 2018. https://townhall.com/tipsheet/mattvespa/2018/02/27/cnn-and-the-curious-case-of-the-full-semiautomatic-rifle-n2454766.

[41] Abigail Tracy "Donald Trump Made Justice Kennedy An Offer He Couldn't Refuse." *Vanity Fair.* June 29, 2018. https://www.vanityfair.com/news/2018/06/donald-trump-justice-anthony-kennedy-retirement.

[42] "Four Examples Showing That Trump Opponents Planned To Attack Any Supreme Court Nominee." *ABC30 St. Louis.* July 10, 2018. https://abcstlouis.com/news/nation-world/four-examples-showing-that-trump-opponents-planned-to-attack-any-supreme-court-nominee.

[43] Chris Cillizza, "How Ruth Bader Ginsburg became the face of the Trump resistance." *CNN.* August 31, 2018. https://www.cnn.com/2018/08/31/politics/ruth-bader-ginsburg-democrats/index.html.

[44] Ibid.

[45] David Davenport, "Democrats finally discover federalism." *Washington Examiner.* April 18, 2018. https://www.washingtonexaminer.com/opinion/democrats-finally-discover-federalism.

[46] "The American Legion v. American Humanist Association." *SCO-TUSblog*. https://www.scotusblog.com/case-files/cases/the-american-legion-v-american-humanist-association/.

[47] Alyssa Milano, Twitter post, March 28, 2019, 9:29 p.m., https://twitter.com/Alyssa_Milano/status/1111440326181322752.

[48] Cristina G. Mittermeier, "Starving-Polar-Bear Photographer Recalls What Went Wrong." *National Geographic*. August 2018. https://www.nationalgeographic.com/magazine/2018/08/explore-through-the-lens-starving-polar-bear-photo/.

[49] Susan J. Crockford, "State of the Polar Bear Report 2018." *The Global Warming Policy Foundation*. February 26, 2019. https://www.thegwpf.org/content/uploads/2019/02/State-of-the-polar-bear2018.pdf.

[50] K. Walker, "Occasional-Cortex Thinks The 'World's Going To End In 12 Years' Because Of 'Climate Change." *ClashDaily*. https://clashdaily.com/2019/01/occasional-cortex-thinks-the-worlds-going-to-end-in-12-years-because-of-climate-change/.

[51] Barack Obama, "Obama's Nomination Victory Speech In St. Paul." *The Huffington Post*. Last modified May 25, 2011. https://www.huffingtonpost.ca/2008/06/03/obamas-nomination-victory_n_105028.html.

[52] Ray Sanchez, "Flint water crisis: Complaint against EPA seeks $220 million in damages." *CNN*. April 26, 2016. https://www.cnn.com/2016/04/26/us/flint-class-action-epa-complaint/index.html.

[53] Mark Esper, "Yes, that letter to the editor about the EPA was published." *Silverton Standard*. August 12, 2015. http://www.silvertonstandard.com/news.php?id=847.

[54] David Bookbinder, "Obama had a chance to really fight climate change. He blew it." *April 29, 2017*. https://www.vox.com/the-big-idea/2017/4/28/15472508/obama-climate-change-legacy-overrated-clean-power.

55 "Al Gore could become the world's first carbon billionaire." *The Telegraph*. November 3, 2009. https://www.telegraph.co.uk/news/earth/energy/6491195/Al-Gore-could-become-worlds-first-carbon-billionaire.html."

56 Geoff Earle, "Climate hawk Bernie Sanders spent $297,000 on private jet travel in ONE MONTH to stump for Democratic candidates." *Daily Mail*. December 5, 2018. https://www.dailymail.co.uk/news/article-6465235/Climate-hawk-Bernie-Sanders-spent-297-000-private-jet-travel-ONE-MONTH.html.

57 Charles C. Mann, "The Book That Incited a Worldwide Fear of Overpopulation." *Smithsonian*. January 8, 2018. https://www.smithsonianmag.com/innovation/book-incited-world-wide-fear-overpopulation-180967499/.

58 "Energy Crisis." *Smithsonian, National Museum of American History*. https://americanhistory.si.edu/american-enterprise-exhibition/consumer-era/energy-crisis.

59 John Tierney, "Fateful Voice of a Generation Still Drowns Out Real Science." *The New York Times*. June 5, 2007. https://www.nytimes.com/2007/06/05/science/earth/05tier.html?module=inline.

60 Peter Gwynne, "The Cooling World." *Newsweek*. April 28, 1975. Accessed on Scribd, March 21 2019. https://www.scribd.com/doc/225798861/Newsweek-s-Global-Cooling-Article-From-April-28-1975.

61 Larry Bell, "Remember The Acid Rain 'Scare'? Global Warming Hysteria Is Pouring Down." *Forbes*. February 11, 2014. https://www.forbes.com/sites/larrybell/2014/02/11/remember-the-acid-rain-scare-global-warming-hysteria-is-pouring-down/#342cc6a053fc.

62 "Nuclear Winter." *Pulitzer Center*. https://pulitzercenter.org/project/nuclear-winter.

63 Mike Ciandella, "Arctic Ice Cap Grows Same Year Al Gore Predicted It Would Disappear, Networks Ignore.: *Newsbusters*. September 2, 2014. https://www.newsbusters.org/blogs/mike-ciandella/2014/09/02/arctic-ice-cap-grows-same-year-al-gore-predicted-it-would-disappear.

[64] Kastalia Medrano, "Climate Change is a Main Cause of the World's Refugee Crisis." *Vice.* June 29, 2017. https://impact.vice.com/en_us/article/pady4y/climate-change-is-a-main-cause-of-the-worlds-refugee-crisis?utm_source=viceadword-sca&utm_medium=cpc.

[65] Alejandra Borunda, "See how a warmer world primed California for larger fires." *National Geographic.* November 15, 2018. https://www.nationalgeographic.com/environment/2018/11/climate-change-california-wildfire/.

[66] "Hurricanes and Climate Change." *Union of Concerned Scientists.* Last updated December 1, 2017. https://www.ucsusa.org/global-warming/science-and-impacts/impacts/hurricanes-and-climate-change.html.

[67] Chris Mooney, "The science behind the U.S.'s strange hurricane 'drought' – and it's sudden end." *The Washington Post.* September 7, 2017. https://www.washingtonpost.com/news/energy-environment/wp/2017/09/07/the-science-behind-the-u-s-s-strange-hurricane-drought-and-its-sudden-end/.

[68] Bill McGuire, "How climate change triggers earthquakes, tsunamis and tornadoes." *The Guardian.* October 16, 2016. https://www.theguardian.com/world/2016/oct/16/climate-change-triggers-earthquakes-tsunamis-volcanoes.

[69] K. Walker, "$29K Is How Much AOC Spent On Rides To Her Office Which Is ONE Minute Away From A Subway." *ClashDaily.* March 4, 2019. https://clashdaily.com/2019/03/29k-is-how-much-aoc-spent-on-rides-to-her-office-which-is-one-minute-away-from-a-subway/.

[70] K. Walker, "Senate Votes 57-0: AOC's GND Is DOA." *ClashDaily.* March 27, 2019. https://clashdaily.com/2019/03/senate-votes-57-0-aocs-gnd-is-doa/.

[71] Wes Walker, "'Hooked On Government Money': Greenpeace Co-Founder Who Mocked AOC Calls 'Green' Scientists Corrupt." March 10, 2019. https://clashdaily.com/2019/03/hooked-on-government-money-greenpeace-co-founder-who-mocked-aoc-calls-green-scientists-corrupt/.

[72] Wes Walker, "Greenpeace Bro Calls Occasional-Cortex A 'POMP-OUS LITTLE TWIT' And It Gets Better." *ClashDaily.* March 4, 2019. https://clashdaily.com/2019/03/greenpeace-green-new-deal-gnd-occasio-cortez/.

[73] Patrick Moore, Twitter post, March 3, 2019, 2:23 p.m. https://twitter.com/EcoSenseNow/status/1102288335572066304.

[74] Patrick Moore, Twitter post, March 3, 2019, 8:09 p.m. https://twitter.com/EcoSenseNow/status/1102375449211023360.

[75] Wes Walker, "'Hooked On Government Money': Greenpeace Co-Founder Who Mocked AOC Calls 'Green' Scientists Corrupt." March 10, 2019. https://clashdaily.com/2019/03/hooked-on-government-money-greenpeace-co-founder-who-mocked-aoc-calls-green-scientists-corrupt/.

[76] K. Walker, "Senate Votes 57-0: AOC's GND Is DOA." *ClashDaily.* March 27, 2019. https://clashdaily.com/2019/03/senate-votes-57-0-aocs-gnd-is-doa/.

[77] Benjamin Storrow, "Global CO2 Emissions Rise after Paris Climate Agreement Signed." *Scientific American.* March 24, 2018. https://www.scientificamerican.com/article/global-co2-emissions-rise-after-paris-climate-agreement-signed/.

[78] Chris Agee, "After Dumping Paris Accords, US Leads World in Reduction of Carbon Emissions." *The Western Journal.* July 18, 2018. https://www.westernjournal.com/after-dumping-paris-accords-us-leads-world-reduction-carbon-emissions/.

[79] Ibid.

[80] "Obama: 'If you like your health care plan, you'll be able to keep your health care plan'." *Politifact.* https://www.politifact.com/obama-like-health-care-keep/.

[81] John Tozzi and Zachary Tracer, "Sky-High Deductibles Broke the U.S. Health Insurance System." *Bloomberg.* June 26, 2018. https://www.bloomberg.com/news/features/2018-06-26/sky-high-deductibles-broke-the-u-s-health-insurance-system.

[82] Jacob Passy, "Businesses eliminated hundreds of thousands of full-time jobs to avoid Obamacare mandate." *MarketWatch*. November 24, 2017. https://www.marketwatch.com/story/businesses-eliminated-hundreds-of-thousands-of-full-time-jobs-to-avoid-obamacare-mandate-2017-11-24.

[83] Alicia Adamczyk, "One-Third of Counties Will Have Just One Obamacare Insurer by 2017." *Money*. August 29, 2016. http://money.com/money/4470574/obamacare-providers-2017/.

[84] Scott Bronstein and Drew Griffin, "Fatal wait: Veterans languish and die on a VA hospital's secret list." *CNN*. April 23, 2014. https://www.cnn.com/2014/04/23/health/veterans-dying-health-care-delays/index.html.

[85] Aurora Banner, "No long MRI waits for furry friends." *York Region News*. February 22, 2011. https://www.yorkregion.com/news-story/1451889-no-long-mri-waits-for-furry-friends/.

[86] "Gard spokesperson: Baby Charlie is effectively 'a prisoner of the state'." *Sky News*. July 16, 2017. https://news.sky.com/story/gard-spokesperson-baby-charlie-is-effectively-a-prisoner-of-the-state-10949732.

[87] Wes Walker, "Little Alfie Evans Is Dead: You Can Thank Socialized Medicine For That." *ClashDaily*. April 28, 2018. https://clashdaily.com/2018/04/little-alfie-evans-dead-can-thank-socialized-medicine/.

[88] Sophie Borland, "'Arrogance' of doctors STILL using banned death pathway because 'they think they know what's best for patients'." *Daily Mail*. December 15, 2015. https://www.dailymail.co.uk/news/article-3361844/Arrogance-doctors-using-banned-death-pathway-think-know-s-best-patients.html.

[89] Gary Rinne, "Appeal board orders OHIP to cover out-of-country medical care." *Thunder Bay News Watch*. January 30, 2019. https://www.tbnewswatch.com/local-news/appeal-board-orders-ohip-to-cover-out-of-country-medical-care-1218166.

[90] Belén Marty, "Inside the Cuban Hospital That Castro Doesn't Want Tourists to See." *Pan Am Post*. October 6, 2015.

https://panampost.com/belen-marty/2015/10/06/inside-the-cuban-hospitals-that-castro-doesnt-want-tourists-to-see/.

[91] "Controversial Cartoons." *Newseum.* January 7, 2015. http://www.newseum.org/2015/01/07/case-study-controversial-cartoons/.

[92] "Western Canadian magazine publishes Muhammad cartoons." *CBC News.* February 13, 2006. https://www.cbc.ca/news/canada/western-canadian-magazine-publishes-muhammad-cartoons-1.591923.

[93] Wes Walker, "Leftists Want A 'New Civil War' – This Post Is Disturbing." *ClashDaily.* April 8, 2018. https://clashdaily.com/2018/04/leftist-want-new-civil-war-post-disturbing/.

[94] "Remarks at the Annual Convention of Kiwanis International." *The Ronald Reagan Presidential Foundation & Institute.* July 6,1987. https://www.reaganfoundation.org/ronald-reagan/reagan-quotes-speeches/remarks-at-the-annual-convention-of-kiwanis-international/.

[95] Kyle Drennen, "Ellen DeGeneres: I Wouldn't Have Trump on Show, He's 'Dangerous for the Country'." *Newsbusters.* September 20, 2017. https://www.newsbusters.org/blogs/nb/kyle-drennen/2017/09/20/ellen-degeneres-wouldnt-have-trump-show-hes-dangerous-country.

[96] Sophia Tesfaye, "'Muslims are a part of the LGBT community, not distinct from it": Watch Dan Savage forcefully push back against Trump's divisive response to Orlando attack." *Salon.* June 15, 2016. https://www.salon.com/2016/06/15/muslims_are_a_part_of_the_lgbt_community_not_distinct_from_it_watch_dan_savage_forcefully_push_back_against_trumps_divisive_response_to_orlando_attack/.

[97] Samantha Allen, "Are Bisexuals Shut Out of the LGBT Club?" *The Daily Beast.* January 3, 2016. https://www.thedailybeast.com/are-bisexuals-shut-out-of-the-lgbt-club.

[98] "5 Common Misconceptions About Sex and Gender." *Teen Vogue* (video). March 29, 2019. https://video.teenvogue.com/watch/5-common-misconceptions-about-sex-and-gender.

[99] Joseph Brean, "Forced to share a room with transgender woman in Toronto shelter, sex abuse victim files human rights complaint." *National Post.* August 2, 2018. https://nationalpost.com/news/canada/kristi-hanna-human-rights-complaint-transgender-woman-toronto-shelter.

[100] Iva Djokovic, "Transgender MMA Fighter Who Broke Female Opponent's Skull. Are We Getting Too 'Politically Correct' With Reality?" *Eastern Europe BJJ.* October 19, 2018. https://www.bjjee.com/articles/transgender-mma-fighter-who-broke-female-opponents-skull-are-we-getting-too-politically-correct-with-reality/.

[101] Martina Navratilova, "The rules on trans athletes reward cheats and punish the innocent." *The Sunday Times.* February 17, 2019. https://www.thetimes.co.uk/article/the-rules-on-trans-athletes-reward-cheats-and-punish-the-innocent-klsrq6h3x.

[102] Valerie Richardson, "Senate Republicans flip script on gay rights by confirming Ric Grenell over Democratic objections." *The Washington Times.* April 27, 2018. https://www.washingtontimes.com/news/2018/apr/27/ric-grenell-gay-conservative-confirmed-us-ambassad/.

[103] Josh Meyer, "The secret backstory of how Obama let Hezbollah off the hook." *Politico.* January 2018. https://www.politico.com/interactives/2017/obama-hezbollah-drug-trafficking-investigation/.

[104] Ibid.

[105] Matthew Lee, "Iran still top state sponsor of terrorism, U.S. report says." *PBS News Hour.* July 19, 2017. https://www.pbs.org/newshour/world/iran-still-top-state-sponsor-terrorism-us-report-says.

[106] Jeffrey Goldberg, "What Obama is Actually Trying to Do in Israel." *The Atlantic.* March 16, 2010. https://www.theatlantic.com/international/archive/2010/03/what-obama-is-actually-trying-to-do-in-israel/37548/.

[107] Jennifer Rubin, "NGO connected to Obama's 2008 campaign used U.S. tax dollars trying to oust Netanyahu." *The Washington Post.* July 12, 2016.

https://www.washingtonpost.com/blogs/right-turn/wp/2016/07/12/ngo-connected-to-obamas-2008-campaign-used-u-s-tax-dollars-trying-to-oust-netanyahu/.

[108] Peter Beaumont, "US abstention allows UN to demand end to Israeli settlements." *The Guardian.* December 23, 1016.
https://www.theguardian.com/world/2016/dec/23/us-abstention-allows-un-to-demand-end-to-israeli-settlements.

[109] Tim Molloy, "When Donald Trump Met Rosa Parks (Photo)." *The Houston Chronicle.* December 1, 2016.
https://www.chron.com/entertainment/the-wrap/article/When-Donald-Trump-Met-Rosa-Parks-Photo-10647898.php.

[110] "Orthodox Child with Rare Ailment is Rescued Aboard Tycoon's Jet." *Jewish Telegraphic Agency.* July 20, 1988.
https://www.jta.org/1988/07/20/archive/orthodox-child-with-rare-ailment-is-rescued-aboard-tycoons-jet.

[111] "Statement by President Trump." *White House.* August 14, 2017.
https://www.whitehouse.gov/briefings-statements/statement-president-trump/.

[112] Mark Berman, "Charlottesville car attacker could be prosecuted as a hate crime, Sessions." August 16, 2017.
https://www.washingtonpost.com/news/post-nation/wp/2017/08/16/sessions-says-charlottesville-car-attack-could-be-prosecuted-as-a-hate-crime/.

[113] Libby Nelson and Kelly Swanson, "Full transcript: Donald Trump's press conference defending the Charlottesville rally." *Vox.* August 15, 2017.
https://www.vox.com/2017/8/15/16154028/trump-press-conference-transcript-charlottesville.

[114] Ilan Ben Zion and Stuart Winer, "Netanyahu hails Donald Trump as a 'true friend' of Israel." *The Times of Israel.* November 9, 2016.
https://www.timesofisrael.com/netanyahu-hails-trump-as-a-true-friend-of-israel/.

[115] Nikki Haley, "Remarks at a U.N. Security Council Briefing on the Middle East." *United States Mission to the United Nations.* December 18, 2018.
https://usun.state.gov/remarks/8869.

[116] Ibid.

[117] Andrew Silow-Carroll, "Who is King Cyrus and why did Netanyahu compare him to Trump?" *The Times of Israel*. March 8, 2018. https://www.timesofisrael.com/who-is-king-cyrus-and-why-is-netanyahu-comparing-him-to-trump/.

[118] Benjamin Netanyahu, Twitter post, March 21, 2019, 1:06 p.m. https://twitter.com/netanyahu/status/1108777011227619329.

[119] Jen Kerns, "Trump's first year in office was the year of the woman." *The Hill*. January 16, 2018. https://thehill.com/opinion/white-house/369112-trumps-first-year-in-office-was-the-year-of-the-woman.

[120] John Gramlich, "Trump has appointed a larger share of female judges than other GOP presidents, but lags Obama." *Pew Research Center*. October 2, 2018. https://www.pewresearch.org/fact-tank/2018/10/02/trump-has-appointed-a-larger-share-of-female-judges-than-other-gop-presidents-but-lags-obama/.

[121] Tessa Stuart, "Ex-Trump Employee Speaks Out on His Treatment of Women." *Rolling Stone*. March 29, 2016. https://www.rollingstone.com/politics/politics-news/ex-trump-employee-speaks-out-on-his-treatment-of-women-104728/.

[122] Josh Meyer, "The secret backstory of how Obama let Hezbollah off the hook." *Politico*. January 2018. https://www.politico.com/interactives/2017/obama-hezbollah-drug-trafficking-investigation/.

[123] Chuck Ross, "Podesta Email: It Would Have Been 'Better' If San Bernardino Shooter Had A Stereotypical White Name." *The Daily Caller*. October 10, 2016. https://dailycaller.com/2016/10/16/podesta-email-it-would-have-been-better-if-san-bernardino-shooter-had-a-stereotypical-white-name/

[124] Jeremy Diamond, "Trump: Paris massacre would have been 'much different' if people had guns." *CNN*. November 14, 2015. https://www.cnn.com/2015/11/14/politics/paris-terror-attacks-donald-trump-guns/index.html.

[125] Jared Keller, "Trump Is Making Good On His Promise To 'Bomb The Sh*t' Out Of Terrorists." *Task & Purpose.* September 13, 2017. https://taskandpurpose.com/trump-bomb-shit-afghanistan-isis.

[126] Ehsan Popalzai and Laura Smith-Spark, "'Mother of all bombs' killed 94 ISIS fighters, Afghan official says." *CNN.* April 15, 2017. https://www.cnn.com/2017/04/15/asia/afghanistan-isis-moab-strike/index.html.

[127] Ryan Pickrell, "Here Are The 17 Prisoners Trump Has Freed Since He Took Office." *The Daily Caller News Foundation.* May 27, 2018. https://dailycaller.com/2018/05/27/president-trump-freed-17-prisoners/.

[128] Wes Walker, "Defamation: 'News' Org Writes Apology To Melania, Pays Damages For Hit Piece." *ClashDaily.* January 26, 2019. https://clashdaily.com/2019/01/defamation-news-org-writes-apology-to-melania-pays-damages-for-hit-piece/.

[129] Doug Giles, "Fake News: Here's All The Bogus 'Missing Melania' Stories Spawned By 'The Media(D)'." *ClashDaily.* June 7, 2018. https://clashdaily.com/2018/06/fake-news-heres-all-the-bogus-missing-melania-stories-spawned-by-the-mediad/.

[130] Katie Rogers, "Melania Trump Returns to the Public Eye (Sort Of)." *The New York Times.* June 4, 2018. https://www.nytimes.com/2018/06/04/us/politics/melania-trump-reappears.html?action=click&module=RelatedCoverage&pgtype=Article&region=Footer.

[131] Stephen A. Crockett, Jr., "Wait, Is That a Melania Trump Look-Alike?" *The Root.* June 5, 2018. https://www.theroot.com/wait-was-that-a-melania-trump-looka-like-1826570407.

[132] Jamil Smith, Twitter post. June 3, 2018, 7:44 a.m. https://twitter.com/JamilSmith/status/1003240956798349316

[133] Annie Karni, "White House silence on Melania stokes conspiracy theories." *Politico.* May 29, 2018. https://www.politico.com/story/2018/05/29/melania-trump-conspiracy-theories-611588.

[134] Andy Ostroy, Twitter post. May 31, 2018, 8:31 a.m. https://twitter.com/AndyOstroy/status/1002165728747892737.

[135] David Frum, Twitter post, June 2, 2018, 2:46 p.m. https://twitter.com/davidfrum/status/1002984804885893122.

[136] Bre Payton, "8 Times Members Of The Media Spread 'Missing Melania' Conspiracy Theories." *The Federalist.* June 7, 2018. https://thefederalist.com/2018/06/07/8-times-members-of-the-media-spread-missing-melania-conspiracy-theories/.

[137] Jerry Dunleavy, Twitter post, June 3, 2018, 9:22 p.m. https://twitter.com/JerryDunleavy/status/1003446964191748097.

[138] Stephanie Grisham, "Melania Trump's spokeswoman speaks out." *CNN.* December 17, 2018. https://www.cnn.com/2018/12/15/opinions/melania-trumps-spokeswoman-speaks-out-grisham/index.html.

[139] Greg Price, "'You Don't Know Me,' Melania Trump Says Of Mika Brzezinski After Twitter Scandal." *Newsweek.* July 3, 2017. https://www.newsweek.com/melania-brzezinski-worst-job-631372.

[140] Stephanie McNeal, "Melania Trump Has Responded To Jokes About Her 'Blood Tree' Christmas Decorations." *Buzzfeed.* November 28, 2018. https://www.buzzfeednews.com/article/stephaniemcneal/melania-trump-christmas-blood-trees.

[141] Joe Concha, "Melania Trump: When it comes to me, media focuses on 'unimportant stuff'." *The Hill.* November 28, 2018. https://thehill.com/homenews/media/418705-melania-trump-when-it-comes-to-me-media-focuses-on-unimportant-stuff.

[142] "Michelle Obama's DNC speech: 'I wake up every morning in a house built by slaves' – video." *The Guardian.* July 26, 2016. https://www.theguardian.com/us-news/video/2016/jul/26/michelle-obama-democratic-convention-video.

[143] NBC News, Twitter post, November 27, 2017, 12:04 p.m. https://twitter.com/nbcnews/status/935192691826143232?lang=en.

[144] Eric Bradner and Patrick Gillespie, "Trump's impossibly ambitious trade promises." *CNN.* July 11, 2017.
https://www.cnn.com/2017/07/11/politics/trump-trade-promises/index.html.

[145] "NATO Says More Members Plan To Reach Spending Goal By 2024." *Radio Free Europe.* February 14, 2018.
https://www.rferl.org/a/fifteen-of-29-nato-members-meet-defense-spending-goal-2-percent-gdp-by-2024-stoltenberg-says-mattis-pressure-brussels-meeting/29038749.html.

[146] Ibid.

[147] Jill Jusko, "America's New Factory Building Frenzy." *Industry Week.* June 15, 2018.
https://www.industryweek.com/leadership/america-s-new-factory-building-frenzy.

[148] Press Release, "Treasury Sanctions Russia-backed Bank Attempting to Circumvent U.S. Sanctions on Venezuela." *Department of the Treasury.* March 11, 2019.
https://home.treasury.gov/news/press-releases/sm622.

[149] "The Old Deluder Satan Act Made Sure Puritan Children Got Educated." *New England Historical Society.*
https://home.treasury.gov/news/press-releases/sm622.

[150] "Humanist Manifesto I" *The American Humanist Association.*
https://americanhumanist.org/what-is-humanism/manifesto1/.

[151] Ramesh Ponnuru, "Betsy DeVos Is Protecting Civil Liberties on Campus." *Bloomberg.* November 20, 2018.
https://www.bloomberg.com/opinion/articles/2018-11-20/trump-and-devos-are-right-on-college-sexual-harassment-rules.

[152] Donald J. Trump, Twitter post, January 28, 2019, 8:21 a.m.
https://twitter.com/realdonaldtrump/status/1089876055224184833?lang=en.

[153] Chuck Ross, "Podesta Email: It Would Have Been 'Better' If San Bernardino Shooter Had A Stereotypical White Name." *The Daily Caller.* October 10, 2016.
https://dailycaller.com/2016/10/16/podesta-email-it-would-have-been-better-if-san-bernardino-shooter-had-a-stereotypical-white-name/.

[154] "Trump: We're going to win so much (2016)." *CNN Politics (Video)*. August 18, 2017. https://www.cnn.com/videos/politics/2017/08/18/trump-albany-rally-winning-sot.cnn.

[155] Paul Krugman, "The Economic Fallout." *The New York Times*. November 9, 2016. https://www.nytimes.com/interactive/projects/cp/opinion/election-night-2016/paul-krugman-the-economic-fallout.

[156] Washington Post Editorial Board, "A President Trump could destroy the world economy." *The Washington Post*. October 5, 2016. https://www.washingtonpost.com/opinions/a-president-trump-could-destroy-the-world-economy/2016/10/05/f70019c0-84df-11e6-92c2-14b64f3d453f_story.html.

[157] Heather Long, "Trump will cause 'protracted recession'." *CNN Business*. June 6, 2016. https://money.cnn.com/2016/06/06/news/economy/donald-trump-recession-larry-summers/index.html.

[158] "What's Warren Buffet buying? $12 billion in stocks in 84 days is huge even for him." *The Financial Post*. January 31, 2017. https://business.financialpost.com/investing/global-investor/warren-buffett-has-bought-12-billion-of-stocks-in-the-past-84-days-hes-just-not-saying-which-stocks.

[159] Yessenia Funes, "US on Track to Meet Obama's Climate Targets Despite Trump Killing Them." *Gizmodo Earther*. October 29, 2018. https://earther.gizmodo.com/us-on-track-to-meet-obamas-climate-targets-despite-trum-1830080106.

[160] "U.S. Leads in Greenhouse Gas Reductions, but Some States Are Falling Behind." *Environmental and Energy Study Institute*. March 27, 2018. https://www.eesi.org/articles/view/u.s.-leads-in-greenhouse-gas-reductions-but-some-states-are-falling-behind.

[161] Lawrence H. Summers, "Trump's budget is simply ludicrous." ^The Washington Post. May 23, 2017. https://www.washingtonpost.com/news/wonk/wp/2017/05/23/larry-summers-trumps-budget-is-simply-ludicrous/.

[162] "Economic Growth Has Reached 3 Percent for the First Time in More than a Decade Thanks to President Donald J. Trump's Policies." *White House.* February 28, 2019.
https://www.whitehouse.gov/briefings-statements/economic-growth-reached-3-percent-first-time-decade-thanks-president-donald-j-trumps-policies/.

[163] Al Root, "Manufacturing Jobs Are Coming Back to the U.S. But is It a Renaissance?" *Barron's.* February 18, 2019.
https://www.barrons.com/articles/manufacturing-jobs-us-renaissance-51550431098.

[164] "Presidential Executive Order Promoting Free Speech and Religious Liberty." *White House.* May 4, 2017.
https://www.whitehouse.gov/presidential-actions/presidential-executive-order-promoting-free-speech-religious-liberty/.

[165] "Muslims in America: Denaturalizing Christian-Centered Narratives of American History." *American History Association.* January 7, 2018.
https://aha.confex.com/aha/2018/webprogram/Session16436.html.

[166] John Winthrop, "A Model of Christian Charity (1630)." *Hanover Historical Texts Collection.* August 1996.
https://history.hanover.edu/texts/winthmod.html.

[167] David Barton, *Original Intent,* (Texas, WallBuilder Press, 2000), 23.

[168] Ibid.

[169] Ibid., 90.

[170] "John Adams." *Faith of Our Fathers.*
http://www.faithofourfathers.net/johnadams.html.

[171] "House Speaker Robert Winthrop Stands for Christ." *Christian Heritage Fellowship.*
https://christianheritagefellowship.com/house-speaker-robert-winthrop-stands-for-christ/.

[172] Barton, *Original Intent,* 117.

[173] "McCain minority staff director Henry Kerner to IRS official Lois Lerner and other IRS officials: 'the solution is to audit so many that it becomes

financially ruinous'." *Judicial Watch.* June 21, 2018.

[174] Dan Merica, "McCain's thumbs down caps contentious relationship with Trump." *CNN.* July 29, 2017. https://www.cnn.com/2017/07/29/politics/mccain-contentious-relationship-with-trump/index.html.

[175] Yvonne Wingett Sanchez, "Sen. John McCain's role in Trump dossier intrigue detailed in deposition." *Ariznoa Central.* March 18, 2019. https://www.azcentral.com/story/news/politics/arizona/2019/03/18/new-details-senator-john-mccain-role-trump-dossier-detailed-deposition-david-kramer/3205658002/.

[176] Mitt Romney, "The president shapes the public character of the nation. Trump's character falls short." *The Washington Post.* January 1, 2019. https://www.washingtonpost.com/opinions/mitt-romney-the-president-shapes-the-public-character-of-the-nation-trumps-character-falls-short/2019/01/01/37a3c8c2-0d1a-11e9-8938-5898adc28fa2_story.html.

[177] Sean Davis, Twitter Post, March 1, 2019, 3:55 p.m. https://twitter.com/seanmdav/status/1101601799902056449?lang=en.

[178] "Presidential Executive Order Promoting Free Speech and Religious Liberty." *White House.* May 4, 2017. https://www.whitehouse.gov/presidential-actions/presidential-executive-order-promoting-free-speech-religious-liberty/.

[179] Vanessa Romo, "Trump Warns Venezuela's Maduro Supporters: 'You Will Lose Everything'." *NPR.* February 18, 2019. https://www.npr.org/2019/02/18/695797870/trump-warns-venezuelas-maduro-supporters-you-will-lose-everything.

[180] "Executive Order 13771 – Reducing Regulation and Controlling Regulatory Costs." *EPA.* February 3, 2017. https://www.epa.gov/laws-regulations/executive-order-13771-reducing-regulation-and-controlling-regulatory-costs.

ISBN 978-164570209-2

US $16.95
51695

9 781645 702092